TL;DR

The Best of Essay Club 2017

Edited by Matthew Broyles

Published by Naïve Books

First printing, February 2018

Essayclub.org

Facebook.com/EssayClub

CONTENTS

○

Foreword

by Matthew Broyles

○

Wow, what a year. I could say that 2017 was more dramatic than the scribes at Essay Club expected, but if you've read last year's compilation, you know that's a lie. We knew it would be crazy, but of the precise flavors brining the stew, we could not speculate with any great detail.

What you see here is 2017 as lived by an assortment of writers from various backgrounds, all contributing their mental efforts to the greater ponderance our planet is undergoing: The Big Think, as it were. Hopefully we create more good than harm.

Ideas are powerful, and as I said in our previous installment, some of the better ones are longer than 140…wait, what's the new Twitter character limit again? Okay, fine, more words don't a more cogent statement make. If we've learned anything this year, that's pretty high on the list.

Still, we here at Essay Club maintain that there is a space for long-form written expression, and I don't mean only for Neal Stephenson. Most every Wednesday in 2017, the title of an as-yet-unwritten essay went out, and every Tuesday, all submissions received from our writers with that title were published.

You may notice that it's a much larger book than last year's. This is owing to a full twelve months of essays vs. only three. Personally, I like having more to read. Helps the bathroom time breeze right by, not to mention the jury duty.

What we try not to do here is prattle, so without further ado, I present to you the Essay Club Class of 2017, in all their literary splendor. While we yet draw breath, we write. As always, we thank you for reading.

If I Had a Million Dollars

If I Had a Million Dollars

by Anna Bardin

If I had a million dollars…

…you would never see or hear from me again.

Sincerely,

Anna

If I Had a Million Dollars

by Ashley Van Arsdel

I am a struggling musician. This will probably never happen to me, therefore, will be something I never have to worry about. However, if I did manage to come into a million, here's what I would do:

I would begin by paying off my debts. Fortunately, I was always pretty smart about not getting credit cards - even though I receive offers for them every day. No, my debts are student loans from art school and medical bills. I would also pay off my car. Be relieved of debt, the American dream. And since my debts seem relatively low in the warm glow of a mil, plenty of change would be left over to roll around in.

Give some to certain family members to repay their generosity.

Buy myself and my daughter a nice, moderate-plus house in whatever area of the country I choose. Maybe upstate New York. Maybe farther north, even, like Canada. Enough space for us to be comfortable and to entertain guests. A quiet area with no annoying neighbors who stick their heads out like cockatiels to say hello to you when you're in your pajamas attempting a quick run to the car. I could live somewhere and live my dream - to not be seen.

In that house, I would build a sound-proofed recording studio. Probably something quite large, like an entire basement, where I could do live band recordings. Top-of-the-line mixing consoles, a hot new keyboard, the best mics I can afford.

A beautiful, mahogany baby grand, which wouldn't grace the studio, but rest in the living room. My guests would enjoy this almost as much I as would. Piano nights by the fire.

A Yamaha tiger-stripe upright, like the one my grandparents have, for my bedroom.

Surround sound speakers and a gigantic TV.

A fully-loaded bar. And maybe guests who halfway know how to make drinks.

Build up my savings. Retirement does not need to be cause for alarm. Neither does whatever college my smart little girl wishes to attend.

Then, contributions to organizations such as the ACLU and NPR. I could say I did my part to keep civil liberties and independent journalism alive. That I did something selfless, something good for the world.

It's easy to speculate, but when the money hits, what do you actually do? You couldn't tell everyone because lots of folks would emerge out of the woodwork: long lost relatives, "friends" and neighbors. No, I do not want to invest in your business. For once, I want to be selfish and invest a little in myself.

Like I said at the beginning, I am a musician and not what you would call a successful one. I do not see myself ever having the "problem" of somehow miraculously acquiring a sum of money that large. But, one quality that I possess which doesn't cost me a dime is my perpetual optimism. It lives in my core, sometimes dormant, and pops out to say hello when I need it most. So, who knows? This is a good drill for preparation; this is a nice dream.

If I Had a Million Dollars

by Bruce Payne

Number One: I'm old enough to instantly retire on such a sum.

So, remain liquid while waiting for the inevitable stock market crash that happens EVERY SINGLE TIME the Republicans gained unfettered control of three branches of government and deregulate the fuck out of what the previous administration enacted to stabilize the economy, then buy low and set up an endowment that pays out enough to live well, if not extravagantly.

Number Two: Set up a small, but meaningful endowment for the Hip Pocket Theatre and Arts Fifth Avenue to assist these worthy organizations with their endeavors.

The Hip Pocket Theatre celebrated its fortieth year of experimental theatre in Fort Worth last summer and capped it with the ultimate staging of *The Lake Worth Monster*. No one is doing anything remotely like this incredibly original and personal theatre.

And Arts Fifth Avenue is a jewel in the Near Southside, serving as an arts anchor at the corner of 5th and Allen. They offer instruction in many disciplines, including tap, guitar, voice, and other performing arts. And they serve as a showplace where local troupes without a permanent home can mount original productions, or new takes on such diversified fare as Shakespeare and Samuel Beckett.

Number Three: Hit the road again.

I want to go back to Europe in the worst way. I want to revisit the same countries as we enjoyed last summer, but with more time for a personized schedule and less "panorama" tours where the bus doesn't stop long enough to disembark and take pictures.

And I want to see Paris, and London, and take in the Irish countryside.

I used to joke that if I had a million dollars, I'd buy a Senator. I don't think that sum would be sufficient in this new age. I think I'd be patted on my head and sent back to the kiddie table. However, the past election made one thing abundantly clear: the two party system has outlived its usefulness as much as the Electoral College. It's time for a true Workers' Party. And free of the burden of "making a living", I could devote as much time as needed to building something that actually helps the working stiff. I am astonished that so many cast their vote for someone who is the antithesis of a working man because the other party lost sight of their pain. That's got to be fixed. The legitimacy of the Bernie Sanders campaign brought so much hope. But we also saw exactly how hard the party would fight to actually nominate a true champion of the working class. And he had the disadvantage of being another old, white guy. (Full disclosure: I'm an old white guy. But I ain't runnin'. I'm just trying to make things better for the next generation. We blew our chance.)

And to literally put my money where my mouth is, I'd raise the ceiling on my own Social Security Tax to pay whatever REALLY should be paid on amounts over $225,000.

Peace,

Bruce

#RESIST!

If I Had a Million Dollars

by Matthew Broyles

"I got 99 problems, and money would solve at least 77 of them."

So reads the meme on my screen. For someone raised lower middle class, and tentatively hanging onto that economic rung in adulthood, the feeling expressed above is painfully familiar.

Yet I know that I have good things within my reach that big piles of money couldn't buy. Abilities, relationships, brought about by quirks of happenstance that dollar amounts cannot quantify. At shows, I've been handed large bills by people who can spare them, and told, "I wish I could do that."

Fiscal disadvantage is less a specifically identifiable set of circumstances than a background noise. A form of tinnitus only heard by those who cannot readily say that if their last paycheck came tomorrow, they would still be able to purchase food a month or two hence. That low-level ringing has been medically shown to increase stress levels, leading to lower life expectancies and a host of ailments. Money may not cure all, but poverty kills, no question.

My late uncle was one of those guys who always had a plan to get rich. These improbable schemes were frequent targets of derision in the family, accompanied by head-shaking and looks of "I know, right?" As I close in on the age he was when I first paid much attention to these criticisms, I find myself stirred to defend him. His skill set was not one that pulled in a ton of money. What other hope for freedom from wage slavery was there than to make a quick million somehow?

It's a thought that floats through my head when I'm in line at the convenience store. When, along with the Kettle chips and a fruit bar for the boy, I think to add, "And one Texas Lotto, please." Do I honestly believe in a world where such impossibly long odds are worth my dollar? For me, at least, that dollar is not so much buying a realistic shot at big money as it is throwing a little spark of magic into an otherwise unremarkable day.

As elephantine demolition crews prepare to lay waste to social safety nets, the better to fatten military budgets and bump CEO bonuses, dotage prospects for the un-moneyed grow increasingly grim. We know that working hard won't change that. Some of the hardest working people I know are at the greatest risk of losing everything in the event of a single prolonged major illness.

We are told by the TED talk set to work smart, not hard. Having served in the dot-com trenches, I can tell you that the difference between a start-up and a pyramid scheme is not as great as aspiring octillionaires would like to believe. Of the companies whose stock options I was once eligible for, none still exist. Who's the gullible uncle now?

When I allow myself to picture a day when checking my bank balance becomes an item of idle interest rather than of heart-pounding suspense, the visions are almost too arresting to behold. Buying houses for friends of mine who are all but homeless, covering studio expenses for penniless bands I believe in, throwing resources into social justice organizations whose work is sorely needed now.

In the age of GoFundMe, how long would my hoard last? Probably not very. Wealth and bleeding hearts are soon parted. I know people who have experienced brief intervals of prosperity, and their propensity for kindness drained the coffers dry in short order. We should not wonder that the one percent is populated so densely with uncaring assholes. How else would they hold onto their money, with such gut-wrenching misery on all sides, woes that only persist for want of a cash wad?

If I had a million dollars, I would first need to somehow avoid telling anyone that I had it. I'm an easy mark already. Emaciated cats and panhandlers never hesitate for a second to hit me up for whatever pitiful largesse I may be able to bestow. If I started handing out Franklins instead of Washingtons, I shudder to imagine the throngs that would gather when next I came blundering down the avenue.

I would probably make far more enemies. Crappy bands I wouldn't fund, sad stories with a dodgy whiff to them, friends of friends who heard about that one time I paid someone's mortgage, and could I just throw a little their way, what's a couple thousand here and there?

As I've often found out to my chagrin, math has no conscience. In a world of 7 billion people, not everyone can be saved, and the cut line has to be drawn, sometimes across the throats of those whose cries are just out of earshot. I feel guilty enough when I have to whittle down my list of doable projects, leaving collaborators hanging, one more good idea shot to hell by the limits of time and energy. Imagine if those endeavors were actually paying someone's bills.

Don't get it twisted, though. I would totally take that million if it came up. Graduating to a higher level of guilt is a price worth paying, if it means I could help even a few of those who I know for a fact need it right now. But I don't spend a whole lot of time worrying about that bargain. If I had a million dollars, the first thing I would probably do is call the paramedics. Unexpected wealth is such a vanishingly rare occurrence in our culture that a heart attack is the only logical response.

Living Forever

Living Forever

by Anna Bardin

My clever nephew spotted something as we were watching an anime the other day. He pointed out that one way you can spot the bad guys immediately is when they offer someone eternal life.

This observation struck me with great force, as someone who was raised in the American Midwest. From my earliest memories, I have been receiving near-constant offers of eternal life. I found one affixed to the doorknob this morning, in fact, after I ignored the knock. Promises of immortality blare at us on all sides, so much so that we hardly ever remark upon them, unless we believe they are true.

Perhaps it's an epiphany I had myself long ago, though I couldn't verbalize it so explicitly. Although I did occasionally press a little, when I was too young not to know better. What do you do forever, in this eternal existence? How do you spend all that time?

The answers were uniformly unimpressive. Singing, praising, shouting hosanna and other improbable words, over and over, for the rest of eternity. As a child, that sounded awful. As an adult, it sounds even worse. I have enough experience with monotony now that the idea of an infinite time loop of adulation chills my blood at the cellular level.

Greek religion (yes, religion, not mythology, o code talkers) is a good indicator that I'm not alone in my suspicions. The gods of old had unbounded spans, and what did they do with them? Coveted, schemed, resented, worked overtime to break the confounded tedium of it all. Eternal life did not give them happiness. More often, it was used to exacerbate punishment, applied to cyclopes and the like. It was not a thing to be prized.

That bit of psychology drives the fear of hell, more or less Tartarus refurnished. Suffering isn't bad enough. No, it must be ETERNAL suffering to be a fit sentence for wickedness. We are given our choice of monotonies, painful or simply boring. I think if the eternal life options were presented in that clear fashion, most of us would opt to just stop existing.

In the words of that old song, what's forever for? I don't know about you, but if I do the same thing for a certain stretch of time, my mind starts scrabbling for the ejection lever. We need variety, or our brains rot. At the risk of overplundering bygone tunes, sure, we like to go where everybody knows our name. But not all the damned time. Without new input, we ossify, and start making lists of who to blame for our entrapment. The only way we want to live forever is if forever keeps us interested.

In this, reincarnation is a curious philosophical adaptation. Eternal life, but different. How many ways are there to live? How many times can we start over, try something else? Yet even in Buddhist thought, there is the idea of parinirvana, the final nirvana. Freedom from the cycle of rebirth. A state that is never fully described by the Buddha himself, as it transcends our understanding.

I've been offered the same arguments on western heavens, that the fulfillment experienced upon ascendance cannot be adequately described to humans stuck in our ambulatory meat wagons.

But isn't that an old trick, too? Can't explain now, just trust me? Don't worry your pretty little head about it, I'll take care of everything? If you saw that in a cartoon, you'd know right away that something was amiss.

I'm willing to accept that there is much about the universe that I don't know. In fact, I have to accept it, because every day I learn something I didn't know. And one thing I don't know is what it would be like to live forever.

I remember when people first started freezing themselves, either wholly or just in head form, in the hope that in a distant future, the frailty of human illness and mortality would find a cure, and they could awaken to life eternal.

That whole badger's nest scared the shit out of me. Still does. What will I wake to? Imagine falling asleep tonight, and the next thing you see upon waking is…what?

That fear sounds paradoxical, given my previously stated craving for novelty, but now we've gone all the way over to the other end of the spectrum. Total unpredictability is no better than its opposite.

Humans are the way we are because we evolved this way. Painstaking, gradual steps. Incremental development. But always forward, sometimes in great wrenching leaps that outpace our imperfect capacity for adaptation. We still seek outrageous quantities of sugar that slowly kill us, our brains struggling to change, to learn that our environment has changed, and our behaviors must follow suit.

Imagine the shock of entering heaven, moments after experiencing the shutdown of a mortal body. Suddenly you have an eternity to fill. No disease, no survival imperatives, no student loan debts. You might at first leap to your feet in praise, certainly.

It's a bit like orgasm in that way. For a moment, it seems as if every problem in the universe has been solved. But it doesn't last forever.

Unless it does. Now, that might be a compelling pitch. Next time those guys knock on the door, I might pry on that topic. Maybe there are a few things I wouldn't mind doing forever. And there, we're back to the Olympians. Even in those matters, infinite variety seems unattainable.

Unless it isn't. I dunno. I'll ask the next 18-year-old missionary I see. That'll give them an eternity of contemplation, no doubt.

Living Forever

by Ashley Van Arsdel

How does one live forever and what does it entail?

Living forever in the sense that your works, whatever they may be, live on after you die. Many artists have not been fully appreciated until after they passed. Van Gogh was thought to be a lunatic in his time. However, posthumously his works were greatly valued. Beethoven, Bach, Mozart, and all the classical composers have works which have remained in our hearts and our ears for centuries. One of my personal aspirations is to leave a large volume of music to be heard after I am gone. Perhaps an alien will find my tunes and jam out to them one thousand years in the future. I can only hope.

Immortality through others - the closest people you knew will always remember you and carry a piece of you with them. When my Dad passed away, I was so devastated. He and I weren't as close as we should have been; we disagreed on a lot of subjects - especially politics and religion - but I loved him still the same. My thought was, over and over again, I will never see my Dad again. And it is true, that in the flesh I have not seen him again, but my mind sees him every single day. My heart sees him every day. He lives in my heart forever and that is his immortality.

Life support is no way to live forever. It's not really living. Who knows what it is really like in one's head. I think the best possible description I have ever heard came from Dalton Trumbo's book, Johnny Got His Gun, in which he narrated the thoughts of a man who could speak, had no arms, legs or sight. The man did learn to communicate through Morse code and was able to request that they allow to him to die. His request was met with no, they wanted to see how long they could keep him alive through science. Like an experiment. And, so I have this in writing, I would like it known that my wishes are DNR (do not resuscitate). Pull the plug.

Forever physically being alive, cognitive and able to function? There are several variations of this. If you were allowed to keep your youth, or stay whatever your current age is, swell. It would open its own hell, though, watching those you love die around you, civilizations burn and there you are, alive with no conclusion. Making new friends and loved ones only to eventually watch them die. Or, having to dwell in a decaying shell which ages. Falling apart around you. Your thoughts living on in a different brain and body? Your memories overtaking that which could've belonged to another. Just for the gratification of occupying some form of life? Does not sound appealing to me. I would much prefer death to this. Death is, at its least and its most, an ending.

Living Forever

by Chris Dashiell

As one of the few people ever to live forever, I wish I could tell you that it's great. But I have to be honest. I'm sick to death of it.

For one thing, I miss being surprised. There's not a thing that could ever surprise me again. Everything people do, say, or write, I have seen before. The most daring and original works of art strike me as hackneyed and boring. To be perfectly frank, I don't want to hear or see anything that tries to express meaning. Believe me, it's meaningless. The only times I'm even close to being content is when I'm sitting in a field or a forest, with no humans in sight and no noises other than the wind or the occasional small animal.

I thought sleeping would be a relief, but of course there are dreams. The same fucking dreams I've had a million times before. There are only so many motifs a single mind can come up with for dreaming. I still get the one about being late for class and then remembering that I haven't done any of the work for an entire semester. I think in the dream, "Oh no, not this dream again." It's been two hundred and thirteen years since I went to school, for Christ's sake.

I am bored with people, and of course they are bored with me. How could I blame them? I'm incapable of showing interest in anything anymore, so talking to me is a dead end. They know I'm old, but of course they don't know exactly how old. I have to keep that a secret, or they'll put me in a psych hospital—no, that would not be a change of pace. Abnormality no longer interests me. When you get down to it, all these psychological aberrations are the same.

Food is disgusting. I only eat occasionally to avoid weakness and a skeletal appearance, which would attract undue attention. I've tasted every possible thing you could taste and now I'm nauseated by tastes and odors. You probably think alcoholic drinks might help, or other drugs. Well, you're wrong. Being high just accentuates the boredom, and getting drunk makes everything seem even more monotonously the same.

Sex? Yecch. What a fraud that is. Everyone's body is like everyone else's, and what was that excitement really about? Special effects. The curve of a back, or a proportion of a waist to a pair of legs: so what? Why should that possibly have an effect on me?

Love? I still love some people, but it's completely abstract at this point. I can imagine my love, and it's perfectly sincere, but to actually be with anyone is torture. I know what they'll do or say before they do. All my original loves, and my spouses and children, are long dead.

Even though I live forever, I still have to excrete waste from my body from time to time. I find it humiliating. I will never graduate from the animal kingdom, with all its blotches and parasites and involuntary flatulence. There has to be a limit, I tell myself. There has to be.

Most of all, I'm sick of myself. The same memories, except they stretch further back. The same personality, habits, tired old jokes, defects of character. Having needs would lend some piquancy to my experiences, but what needs could I have, since this life will never end? The need to be held, the need for love, the need for respect: these only meant something when there was a time for it all to end. Running out of time lent my life a sense of urgency. But I've got all the time in the world and I don't need anything.

What am I, anyway? I'm just a bookmark, a place holder, a symbol for a particular vantage point of experience. An ego is a complete liability when you live forever. Personal drama, for instance: what is my career, who am I fucking, what have I achieved? These questions are pure nonsense.

The only thing I ever want anymore, the only thing that could make me happy, would be to die. Yeah, I know, I wouldn't really be happy after I'm dead, but isn't that the point? There has to be nothing for me to care about anything. So if you can figure out a way to kill me, please do. We'll make it look like a suicide so you won't get in trouble. I promise I'll be grateful to you for the rest of my life.

Living Forever

by Doremus Jessup

In Jonathan Swift's book *Gulliver's Travels*, we find the Struldbrug. These citizens of Luggnagg are born seemingly normal, average human beings. They are, in fact, immortal. There is one catch though - and of all the various immortality concepts in literature this is my favorite - they don't stop aging. It gets worse. At age 30, knowing their immortality, they become dejected. Why? Because they know what is coming. At age 80, they are declared legally dead. Think about that. Stripped of all protections, because you'll never die.

Between this and feasting on Irish children, Jonathan Swift was a lot heavier than people think.

The Struldbrugs are even denied the right to own property after 80:

"As soon as they have completed the term of eighty years, they are looked on as dead in law; their heirs immediately succeed to their estates; only a small pittance is reserved for their support; and the poor ones are maintained at the public charge. After that period, they are held incapable of any employment of trust or profit; they cannot purchase lands, or take leases; neither are they allowed to be witnesses in any cause, either civil or criminal, not even for the decision of meers (metes) and bounds."

Why, you ask? Why would any man, even in 1726, want to remove the rights and liberties of those still alive? What fuckery is this Swift proposes? Simple.

"Otherwise, as avarice is the necessary consequence of old age, those immortals would in time become proprietors of the whole nation, and engross the civil power, which, for want of abilities to manage, must end in the ruin of the public."

I tell you, Swift had refined and mastered the twin arts of sarcasm and satire in a way rarely seen.

So many of our more modern tales of immortality involve blood, beheading, or compulsive consumption. There is an element of magic, or the unknown attached to them. The tragedy of never being able to know true love, having to watch those around you grow old and die, having to drink blood and the cheesy conundra which have been born of that trope, mindless driven consumption of the living…they all have an aspect of the supernatural which makes suspension of disbelief, and suspension of introspection easy.

Not so with the Struldbrugs. They represent an immortality so mundane, so Herzogianly bleak, as to make it more believable, more approachable. Struldbrugs show the truth of human existence. It is not some grand struggle, or fight. It is a bore. It is mundane. It is an eternity of waiting in line.

You can keep your sparkly emo-pires, and your ambulatory deceased, and your singular individual and all the attendant woo woo fluff that keeps you numbed to the deeper meaning of your entertainment. Me, I'll go with the boring, the mundane, the dismal, and the direct.

Living Forever

by Eva Moon

The chime on Jula Karell's door rang softly. She checked her comm. Avic Daser waited patiently outside, his calm, smooth face pleasant and impassive. She pressed the button and the door slid open soundlessly.

"Avic. Please come in."

"Greetings, Captain Karell."

"No need for formality, Avic. Please sit."

Avic sat. Jula materialized tea and they rested, sipping it in easy, unhurried silence for a long moment.

"It's good to see you. I assume there is some reason you made the effort to come in person?"

"Yes, Ca-- Jula. I wanted to let you know we've captured one."

"You've captured… you mean one of the… before he…?"

"Yes. We removed his cube before it could activate."

Avic leaned forward and placed the cube on her desk. It was small and benign looking, for something so unimaginable. She hesitated to touch it.

"Oh, it's safe to touch. It's harmless unless it's properly affixed."

Jula picked it up. It was a smooth, pale blue cube about a centimeter on a side. The only discernible feature was two hair-wide slits on one side. An almost invisible wire lay in each slit. So this was the terrible thing that was causing so much trouble. Hard to believe!

For the past few months individuals had been… vanishing? Ceasing to be detectable in the Lattice? There wasn't even a word for it. It might even be permanent. No one had ever come back and until now, no one had been apprehended prior to - whatever it was. She shivered slightly. Avic waited patiently.

"I will speak with him."

"Of course. I've already sent you his coordinates."

"Thank you."

Avic started to rise.

"Avic. Do you have any thoughts of your own about what's behind this? I mean, I've read the reports but what do you think? Why would anyone want to…" She trailed off partly out of reluctance to voice it and partly out of sheer lack of vocabulary.

"I don't know. But it must be pretty… attractive? It's hard to call it addictive when it's just the one time. This fad, if you will, is growing fast. You've seen the stats. But, me? I've got no clue."

Jula nodded. "Well, thank you. I'll speak with him."

Avic left. Jula checked her comm and tapped on the coordinates. In a moment she was seated at a table in a nondescript cell. The man sat at the other side of the table. He looked normal, but at the same time, not. She couldn't put her finger on it. He seemed to almost radiate some kind of energy.

"Hello…" she tapped her comm, "Malik Steek. I am Captain Jula Karell."

He remained silent.

"Nothing's going to happen to you. There's no punishment and you'll be free to go shortly. But I'd like to talk with you first, if I may? We're trying to understand what… this is." She held up the cube. His pupils dilated at the sight of it but he made no move to take it from her. "Please. We can wait as long as you like."

Malik tensed for a moment and then sighed and slumped. "It's Death."

"I'm not familiar with that word." Jula tapped her comm.

"Death… ceasing to exist… permanently. The word used to exist."

"I've checked and there's no listing for the word."

"It existed before. Before the Lattice."

Jula chuckled. "A religious one, are you? I've heard about people with such ideas but scientists have shown there was nothing before the Lattice. There's nothing outside the Lattice and it will continue on. We've always been just as we are. It's a closed, static system."

Malik leaned forward. "Are you sure? If there's nothing but the Lattice, where do the dead go?"

"Dead. Is that your word for people who… " she indicated the cube. "How does it work?"

"You attach it," he pointed to a spot on the back of his neck. "Here."

"And then what?"

"Then you go on living. Until it activates."

"And how long does it take to… activate?"

"There's no way to know. It could be right away. Or it could be a year. Or fifty. Or a hundred."

"And after?"

"Nothing. No existence. Death."

Jula struggled with this thought. "I don't understand. For how long?"

"Forever."

Jula shuddered. "Why would you choose this?"

Malik tapped his fingers on the table and made several false starts at speaking. When he spoke at last, it was with great intensity, looking her straight in the eyes with an unwavering gaze.

"Have you ever wondered what the Lattice is? Really is? Why are we here? There's no beginning and no end - a static system. You drift along forever. Nothing is urgent. Ever. There's no reason to do - or not do - anything. No reason to make art. No reason to invent anything. No reason to fall in love. Death… is a deadline. I don't… didn't… know how long I had left and it gave a shape to time and made every moment unbelievably precious. I wanted to dance and write and fuck. I wanted to see everything and eat up life in whatever time I had left. I was never so happy before. I was never happy. What is happy when there's nothing to compare it to? Have you ever felt… anything?"

Malik stopped speaking, but his eyes were still fastened on hers and he seemed to vibrate with vitality. It made her uneasy. She turned away and tapped her comm.

"Thank you, Malik. I've arranged for you to be reconditioned."

"No!!"

"I can see you're in a lot of distress. It's not good to be this… worked up. Really, there's nothing to fear. It's completely painless and you won't remember a thing!"

"No! Please! Let me have it. Please, I need it!"

The door slid open and two orderlies entered. He jumped up and backed away.

"What do you think the Lattice is, anyway? A reward? Eternal life for the blessed? It was designed as a punishment!"

"Please be calm and let the orderlies help you. Life as a punishment is a ridiculous idea. Life is neither a reward nor a punishment. It simply is."

He struggled against the orderlies as they tried to subdue him.

"You're wrong. It was the worst torture they could devise! Eternal existence with no purpose. Forever and ever!"

One of the orderlies finally administered the sedative and Malik slumped. The second orderly pressed a button on his chest and they winked away.

The blue cube sat on Jula's desk for two weeks before she pressed it to the back of her neck.

Living Forever

by Matthew Broyles

Every so often, I spot another article about extending human lifespans beyond the already advanced level they have achieved in the past few decades. It isn't a popular opinion, but in a culture where one is prevented by law from deciding when they want to die, such medical advances can seem more like horrific threats than good news.

In my paternal grandfather's 95th year, he kept not dying. Something would flare up, they'd rush him to the hospital, and he would wake up still alive. He had lost much of his mobility by that point, and was not longer able to work on the beloved stained glass projects that kept his mind alive.

About the umpteenth time he woke up in the hospital again, feeling terrible but still not dead, he told my father, "You know, I really don't mind if I go next time. I'm ready." When at last one day he did not revive, it was of course painful for the rest of us, but I felt quite a bit of relief knowing that he was no longer in pain.

We have fairly frank discussions of death in my family. When I was a teenager, my old man explained to us that his life insurance paid double if he died on the way to work. We were instructed that if he ever died at home, it was our responsibility to load him up in the driver's seat of his truck and run him off the road to collect our full share of the payoff. Death has never been treated gingerly or sentimentally by my clan. It's a thing that's going to happen one day, so you'd better have a plan.

It's increasingly hard to make plans when you honestly have no idea how long you're going to be old. My mother's mom, the only grandparent I have remaining, is 98 years old, and has survived two broken hips over the past year. All of her 12 siblings have been dead for decades now, as have most of her friends. Her house, a lovely structure in its day, is now held together by the barest threads, hanging on as long as she needs it, which for all we know could be another ten years.

We know now that my generation will have far fewer safety nets in our dotage than hers. Leafing through my retirement kitty, a knot forms in my stomach, wondering if, even supposing I can work till 70, as the GOP believes I should, I can pay my bills another decade after that. And that only gets me to 80. Suppose, like my grandmother, I'll have another 18 years or more on top of that? Hearing the flies buzzing in my piggy bank, the prospect is not terribly inviting.

In the abstract, no one wants to die. We want to see our kids grow up, watch history unfold, catch the next season of Sherlock, and do the things that make us feel alive. I certainly do.

But I know there will come a time when that might change. Last summer, I had a terrible stomach condition that prevented me from eating much. I lost 50 pounds in a month, and felt like a ghost drifting through my own life, watching but not really able to participate the way I would want to. Thankfully, being in relatively good middle-aged health, I got to the other side of that illness and began enjoying life again.

What if I hadn't? If I'd been forced to live another four or five decades half-conscious, all for the supposition that everyone would always rather be alive than dead, it would have felt like prison. It would have been hell.

I know people who suffer from far worse conditions. I see them fight, trying to gain back the parts of their lives that were stolen from them, and a fair amount of the time, they succeed. But sometimes they don't, and keep dragging on, more for the sake of loved ones than for themselves. If someone who did not have a dog in the fight asked them if they wanted to live forever like that, I feel fairly confident they would say no.

Options are good. The option to rid oneself of disease and have a chance at seeing a few more years is certainly valuable. However, we must not forget to leave other options on the table. People are different. Situations vary. Not everyone is the happy centenarian at a winning Cubs game. Some of us might be more like Old Yeller, in desperate need of someone to put us out of our misery.

Don't go emailing me asking if everything's okay. Approaching 43, I'm in no hurry to shuffle off. Books to write, gigs to play, people to love. But if you ask again by century's middle, you might get a different answer. I don't know any more than anyone else how things will be going, for me or the world at large by then. However, in remembering the lives of those now passed, we have to be honest about the fact that sometimes death is the best option.

We have to realize that surviving forever and living forever are two different things.

Also, don't run my corpse off the road for extra payout. That's insurance fraud, for which life is definitely too short.

○

Poor Lives Matter

○

Poor Lives Matter

by Anna Bardin

This morning, in a rush to get all my very important errands run before my very important scheduled activities in my very important day, I walked up to the line for the pharmacy counter just a few seconds before a stooped, elderly gentleman shuffled up behind me. He held onto his cane with trembling hands, and it was clear the effort to remain upright was taking all the energy he had in his frail body. Though the clock ticked inside my head, and the lady in front of us asked an interminable array of questions about her coupons, I felt the presence of the old man like a hot iron in my conscience.

Were that me in line, I thought, I would want to get this business over with as soon as possible. When the coupon lady was done, I turned to the gentleman and said, "Please, you can go ahead. I'm not in a hurry." The relief in his eyes was palpable, in amongst a tug of old-world shame at being the beneficiary of a woman's consideration. He thanked me quietly, and toddled slowly up to get his prescriptions. The clock's loud tocking faded in my head. To hell with efficiency, I scolded myself. Dammit, you've got to be kind.

Many of us have a condition we are not aware of: TAB, which stands for Temporarily Able Bodied. We may have a few hitches in our getalong, but by and large we are able to perform the tasks that life demands of us, with some energy left over for those pursuits we enjoy. Any time spent with our elders reminds us that one day, this will not be entirely the case. We will need help sometimes doing things we don't even think about now. Bathing, picking up objects from the ground, going to the pharmacy.

As self-evident as this is, there is yet another pre-existing condition that a lot of us carry, and which we do not speak of: TNP, that being Temporarily Not Poor.

What qualifies as poverty is a moving target, based more on individual circumstance than broad numbers. Let us posit for the moment that if you have only one job, and your bills get paid every month, then for the purposes of this essay, you are not poor. Because there are plenty of people for whom the above conditions do not apply.

Using the terms above, I am not poor, and have not been for some time. Certainly not wealthy, but I owe no souls to the company store. Yet, like many Americans, it really wouldn't take very much to change that situation. A major illness, a prolonged financial downturn in an area of the economy upon which my employment depends, being stuck on a jury for the next OJ case…Scenarios abound.

Thus, my status isn't Not Poor. It is Temporarily Not Poor. Because no one can reliably say that terrible things won't happen to knock me down the rungs, closer to the abyss. And if I should end up there, I don't want the other people who remain in my present TNP cohort to treat me like I see them treat the poor.

Co-workers with salaries equivalent to mine expound on their moral fiber, using their TNP status to hoist themselves above the rabble, blaming the unfortunate for their circumstances. Because that's what the poor need, really, is more people disrespecting them. That does wonders for their morale, to hear pundits and politicians speak of poverty as a genetic abomination, curable only by even more suffering, to motivate them to excel, something they would clearly be doing if being poor weren't so goddamned awesome.

It is remarkable, in a society which prides itself on an affinity with a penniless Israeli mystic, that our attitudes towards the poor are so cruel. Not always actively malicious, but indolently so. I have heard TNP associates, considering homeless people sleeping under a bridge in subzero weather, speaking of their fellow humans as if they were stray cats. It's a kindness, allowing nature to thin the herd, take them out of their misery. I take careful note of those who say these things, for I know they will be the last ones I can count on if my TNP status loses its first two letters.

We talk of the poor this way because we truly believe that we are not the same. Some different species, like Neanderthals, an evolutionary mistake that Darwin will correct in that efficient way of his. We do not see familiar faces when we are asked for spare change. We see aliens, people who we couldn't possibly be, and we treat them accordingly. Because we honestly believe we are better.

Why? Because we put the pieces together like we were told. Because we understood the instructions. Because we had two hands to do so. Because our functional bodies and brains allowed us to.

I don't like to, but if I listen, sometimes I swear I can hear them: Little microscopic villains, creeping around in my bloodstream. Waiting for their chance to strike. To knock me down, and take everything I've worked for. To siphon it away into the wallets of specialists and imaging centers. To fund the TNP/TAB lifestyles of those who benefit from our criminalization of poverty.

We walk such a thin line. One misstep, and we become what we fear. Them. The poor. It chills the blood to think of it.

So why not, while we are in a position to do so, help cushion the path for those in that situation? Because it is always possible that, without warning, the poor will suddenly include us.

Poor Lives Matter

by Bruce Payne

Full disclosure: I'm not poor. Poor folks don't know where their next meal is coming from. Poor folks may not have a roof over their heads. Or a car. I've never made $40,000 in a year, but I'm not poor.

I have been in the past, usually by choice. I've lived without hot water, without electricity. But I've never gone to bed hungry. So I've never been truly poor.

The reason poor lives matter? Because no one speaks for them. Absolutely no one. That may change. Sooner than we think. We're only one uncontrollable economic downturn from ALL of us being in the bread line at a soup kitchen, modern reflections of those grey souls that haunt the photographs from the Great Depression.

Have you ever studied those faces? I mean taken an hour and poured over the details? The lines and eyes sunken deep into skull-like sockets borne of worry? Have you seen the dust that they no longer shake from their clothes? Have you seen that endless line of humanity waiting for just enough food to survive? Some of them looked almost like concentration camp victims, they were so slight of build.

Here we think of India as an enlightened country. But their caste system is almost impenetrable, the layers defined so unflinching and unyielding that they might as well be strata in sedimentary rock. Not even god helps the untouchables.

I hardly ever carry cash anymore, a result of having been robbed at gunpoint while working for FedEx in Houston. I saw people on my route who were right up against it: one unexpected bill away from being thrown out of the shittiest apartments you've ever seen. But their kids were friendly. "Hi, mister! Is that for me?"

When I was young, money didn't mean much to me. I worked, hard enough to have money, but I never had any left by payday. I had a few friends who weren't good with money either. But we shared. Food, beer, a joint, a couch. Pretty much the quintessential damn, commie hippies in the flesh. I never got the whole "not bathing" thing, though. Even when the water wasn't hot, we showered.

Money just never was the driving force for our existence. It shouldn't be for anyone. I thought greater thoughts, unencumbered by the endless need to pay my bills. One job I had that didn't pay squat was delivering circulars for the Star-Telegram. I listened to KERA all the time back then, with Abby Goldstein and Gabrielle West guiding me through hours of life-affirming music I'd have otherwise never been exposed to. (Poor folk don't give a damn about dangling participles, either, let me tell you what.)

And when they added an hour of "Fresh Air" with Terri Gross, the conversation elevated my consciousness at a time when I most needed it. Together, somehow it confirmed to me my self-worth. I felt spiritually enlightened almost every day, making a wage to walk all day, lost in thought. I still miss those days at times. Walking puts you in touch with the proper cadence of life. Bonnie Raitt talked about it one day on that very show, and it stuck with me. She said that a lot of the rhythms in her music were walking rhythms, in time with your steps and the beatings of your heart. I never forgot that. Obviously.

My grandparents and great-grandparents were probably some of the poorest people I ever met. But they'd managed to guide their families safely through that depression. And I never once heard them complain or worry about money. They worked and cooked and cleaned and prayed at the Baptist church in Kaufman. They lived for their grandkids, at least when I knew them. And they gave 10% of whatever they had away, just like Jesus told them to in the Bible.

I don't put much stock in judging people. I don't judge their clothes or hair or job or cars. Because I still really don't care about any of that shit. When someone close to me whines about something someone else has or does, my standard reply is good for them. What has that got to do with us?

The same person who frets about that stuff is the one who unfailingly gives something to every homeless person she encounters. She's the first to know their names, their stories. What they like to eat and where they go when it gets too cold on the street. She tracked down what happened to a lady who used to frequent the bus stop in front of the 7-11 at Berry and University by asking one of the cops about her. (She'd had a medical event and they'd taken her to Petersmith. She has not reappeared since that day, a few years back, but the cop said she'd recovered.) She opened my eyes to them and I love her for that.

All I'm saying here is that sometimes folks will find themselves without adequate resources at times. Doesn't make them bad, or lazy. It makes them human. What makes US human, is how we react to them.

Poor Lives Matter

by Matthew Broyles

As I write this, the elected representatives of my fellow citizens (for they're certainly not mine) are expending every effort to dismantle a law intended to provide health insurance for all Americans.

To be clear, the Affordable Care Act was not the law it needed to be. A single payer system that eliminates the health insurance industry entirely is my Bolshevik preference. Because we have proven that we can't have nice things, though, I won't spend any time pining for that.

Instead, I will swallow the lump in my throat as I take a moment to consider all the people I know for whom the absence of health coverage is a stalking predator, always on their path, waiting for its moment to strike them down.

When we hear debates about the merits of universal care, whose voices are we hearing? People who are covered. How many uninsured pundits are there? Make a wild guess, and it won't be low enough. Just as the poor are told how to be rich by those who have never known poverty, so too are the uninsured being told how best to be insured by those who have never darkened the door of an overcrowded county ER.

Illness isn't a choice. If it were, no one would get sick. Likewise, being born into poverty is not a conscious decision. You can tell me the rags to riches stories, and I'll show you the odds against those, which are staggering. Even as relatively sheltered as my childhood was, I remember how hard it can be to truly cast off the social norms and assumptions of the peer groups we all find ourselves in. Harder still to get a loan.

And when we fail to achieve escape velocity, where does the blame fall? Always on the battered backs of the ones who dared to try. Thus are the laws of our moral universe enforced: Those who are poor deserve to be. Those who are rich have earned it.

This, despite mountainous evidence to the contrary. Miles from my house, a scion of the Walton family bathes in unfathomable economic security. She didn't earn it, any more than the fresh-faced partiers I wade through in Uptown Dallas have. Yet I hear them opine on the obvious mistakes of the poor, with me in earshot, not recognizing the interloper in their midst.

I always call myself lower middle class, because I know people who have way less than I do. Orders of magnitude less, in fact, so to call myself poor seems like an exaggeration. Yet there is less separating my circumstance from the truly poor than I'm comfortable with.

That chasm yawns below, and being on a slightly higher viewing platform—no rails, mind you, like a damned Star Destroyer—doesn't give me a whole lot of confidence, should the rocks start pelting from above.

And now here come those hefty stones, lobbed by those who believe they have earned the right to decide my future and those of the people below me. Worse, the underpinning of their belief is that it is a zero-sum game. That it's either me or them. If I truly believed that, I might act similarly.

The biggest victory ever achieved by the oligarchs was to split the poor into teams. Poor urbanites, poor rural dwellers, poor Christians, poor atheists, poor whites, poor minorities, poor men, poor women…

Surely the pattern must be obvious.

What is the thing that separates all these groups from their rulers? The one thing they have in common. The one thing they carry like a badge of shame, and will not acknowledge, lest it reflect on their moral character. Because of all the sins one can commit in our culture, being financially unsuccessful is the most unspeakable.

This is what keeps us from speaking up. From saying that poor lives matter. Because in doing so, we must first admit that we are poor. Lower middle class I may be at this very moment, but in one reversal in fortune, I am almost instantaneously poor. So in truth, my economic status is mere window dressing, as easily torched as a set of curtains, bringing the whole house down with it. If I'm honest, I am poor.

How many of us are willing to say that? To shout out the villains on high (can we start with the one who has a goddamn GOLDEN TOILET, fer chrissakes?), marking ourselves as their clear target, because we recognize just how weak our grip on solvency is? Until we do, they will pit us against each other, and we will continue losing.

Is it too much to hope that if I were to say Poor Lives Matter, my inbox wouldn't be inundated with "All Lives Matter!" retorts, indignant that I dare put the concerns of the economically disadvantaged on a higher footing than the big wheels? If the fat cats make a mistake, they can't afford a new yacht. If a poor person errs, they end up on the street. There is no equivalency.

Poor Lives Matter. That shouldn't be a controversial statement. Yet in this new season of *The Apprentice: Hunger Games Edition*, it is. We fear to criticize a class we aspire to join. Even when the truth is that most of us are a whole lot more likely to wind up shifting status in an entirely different direction. Be careful where you make your enemies.

Poor Lives Matter

by MC Dalet

If the reader's experience is anything like my own, (s)he has had the discomfort of seeing his or her existence reduced to a dismal set of numbers. Are those numbers an accurate expression of our *being*? They are one aspect of our material existence according to one set of rigidly focused measurements. Now consider how many more variables aside from your earnings, account balance, and credit score must be taken into account to even begin to compose an accurate description of YOU, your essence, who you *are*. These fiscal numbers are maybe 1% of the full reality of your life. The material itself is probably 1%. Yes, it is the most tangible, the most quantifiable. But only the intangible elements like the love and pain we experience, our talents and preferences, and even the experiences we have that are so personalized that they cannot be externally measured can begin to give us the picture of who we really are. We can be poor in any area of our lives – financial, emotional, psychological, spiritual. And the less we have in each of these and countless other areas, the more we can gain.

A full vessel overflows if new material is poured into it, but an empty vessel has a capacity to receive everything. A "poor" person, then, has the opportunity to manifest anything. This is particularly true of those who are denied dignity in the 1% material reality.

This is a spiritual law, but it presents material evidence. Consider all of the art that grows out of or responds to poverty, or even to finding one's self "poor" in social currency. My academic work argues, for example, that the American slave narrative shapes the trajectory of American literature at large. From a denial of human dignity came such a profound calling of a people into human existence that it shaped the expression of a nation. From the struggles of the working class came such classics as *The Grapes of Wrath* and *Death of a Salesman*. Denials of agency, space, and voice gave rise to street art. From war comes nearly all else. The absence of peace connects us to a strong desire to create it in any way we can.

To see the potential for great Light to be revealed from such Darkness takes spiritual sight. The bottom line is this: to see with spiritual eyes we must look beyond the material *is* and actively seek the potential for good in all things. This is challenging to say the least. Remember, that 1% reality is in your face. Numbers, completely measurable and thus, fixed. Potential, however, is always in flux, and *it* can change in an instant. There's always a chance to win big!

There are two wisdoms which help me occasionally see through the 1% illusion: the spiritual wisdom of Kabbalah and the tapestry of stories, both sacred and secular, that humanity has manifested. My practice in kabbalah is in part guided by my use of the siddur, or prayer book, while my reading of story is informed by Joseph Campbell's monomythic hero's journey. It is incredible that kabbalah's wisdom and Campbell's intellectual pursuits reveal the same truth: one must become "poor" to transform and grow into one's true greatness.

My prayer book carries the title *Prayer of the Poor*. The introduction explains that, according to the kabbalistic texts, "as soon as the poor man says his prayer, the Holy One, blessed be He, opens all the windows of the Firmament. . .there exists no other prayer in the world to which the Holy One, blessed be He, will give His immediate attention." What does it mean? A rich person cannot be spiritual. No. The wisdom suggests that when we cling to what we have, we will never know what we *could* have, which is ALL there, in a state of potential within our soul's true desire. Ready-made fulfillment waits if only we choose to undertake the hero's journey.

Joseph Campbell was a brilliant scholar who sought spiritual truth by means of intellectual pursuit. He did so by consuming and synthesizing the world's great myths. In so doing, he discovered a singular pattern which all great heroes undergo. He dubbed the singularity the *monomyth* and this pattern of ascension the *hero's journey*. The hero's journey begins with the focal character in a fixed status quo, and they are comfortable, if not satisfied, there. They are the center of their own world. They are then told that they are simultaneously insignificant and limitlessly powerful. The hero completes the journey only by internalizing this fact. The hero must, in their deepest knowing, understand that *they* are presently powerless, but more importantly believe that they do have the potential to transcend all rational (and quantifiable) limits.

The hero must realize she is – or what is more must make himself – poor *while* realizing that (s)he can be infinitely rich. But this richness hardly if ever comes in the form of material wealth.

Why? Are we back to the question of money versus virtue?

In our stories – which represent the core of our immeasurable desires – material wealth is just not particularly valued. It is a wealth of character, of valor, of integrity, of perseverance, of love, of ability, of drive that we crave. Whether it is Neo losing his entire reality to learn the Truth or the consummately humble Moses splitting the Red Sea, our hero has connected so fully to these desires of the soul, freedom from the constraints of the material 1% that the Hero is capable of creating miracles. Yet they realize that nothing is really *theirs*, that whatever their limited number, they are part of the great All-That-Is. And that is always enough.

○

Outbreak:

Spreading the Human Condition to the Stars

○

Outbreak: Spreading the Human Condition to the Stars

by Anna Bardin

In science fiction, there is a recurring theme. Humans spread out amongst the stars, and set up different planetary utopias, giving ourselves entire worlds upon which to build our ideological fantasies.

This is, of course, partially based on history. Puritans and idealists of all sorts gazed at the great untilled continents to the west and saw visions of their perfect Eden, the place where at last, all of their stymied longings could be acted upon without interference from the corrupt powers that be.

It is just possible that, when at last humankind leaves harbor, we will see a proliferation of utopian societies, safely separated from their opposite numbers by light-years of dark matter and quantum foam.

Will we be happy then? Is that what it takes to satisfy our boundless quest for contentment? The removal of all whose ideas give us unease, forcing us to defend our wants, keeping us from declaring them universally as needs?

Of course I dream of it, too. Building a world of free sexual expression appeals greatly to me, and if offered an entire planet upon which to found such a society, I would be hard-pressed to turn it down. I long to set up entirely different expectations from those I was raised on, and pass those defaults on to a grateful posterity.

Yet what happens when a child is born into one of these idealized enclaves whose personality does not fit into their parents' immaculate design? The job of the next generation is to question the previous one. And so the enemy will lie in our midst, agitating and breaking up the finely formed clay in which our pure roots grip so tightly. Once again, we will be at war with ourselves.

The human condition is pre-existing. There is no known cure at present, and most likely, as our bodies and societies evolve, the tangle will become even denser, with new problems arising to fill the void left by those made obsolete. Who will we be by the time that first colony ship is launched? Who will dare to embark on such a journey, and who will stay, enjoying the absence of the zealots as they rocket out to carve their egos into fresh stone?

It's at times like these when I wish for an intervention of some kind. A wise voice from the cosmic beyond to lay hand on us and say, before you go, know what you are taking with you. Know thyself, and then make your decision to leave or remain.

I've often said that if anyone who truly knows themselves isn't at least a little frightened by what they discover, then they aren't paying attention. We are still animals, with all the savagery and unpredictability of a caged gorilla, channeled through an enormous brain that, most of the time, has no idea what to do with itself, how to fill the hours upon hours of its existence.

To quote Michael Cunningham:

"To look life in the face. Always to look life in the face and to know it for what it is. At last to know it. To love it for what it is, and then, to put it away. Always the years between us. Always the years. Always the love. Always the hours."

Having looked thus, do we trust that our otherworldly paradise will live up to our expectations? I cannot help but doubt it.

Still, we hope. We cannot but hope, floating as we do in an infinite vacuum that cares as little for our predilections as we do for its opinion of our tiny lives. Dreams keep us alive just as surely as air and water. Without our fantasies of perfect worlds, are we still human? Is that aspiration so deeply ingrained that its removal would render our spark null, driving us back to the trees and caves from whence we emerged, stars in our eyes, the entire world a shiny tool not yet forged?

Perhaps it is who we are. And if we can keep from destroying ourselves, we will inevitably reach out and touch the distant heavens. And as on Earth, what we find will depend entirely upon what we take with us. I ask only that we do a thorough inventory before launch. Extra baggage is heavy, and maybe jettisoning that which we do not truly need will open us up to receive gifts unimagined.

Outbreak: Spreading the Human Condition to the Stars

by Bruce Payne

I'm going to begin this essay by telling a story I've not heard, nor repeated since the fifth grade. Mrs. Frazier, a Music teacher, rather than English or Creative Writing teacher, would sometimes read to us as part her duties as a home room teacher. And, while this story may have been designed for younger listeners than fifth graders, I have never forgotten it.

A young lad was taken prisoner by a wizard and placed in a cage made of equal parts windows and mirrors. His only companion was a bird in another, smaller cage that sat in the corner of the boy's large one. The boy examined his cell completely, unaware of how he'd come to be here, and found a table with food and drink, which was replenished several times each day, a bed, a water closet with a tub for cleaning himself, some toys, a closet full of the most beautiful clothes he'd ever seen.

He tried on the clothes and positioned himself where he could see the most complete reflection in one of the many mirrors. As he admired his image, the mirrors imperceptibly grew and the windows shrank in proportion.

And so their days went, the boy preening and posing, the bird singing less and less, neither of them wanting for food or nourishment. And each day, there were more and more spaces to see his beautiful reflection wearing ever more magnificent clothes, while the windows became smaller and smaller, until only the smallest single crack remained.

As he walked past the crack, he noticed a sunset. Pressing his eyes against the tiny window, he saw the way the dimming light played on the trees, the grass, and broke across the brook. He gasped in awe at its beauty. And the bird chirped for the first time in days.

"Oh, bird! Come and see! Come and see!"

He ran and grabbed the cage and held it to the crack for the bird to see the sun.

And the window grew imperceptibly.

Now, think of the earth and its people. When I was young, I could see the Milky Way every night from our backyard in Wedgwood. I could see Jupiter, and Venus, and Saturn with the naked eye every night. There were billions of stars to ponder, to inspire our dreams.

And then "stuff" got in the way. As the cities became brighter, the stars grew dim, forgotten by the children who dreamed of reaching them, of becoming the heroes of novels written by Jules Verne, by Asimov, of Heinlein.

Who rode the great sandworms like Muad Dib. Who walked the sky with Skywalker.

But as the mirror of civilization blots out our window to the stars, as we grow ever more enamored of our earthly reflection, what will drive us to share what we can no longer see?

I fear, without that chance beam of light that catches our attention, that forces us to behold a beauty almost without comprehension that is so great that we must share it, that there will never be an outbreak.

In the story, the windows kept growing until nothing of the mirrors remained and the boy and bird were freed.

We need bigger windows.

Outbreak: Spreading the Human Condition to the Stars

by Cristee Cook

I'm thinking about astronomer Carl Sagan. There's a popular quote of his that I see pop up in inspirational graphics online: "The cosmos is within us. We are made of star-stuff. We are a way for the universe to know itself."

It's a nice quote if you need inspiration about your own purpose in the world. But after some research, and reading the quote in context, it is basically a beautiful way to highlight one effect of The Big Bang. The quote comes from an episode of Sagan's 1980 *Cosmos* series, during which he explains elements present in the universe at the time of The Big Bang. They are the same elements present not only in the human body, but all forms of life on Earth. Sagan's eloquent words aren't hyperbole. We are made of stars.

If true, we should be limitless. The illusion that there is any separation between anything is shattered. Where did the idea (and subsequent actions) of separation come from? Are our limitations part of our DNA?

Sagan's speech, "Pale Blue Dot," also comes to mind. In it, he describes the reality of our planet: a pale, isolated, blue dot. He examines the famous photograph with a palpable awe of astronomy, and a sad awareness of humanity's limitations. In the speech he states, "Our posturing, our imagined self-importance, the delusion that we have some privileged position in the Universe, are challenged by this point of pale light. Our planet is a lonely speck in the great enveloping cosmic dark. In our obscurity, in all this vastness, there is no hint that help will come from elsewhere to save us from ourselves."

Ouch.

I'm also thinking about Eckhart Tolle. In 2008 I was introduced to his bestseller *A New Earth: Awakening to your Life's Purpose*. I was excited to dive in, hoping to gain a deeper understanding or some helpful insights about how to elevate the meditation practice I had begun the previous year. My friend, the teacher of my meditation class, suggested the book with a caveat that it wasn't so much about how to meditate, but more what to meditate on. I was thinking I would learn more information about the practice of meditation and have a clearer picture on how to progress as a spiritual person in my daily life. I had no idea what the book was actually about, and I see now that I was naïve about what I had agreed to read.

In the opening chapter of his book, Tolle describes the limitations of human perspective. He addresses the barbarous consciousness from which we seem to operate. He makes a grave statement: "Humanity is now faced with a stark choice: evolve or die. If the structures of the human mind remain unchanged, we will always end up re-creating the same world, the same evils, the same dysfunction."

The book changed the trajectory of my thought process about humanity's purpose and my place within the whole. I was inspired and terrified.

The past few weeks I have felt paralyzed by what I view as a dead-end: I must do something, anything, to help the situation, and if I do anything it will make the situation worse. I think about Sagan and Tolle, each presenting the paradox that we are concurrently tiny specks in a vast and unpredictable cosmos, and completely responsible for our personal contribution to the whole. They both posit that in our miniscule existence, we have the power to change the world, that we are the world.

In this moment, I find my thoughts almost impossible to verbalize, which is a challenge for someone trying to be a writer. Whether my glimmer of understanding comes from a scientist or a metaphysical author, I've come to the conclusion that human beings have created the mess we find ourselves in, and it is human beings who must correct it. No one is coming to save us, and there's nowhere else for us to go.

If, as Sagan states, "we are a way for the Universe to know itself," then, despite the illusion of utter chaos, the process of our existence is absolutely perfect. The alternative is that it's all meaningless and we are heading straight for an implosion. I don't want the latter to be the truth. I hope we can change. I want to see us triumph.

Outbreak: Spreading the Human Condition to the Stars

by Eva Moon

"He's lost weight since his last check up."

Martina looked at her baby. He was plump, rosy and smiling.

"How can that be? Look at him!"

It was true. He was clearly thriving and yet... he had definitely lost weight.

"Maybe try to nurse a little more often."

That evening Martina cooked dinner. On TV, a parade of world news: Another suicide bomber. Another unarmed black boy shot by police. A synagogue torched. A riot. Then, a story about an epidemic of unexplained weight loss in infants. She looked her her son. Ernesto bounced in his baby walker. His fat little legs pushed off the floor, sending him high with ease.

"That doctor must be crazy. Look at you! My strong little man!"

Far away, in a war-ravaged city, a ragged young couple looked into their daughter's cradle.

"Ali, I'm worried. She weighs nothing!"

Ali tickled the baby and she giggled. Her skin seemed to glow with a golden sheen.

"You're my dainty little girl, aren't you? Light as a feather!"

Outside, an eruption of mortar fire rattled the shutters, showing them with plaster dust. Ali plucked his daughter from her cradle and held her to his chest as they ran. Was she lighter than last week?

The news anchor read from the teleprompter.

"The epidemic is spreading. Across the globe infants, outwardly healthy, continue to lose weight. The CDC has found no vector or identified a country of origin. Some affected infants have begun to show skin changes as well. Check your children for hardened, yellow areas, which can appear anywhere on the body."

The video cut to images of babies covered with patches of a shiny, yellowish film. The anchor winced and thought of her son at home. Did he have any symptoms?

"If you notice any of these symptoms, please see your doctor immediately. Next up, protests across the country turn violent. We'll be right back after these messages."

As soon as the light turned red, she reached for her cell phone.

At the orphanage, Wei had one more problem. Sixteen babies would not stay in their cribs at nap time. She'd get them settled down, go to the kitchen to prepare bottles - watered down because there was never enough formula - and by the time she got back, babies out of cribs everywhere! She solved it by tying their blankets to the slats, holding them firmly in their cribs.

"Try to escape now, little monkeys!"

Dr. Patel sat in gridlock traffic and thought about his last patient of the day. Seven months old, seemingly healthy, in no distress. And yet she weighed a fraction of what she should have. Most worrying was the yellowish crust covering about 60% of her skin, even on her face. It was pliable at the edges, but the thickest areas were growing hard. Almost like shellac.

There was no way to remove it without injuring the child: it was integrated with her skin. He could do nothing beyond admitting her for observation.

He turned on the car radio to see if there was any explanation for the traffic.

He couldn't forget the mother's haunted face as she pleaded with him. "What if it covers her face? What if she can't breathe?"

The one bright spot in this whole mess was no infant had died of it. Yet.

The radio reported an explosion had closed the bridge ahead. He cursed. It would be hours before he got home.

Martina had to improvise. Ernesto now weighed nothing at all. If she didn't run a string from his foot to her wrist, she could turn away for one minute and turn back to find him asleep on the mantlepiece. He slept most of the time now and the… rash, or whatever it was, had spread so much, he was getting stiff.

She'd be more concerned if Ernesto didn't seem so calm and happy. She wished her husband would help. He was home all the time since the factory shut down. But he just sat on the porch, drinking.

She turned to check on the baby and gasped. The end of his string lay untied on the floor.

Wei carried the tray of bottles to the dormitory. It was time to rouse her charges. Not that they could do much anymore. Most of them were too stiff with that yellow… shell? They curled quietly under tightly tucked blankets. It was strange, but frankly, it made her job easier. They no longer cried constantly with hunger.

She pushed open the door with her hip and entered. A second later the tray of bottles crashed to the floor and she screamed. One by one, the babies were drifting out the open window and up into the sky.

She got to the window in time to grab the last one and pull her back. When she looked out, thousands tiny dots drifted upward as far as she could see, like dandelion seeds in summer.

The news anchor took slow, deep breaths and waited for the green light. When it flicked on, she looked gravely at the camera and spoke in a steady voice.

"Reports are flooding in from across the globe. Affected infants are… levitating. Efforts are being made to retrieve them, but thousands are slipping past rescuers. There's no indication of an upward limit. At a press conference today, the president blamed a Chinese plot and has put the military on high alert. Around the world, governments are mobilizing forces."

Ernesto floated peacefully through the stratosphere, snug in his amber chrysalis. He was surrounded by many thousands like him. Far below, white plumes of rockets streaked across the blue expanse of ocean but it was of no interest to him. He gazed at the vast, glittering expanse of stars above.

Outbreak: Spreading the Human Condition to the Stars

by Matthew Broyles

When my son was three years old, he became fascinated by our car. Anything with wheels generally, but more specifically the controls he watched me manipulate when I would drive him places. Finally he asked me to show him what they all did. Parking the car and removing the key, I gave him the rundown, even though he couldn't reach the pedals and certainly couldn't see over the dashboard. But he grasped the functions of the gear shift, steering wheel, even the blinkers and windshield wipers. We would sit in the car at least once a day and he would go through the motions, practicing.

One day he turned to me and said, "Okay, Daddy. We drive now."

I laughed and told him that yes, one day he would. He gave me a look of impatience, and pointed to the keys. As far as he was concerned, he was ready. He knew how the car worked, and the logical next step was to turn the damn thing on and go for it.

Increasingly, I see this sort of thinking at play in the adult world. Look, we understand the basic principles of a thing. Why the hell not, let's just push the button and see what happens.

Nuclear power, for instance. Even now, huge stockpiles of radioactive waste sit relatively unsecured, with absolutely no viable plan for their disposal, though they will remain dangerously radioactive for years to come. One would have thought that such planning would come before the construction of the weapons and power plants, but one would be wrong.

Likewise with space junk. Right now, a mission is underway to clean up the vast sea of flotsam left behind by all the launches we've sent up for the past half century. Recently, a window on the International Space Station was nearly cracked by a small chunk of debris hurtling through low orbit at thousands of miles per hour.

We shit our nests all the time. Basic things, like clean water. My family had to abandon the house we lived in two years ago because the groundwater had been utterly corrupted by the mining and dumping taking place on all sides. An entire subdivision of homes lost because no one cared enough to make sure one bit of human activity didn't ruin another.

So when I hear people talk about colonizing worlds light-years from Earth, I get a little nervous. How easy would it be to say oh well, we have this backup planet now, why do we need to be careful about this old rock? I think we know ourselves well enough to guarantee that line of thinking. And of course the settlers on the new planet would see the vast unspoiled sphere as a blank canvas, upon which they could paint any sort of "progress" they wanted, heedless of consequences for at least a few hundred years, by which point they themselves would be dead.

Humans are just clever enough to divine the secrets of the cosmos, but we always seem to stop short of considering how our actions will affect our descendants. These young souls who we spend so much time defending from people whose lifestyles we disapprove of, yet cannot bring ourselves to make sure that they aren't left with a giant cesspool of slop as their inheritance when we're gone.

If I were an alien, observing Earth's interstellar ambitions, I might be tempted to go back to my other alien friends and say, look, I dunno if I want these assholes out here tearing the joint up. It's not like they'll figure it out. The pattern is demonstrably locked in, so it's gotta be congenital. Can we talk about containment here?

I've found that I regard humanity at large much the same as I regard white dudes. I know I'm one of both, and frankly I'm tired of our shit. So much hand-wringing over the wrong things. Who's schtupping who, what group of overpaid ball-kickers is beating another, do I look like a wuss driving this economy car…WHERE ARE THE REAL THINGS? Survival of our beloved offspring, conserving precious and finite resources, not completely jacking up the planet that is presently our only lifeboat in a vast sea of empty, indifferent space.

We have no perspective. That is our chief sin. We say we want justice, but what we mean is justice for people we know, or could know, because they look like us. We say we want prosperity, but we look no further than next quarter's earnings. If humanity could gain just a damned ounce of broad, long-term perspective, we would recognize our foolishness and behave entirely differently.

I do not want us to colonize the stars. Not while we are three-year-olds playing with Daddy's car, which is a deadly weapon in the hands of a child. We must grow up first, and at present, we're doing a damned poor job of that. If we level up in future, and develop at least something approaching responsibility for our everyday decisions, then let's talk about putting the keys in and going for a drive.

For now, I want us grounded. Send the robots to do our exploring. They, at least, don't shit where they eat.

Outbreak: Spreading the Human Condition to the Stars

by MC Dalet

Every night my one-and-a-half-year-old son pulls himself to standing and toddles to the back door. With an open palm, he pounds on it, points, and "hollers," asking to go out. He points to the door again, looking back to meet my gaze. His hair is long and wild, his countenance joyfully serious.

Each night, I assist him with the door and carry him into the back yard. His first objective is to locate the moon. If it is visible, he immediately locates it, points explosively, and lets out a man cub howl. In truth, it is clearly more of a word than a howl; but it is a word so indecipherably honest and full of wonder that the adult mind literally cannot hear it. I mean, his "burr" is *bird,* his "stah" is *star*, but this moon word has nothing of the *m-o-o-n* pronunciation about it. It is something beyond identification. It is recognition, a desire. It is uttered with the same tone and volume he uses when he really, really wants something.

"You wanna go there, bubba?"

He looks at me briefly, then turns his gaze back to the night sky, to *Space*, now revealed by the sun's absence. For the adult, this is science. To a child, a new sky has magically appeared, and with it, heavenly bodies that become objects of desire. Destinations.

As a child, I wanted to go there. To the moon. To beyond the moon. To places of unimaginable beauty, mystery, and danger. By night, I dreamed of space travel. In my waking hours, I played at being in space, a part of me truly believing I was there.

This sense of play, of exploration for its own sake, this sense of wonder – that's what gets us up there, right? At the seed level of our spacefaring adventures, these are the qualities we take with us as we boldly go beyond the pull of our home planet. They must be. Sure, the Space Race made it all political and competitive, but once you get out there for real, space don't take no guff. It's a good socio-political referee. No one is on their own turf in space -- not yet.

Space doesn't allow for a lot of bullshit. It is dangerous, formidable, new. We are at the mercy of the great Expanse. We've got a foot in: astronauts, probes, a station. But beyond our meager inroads, we don't *really* know what's out there. What is more, we don't know *who we will be* out there. Our going seems inevitable. If we survive long enough, we will become a spacefaring species. Who will we be when we go? The rapt child gazing up at the stars? Or will we go as the adult, who sees the facts and not the fancy, who has too much on his mind to let wonder in, who is hardened by decades of dreams lost in favor of calculated agendas?

Again, Space doesn't recognize our agendas.

If we're going, we have to leave some stuff behind. I'm no rocket scientist, but I know it takes a gangload of propulsive force to escape the gravitational pull of the Earth – the place where our constructs and concerns reign. It's a perfect metaphor. To achieve space flight, we must leave everything unnecessary behind. It's too weighty. Too costly to carry. These things – our policies, politics, and prejudices – they limit us. Space is not limited. It is infinite. There's no telling what we will find or who we will become there. But first, we have to get there by defying our own gravity. Then, we have to survive there by working together. Everyone.

Dalet, you say, *you're a dreamer*. Yes. But I am not naïve. Cite the "state of the world" all you want, amidst the unrest and uncertainty of the 1960s, a lot of positivity was revealed. Regarding space, two things occurred: human beings actually went into space, and Gene Roddenberry created *Star Trek*, a damn near utopic view of humans in space. On the bridge of his iconic Enterprise are men and women, some people of color, and incredibly, a Russian, one of the folks we were racing against (and afraid of) in the primary world. This united version of humanity does not come easily, even in the world of *Star Trek*. In the *Trek* universe, the events of the beloved series occur after a third world war nearly decimates the human race. From the weight of man-made calamity, people band together, exceed their known limits, create warp drive, and explore the universe together. This takes a childlike sensibility.

Children are not bound by adult limits. The child has no addictions. The child does not know money. The child does not see race. The child is free of spirit, ready to play. The child's only job is to do and to learn, to discover. This better part of our nature, the proverbial "right stuff," the sensibility we need to survive and to thrive off planet is not something we must acquire, but something we must remember. In a constant state of discovery, there is no right and wrong. Only wonder.

Holding my boy, makes me want to defy gravity. I want to hear his address to the moon. And when he goes there, I want him to take me too.

o

Didn't See THAT Coming

o

Didn't See THAT Coming

by Anna Bardin

Why was it you?

You, who got all the girls, and had all the nice things. Whose smile lit up the room.

You, the blue-eyed, sandy-haired Adonis that no one else could be.

You, who kept so much on the inside that no one could see how much you were hurting. Who I would have moved heaven and earth to help, to be there for you, if I had known.

You, whose name was spoken into my ear by a friend in an early morning telephone call, amid sobs of disbelief.

You, who hurt so badly that you ended the pain yourself late on a September night, alone and miserable with the person you hated so much. The one you couldn't escape, because he lived inside your head.

You, who would never see the outpouring of grief on your behalf, from everyone who loved you. So many hearts broken, but none as much as your own.

Why was it you? Surrounded by the most troubled of the misfit toys, you judged yourself the least fit, and removed yourself from this world.

And because you never spoke of your pain, I will never know exactly why. What I could have done. Maybe nothing. But I would like to have tried.

Because I loved you. And I don't know if you knew that. I was afraid to say so. Too many girls loved you, what was one more? But I felt like we had something. That just maybe, we could be special together, after all those nights we had talked and laughed about outrageous dreams, ridiculous people…none of it what you were really thinking about, as it happened.

I loved you, more than you loved yourself. Perhaps that would always have been the case, and the spikes that drove themselves through my heart that day would have killed me, too, if you had been mine to lose. Nonetheless, I still regret never telling you. To this day, that memory of unspoken desire drives me to be fearless, to take chances on love, rejection be damned. That's the gift you gave me, though you couldn't have known it.

Of all the things I never saw coming, that night remains foremost. It's been two decades, and nothing has ever hurt so much since. Not that it ever stops hurting, if I think about it. Most days I don't. I have a life, a good one, with passion and love aplenty.

But there are days, dark days, when I swear I would give it all up to be there with you, in the car on that night, holding you close, expending every ounce of my body and soul to show you how much I wanted you to stay.

Maybe it would only have delayed the inevitable. Maybe I don't care.

Why was it you? Because it was. There are no other answers. Only memories, and a pang in my chest, forcing these words to the surface of my consciousness. We are vessels for all the life that has ever passed through us. Yours was precious, and I will cherish it for the rest of my days. You still live, somewhere inside me, and one day I will take what is left of you to the grave, to still your restless soul forever.

I miss you, Scott.

I always will.

Didn't See THAT Coming

by Bruce Payne

Yesterday, I stood with a crowd at DFW in defense of the victims of an outrageous act of discrimination by a nation founded on principles those currently in power evidently cannot understand.

This action detained, among others, a septuagenarian grandmother, an infant less than a year old, and at least two people who required wheelchairs fir ambulation.

My wife and I went because we'd become energized at an organizational meeting a week ago after the inauguration. We went because it was history. But mostly we went because it was the right thing to do.

As we approached Gate 21 Arrivals, our anticipation quickened our steps. We could faintly hear chants and drums. I was a bit wary, because the opposition to the resistance certainly knew of this event. They'd had an entire day to organize their counter-event.

The elevator doors opened. We immediately saw two friends who were leaving, expressions of flushed excitement on their faces. We embraced (the first of many that day) and exchanged pleasantries and Billy handed his sign to my wife. They told us it would be fantastic.

And it was. Fox News estimated the crowd as 1,000 strong. Other more sympathetic estimates ranged as high as 3,000. The chants were non-stop, save to hear bullhorned updates about the status of the passengers we were rallying to assist.

Best was: HANDS TOO SMALL. CAN'T BUILD WALL

We were there 4 hours.

I'm facing a temporal deadline, so I'll be brief.

I have never had a more profound interaction with strangers of all races, creeds, religions, ethnicities, and country of origins than yesterday afternoon. Each arriving flight, even those not affected by the heinous ban, discharged passengers who were astonished by the outpouring of love from a country that has officially become more and more unwelcoming of "the other".

They shook our hands. They peered deeply into our eyes. They hugged us as long lost friends. They wept with us. We saw their humanity and they saw ours.

And one boy handed out Thank You notes that read:

When I was a little boy and I would see scary things, my mother would say to me, "Look for the helpers. You will always find people who are helping. –Fred Rogers

Handwritten below:

THANK YOU FOR HELPING

Didn't See THAT Coming

by Cristee Cook

I used to think that I was a focused person. Maybe in my younger days of less responsibility, I simply had more free time. I'm not sure if I have changed, or if I just had fewer distractions.

Today, the distractions in my life are numerous. I'm distracted by household chores, keeping up with the bills, maintaining friendships, and general work. I'm distracted by Facebook posts, Instagram pictures, and my Twitter feed.

This week, the distractions have been impossible to ignore: government agencies silenced, the education of the nations' children in the hands of a zealot, and an unconstitutional immigration ban.

I started to share some thoughts about the aforementioned bullet points, but then realized they are tangential and I'm not sure I am capable of discussing our regime change with reason or maturity.

The truth is that I haven't engaged in politics much the past few years. I lost track of the issues. I felt overwhelmed by the amount of arguing in the name of freedom. This year I engaged in the voting process beginning with the primary votes, and I dug deep to understand the issue. I want to be an informed voter. I knew the potential for an amp-up of the dark and scary times was present, but I didn't think we'd actually choose a demagogue. It's hard not to be distracted by the thoughts that stem from THAT realization.

I think I have to find a new way to categorize and define what I consider distractions. What is my most important work? What, exactly, do I bring to the proverbial table that only I can bring? How do I focus on what deserves my attention and what belongs in the garbage can?

This weekend I played with my kids a lot. I spent a few hours with one of my best friends. I watched a little television that made me laugh. I tried, without much success, to distract myself from the drama. It didn't work as well as I had hoped, especially on Saturday when the ban hit and the protests started. I had an anxiety attack. I tried to sleep it all off. I woke up Sunday feeling as though I'd once again wasted my precious energy on things I can't control. The thought cycle of what I should focus on, how to focus, what is most important to me began again. You get the picture.

And it's funny. I did all of this while an ever-present awareness lurked under the surface, chanting softly at first, then screaming: You should be writing.

Didn't See THAT Coming

by Eva Moon

A child grows up in hard circumstances: absent father, neglecting mother, poor diet, crime-filled neighborhood. Most children would not thrive in such an environment. Some won't survive. And yet there are always a few who defy terrible odds and surprise us with their accomplishments.

— Jim Carrey dropped out of school to support his family and at one point was reduced to homelessness.

— Bethany Hamilton was back on her surf board a month after losing her arm to a shark and two years after that, she won first place in a national championship.

— Benjamin Franklin's family couldn't afford to keep him in school past age ten.

— Oprah Winfrey was sexually abused by a relative, ran away from home and lost a baby at age 14.

— Charlize Theron witnessed her mother shoot her alcoholic father when she was a young teen.

And yet our urban streets and jails are full of people who came from similar circumstances (well, maybe not Bethany). What makes the difference between a poor mother on welfare and Oprah Winfrey?

There are, of course, many factors, but a critical one is resilience: the capacity to recover quickly from difficulties.

We are all faced with events in our lives that we didn't see coming. In my own case, it was learning that I carry the BRCA1 genetic mutation that gave me an 87% chance of breast cancer and a 55% chance of ovarian cancer. With a single word, my life turned upside down and all my plans went on hold - some never to be resumed. But it turned out to be a springboard to a life and a voice in the arts and a depth of self-knowledge that I couldn't have imagined before.

I will admit I had many advantages: a loving and supportive family, good insurance, financial stability. But I also learned that I am resilient. I don't spend time thinking about past losses. My focus is naturally forward.

Some people seem to be blessed with an abundance of natural resilience, but you can increase your ability to turn life's unpleasant surprises into positive outcomes.

— Expect change. No one gets out of here without ups and downs, so why be shocked when it happens? Practice facing small upsets with grace. An attitude of acceptance rather than blaming or resentment in small things will give you habits you can rely on to face bigger problems.

Learn from experience. Think about times in the past when you were faced with challenges. Did you handle it well? Take pride in that. Were there things you'd do differently? Take note of those. It's hard to change negative patterns if you aren't aware of them.

— Don't judge. Keep an open mind. Sometimes a situation that seems entirely negative can lead to great things. Remember the story about the optimist child digging happily in a room full of manure, sure there must be a pony in there somewhere! Don't judge yourself either! You'll stumble, you'll fall, you'll react badly. You're not a failure - you're human.

— Nurture connections. Find your tribe. It could be family, old friends, new friends, coworkers, allies. You don't need a thousand friends. But you do need a few. If you don't have at least three friends you spend time with on a regular basis, seek them now. Be there for them. It can be hard to reach out to others when we need support, but if your friend needed you, wouldn't you want to help them? Are you any less deserving?

— Stay healthy. Frail people are always the most vulnerable. This is true for mental frailty as well as physical. Make time to exercise, eat well, sleep, unwind, talk to a counselor. Whatever works for you, go do it! Do you want to be the straggling elk when wolves are hunting?

Pursue your passions. What is it that makes you forget the clock, that fills you with a sense of joy and a sense of purpose, that you bore people talking about it? Do more of that. Never stop learning and exploring. Your passions will always be something you can turn to, something to remind you that life is precious and valuable.

— Laugh and play! Children know how critical playtime is. But we forget it - or reject it as frivolous. But it's proven that play and laughter is healing and necessary. People who find time to laugh are more resilient than those who don't. Do you feel guilty about joking when the situation is dire? Ask an ER doctor or nurse - they'll tell you they couldn't survive if they didn't laugh. It's not weak or wrong to take a break from unrelenting drama. Trust me, the drama will still be there when break time is over. And you'll come back to it refreshed.

We are living in tumultuous times. I'm as susceptible to despair as anyone I know. But

I also believe that no matter how hard it gets, there will also be wonderful things that I totally didn't see coming.

Didn't See THAT Coming

by Matthew Broyles

1992. Mineral Wells, Texas. Inside a ramshackle building dubbed the Westside Teen Club, three teenagers set up a hastily cobbled assortment of music and audio gear. None of them has ever done this before, but they've watched enough concert videos to at least know more or less what it's supposed to look like.

All around them, fellow teens chitter noisily in the way that these studious ones do not. The erstwhile musicians largely ignore them, waiting for their cue from the venue owners to switch on and be the unquestioned center of attention. The signal is given, and the overhead music dies. Stepping up to the mic, the gangly one attempts a lame introduction, swallowed by the indifferent yammering of the crowd. The diminutive keyboard player hits the low opening note, and the band prepares to blow everyone's mind.

And then they don't. The clunky musical fumblings of these nascent pretention kings are unwieldy in such a raging sea of blindly surging hormones and frantic posing. The audience's volume rises to dwarf the tiny combo, and thus do these aspiring world-changers receive their initiation into How It Is.

That was me. That was I. That was the writer of this essay.

Thing is, any one of you reading could have predicted the outcome easily. The one who didn't twig it was me. Because, true story, I am unutterably horrible at forecasting human behavior.

Self-absorption has benefits. You approach things from unusual angles, which can bring about useful observations and keep you out of a lot of unnecessary trouble. But it also has the effect of isolating one from the culture at large, and for someone whose livelihood depends on interfacing with that culture, that can be fatal.

I am the grand lord poobah of unprofitable ideas. Skewed notions that I and my weirdo friends think would be super cool, which then receive frowns of confusion upon presentation to the rest of the world. That has been the story of my creative career, and continues to be, this essay project providing just the latest example.

Yet, unaccountably, this wrinkling of the public brow continues to surprise me. I don't really know why. Some part of me still says, okay, THIS will be interesting to more than a few people, surely. It's like Lucy with the football, except no one outside of my own head ever puts the damn pigskin out for me to kick. That's all me.

The truth, though, is that I'm not sorry I did any of it. Those who like it really like it, and since that includes me, it feels worthwhile, as otherwise I'd just have watched teevee and woken up one day wondering if I should've done all that crazy crap I kept coming up with. I know that commercial failure does not constitute artistic failure, as evidenced by all the good stuff I love made by others that has likewise failed to provide them a sustainable living.

Still, the surprise hurts. That's the bit that confuses me, because I really should know better by now. Make a thing, get a few hits on it, occasionally more than a few, and move on to the next thing. Clockwork, predictable. No need to get all crazy with the expectations. Siddhartha was more than right about that.

Somewhere in my head is a little stage hand. He only has one job, and that is to raise the curtain and leap out when a new project is ready for release. I'm not constitutionally built for effective self-promotion, so he's kinda crap at his job, but he's union and unreplaceable, so when he yanks that curtain up and goes, "TAA DAAAAAAA!!!" and the slow claps trickle in…well, he always gets his tender feelings hurt a bit. He doesn't learn, even when the writer and performer and accountant and all the other hirelings I employ in my crowded cranium keep telling him to back the hell up with the overwrought presumption. He just can't help himself, and part of me sort of likes that. Might depend on it, in fact, to keep creating, in hopes that one day the dude can finally have his big afterparty.

It sounds like bitching, but I promise it's not. I know many of the folks reading this have similar experiences, and it's comforting to know we're not alone in this confounding world. For what it's worth, even the normals seem to have trouble figuring out what the hell is going on.

A few years ago, at a low point, I made a promise to myself. To keep creating even if I knew it wouldn't sell. This hasn't been a difficult vow to keep, since coming up with cockamamie ideas is as instinctive as breathing. Concurrent to that, though, I pledged not to build up fantasies of commercial breakthroughs, the better to take everything in stride and not fall into postpartum pits of creative afterbirth. That stipulation has been less enforceable, and I occasionally find myself in the hole, my private world once again bashing heads with the real one that's right there in front of me all the time, easily discernable if only I possessed the right lens with which to see it.

But I don't, and I suppose that's why I never see it coming. To be okay with that constant surprise is an ongoing endeavor. Here's to all who keep kicking that invisible football.

○

Just Say No

○

Just Say No

by Anna Bardin

As much as I talk about saying yes to life, it must be acknowledged that there are times when we must say no.

It always hurts a little, that rip where one universe splits off into another. I occasionally look back and wonder what Alternate Me is doing in that other timeline where I said yes instead of no.

Somewhere, there is an Anna who got married to the most persistent suitor, despite her doubts. If she said yes to that, then she was probably talked into reproducing, and there are little Annas or Andys running around, possibly with new step-parents after the inevitable flameout. To be honest, that's an Anna I'm not eager to meet.

The Anna who finished her Master's degree in Liberal Arts might be interesting to catch up with. It's difficult to say whether she's still teaching, or whether her proclivity for solitude drove her into a research position somewhere in a cube not dissimilar to the one I presently occupy. We would have a lot to talk about.

Less so the Anna who dropped out of school after her dad died, buckling under the emotional weight and ensuing family chaos. The one who stayed to look after her mother, watching her go insane in bright Technicolor. Maybe that Anna kept her mom out of the welcoming arms of the fundies and their promises of an afterlife reunion, Dad's borderline apostasy notwithstanding. Maybe that Anna went bonkers, too. Yeah, let's not go to that universe.

Now, the Anna who took the big crazy job in Chicago, leaving behind her beloved bf, niece and nephew…she could be fun. Possibly less tightly wound, although who knows what new trouble she's managed to get herself into. I'd like to hear about it, in any case. I wonder if she has regrets.

Speaking of regrets, I never can quite shake the vision of the Anna who decided to follow Mr. Rockstar out on the road, at his rather tempting invitation. I guarantee she has way better stories than I do, although I know how they end, if said rockstar's tortured Facebook page is any indication. I know she has regrets, but then, I kinda do, too. We could hang.

Really, I can't imagine a universe in which any Anna does not wonder about what might have been had she made different choices. Lost timelines are a cornerstone of the human condition, without which we would be gods, able to alter past events to satisfy our curiosity.

And isn't that what writers do? Pull the world into our heads and twist it in ways we couldn't when the decisive moment came? We play dress-up dollies with the people in our past, making them do this instead of that, fixing their bad decisions along with ours. Thank goodness we don't have time machines.

But what if we do? What if some future iteration of me came back and switched a few conditions to put me on this path rather than another, promptly vanishing into a puff of obsolescence once her task had been performed? And here I sit, ungratefully typing out gripes about why I am where I am, unaware of the calamity I've been heroically saved from living.

Gut instinct is tricky. When we listen to it, and say no, often it is in defiance of perfectly reasonable evidence that we should say yes. And certainly the opposite is true. Uncountable times my gut made me say yes when my mind knew damn well to say no, and things predictably went south.

Yet there is part of me that believes in the power of patterns. If we say no too often, we become accustomed to it. No becomes our default, more instinctive than yes. How many opportunities do we miss when no outnumbers yes? Of course, the reverse argument could be made.

It all has to do with one's outlook on serendipity, I suppose. Despite having been burned, I nonetheless tend to trust the universe when it puts things in my path. Perhaps that's naïve. Lord knows I have the scars to prove it. But I also have treasured memories of chances taken, life experienced. And even when the yes didn't meet my expectations, I still believe the failed attempt was better than an outright no.

Maybe that's because I've been lucky, unlike some of the Annas postulated above. Or maybe I've made my own luck by saying yes where others might have said no. It's impossible to say, and I'm certainly not going to suggest that everything turns out peachy keen by hurling oneself at every shiny potentiality that flashes on the scanner. But it does keep life interesting.

However, were I a television therapist or some such—and thank heaven I'm not—I might recommend at least entertaining a temporary maybe when a bogey starts blipping. You might ultimately say no, but the act of considering a yes is worth something. A vision of an alternate universe, a different you.

Who might be a miserable cow, I dunno. But it's good to dream. Said the writer who lives in her own head half the time. Take it with a grain of salt. And maybe a little spoonful of yes.

Just Say No

by Chris Dashiell

In the vacuum left by repressive organized religion, positive thinking rushed in to fill the needs of the more intelligent spiritual seekers. In practice, this was a lot more than positive thinking—a wide range of beliefs that came to be rather clumsily labeled as "New Age" rose to prominence. And the New Age quickly became an easy target for knowing scoffers. Channeling, crystals, angels, spirit guides, and so on: all so ridiculous, so infantile, not like virgin births, cripples cutting capers, and adults raving in tongues that no one ever heard of. But if for an instant one takes a look at this phenomenon with a sense of fairness, it's clear that it answers a need for something good, loving, and wholesome, something to inspire and give meaning in a world ravaged by cruel fundamentalist myths. To experience loving emotional support in a community, to give voice to joy with singing and dancing, to actually practice kindness and understanding instead of just paying it lip service: it's no wonder people would seek spirituality in such a form.

Even this way of light and love must, however, cast a shadow. If a group or belief system tries to deny the shadow, attempting, for instance, to require happiness all the time, you have the makings of cult. But with acknowledgment of grief, sorrow, and anger as necessary aspects of experience, this can be avoided. Freedom, in a real sense, is possible, yet only (and this is a sort of paradox) through hard work.

Social and political conditions present the greatest challenge to any spiritual vantage point. And I cannot escape the observation that, as far as I can tell, all the vantage points have failed. Political and economic organization on the mass level is separated from effective spiritual practices by a thick wall. The public sphere is dominated by fear, greed, and exploitation. In the United States, conditions have deteriorated to the point of incipient fascism. Society itself, as a cohesive whole rather than an assortment of atomized ego-based interests, is crumbling.

It is precisely here that I must find fault with the newer religions of love, peace and positive thinking. They are most prominent among people of progressive tendencies, many of whom are nevertheless uninterested or detached from politics. In other words, they are progressive in terms of their social attitudes, their liberality of spirit, but not in concrete political terms. Now, when an authoritarian tendency threatens the world with destruction, I still hear objections when I protest and say "No" to the policies, institutions, and prominent people who are threatening us. "I choose to live in love and not emphasize negativity." "I try to foster understanding and peace within rather than participate in this turmoil and divisiveness." I'm paraphrasing hundreds of different arguments that I've heard along these lines over the years. And they sound good. They seem plausible. It certainly feels better to be loving, positive and respectful. How wonderful if such an approach could work to change the world.

Unfortunately, it doesn't work.

My experience has been that a strictly "positive" approach ends up being a passive acquiescence in injustice. Those who are operating strictly from fear, greed, and the drive for power, are rarely able to learn from example in this way. These forces can become so big, and so corrupt, that being met with love and acceptance only provides permission to exploit further. Someone who wants to kill you and steal your home, for instance, will do so even more readily when all you're doing is sitting in the lotus position being "centered."

Even for the sake of our own internal process, and especially in the context of public life, it is often necessary to say "No" before one can adequately say "Yes." Saying no to slavery is part of saying yes to freedom. The internal part is realizing that these conditions are not acceptable, which allows one to discover gradually what conditions could be. The No and the Yes are, in effect, a necessary push-and-pull action to effect change. The No pushes against oppression, the Yes pushes forward to more creative forms of freedom.

A lot of the arguments I hear on this subject come down to a need for mental health. Negativity, as it's called, becomes a drag on the spirit. This is a reality. Activists get exhausted by their anger, their frustration. They lose sleep, and sometimes they lose hope. Here's where spirituality has something to teach us. It doesn't need to be theistic or dogmatic, it just involves a recognition of the inner realm as precious and important. Being able to enjoy living in the present moment (redundant, really, because when else are we living?) in an autonomous way, not relying too much on external validation—this is actually a good starting point for activism. We are fighting for ourselves and for loved ones and humanity as such. We are only fighting against something because of this underlying reality of *fighting for*. We can just say no to oppression in all its forms, and keep saying no vigorously, while living in a yes to love as our condition.

This is more realistic, and I think much more effective than retreating into a vapid loving state that has no energy to oppose wrongs. This is just the kind of balance we are going to need to move forward.

Just Say No

by Matthew Broyles

This is going to sound odd, but I'm just going to say it: I used to feel a lot like Nancy Reagan.

Not because I was married to a loopy old chief executive—although one day, who knows—but because, like the most prominent First Lady of my childhood, I believed very firmly in uncrossable lines.

If I said, "I will never do _____," then that was it. No reconsideration, no retractions, my line was drawn in the sand, and you might as well pour concrete on that sucker, because it ain't going anywhere.

Funny thing, though, erosion. It happens whether you're aware of it or not. As adulthood unfolded, I found that the solid foundations upon which I stood would occasionally shift, causing me to flail about, dancing from conclusion to conclusion as if an old west bandit were shooting at my feet. I had to start changing my mind. And for me, that was a big deal.

We are told that consistency is a virtue. This actually makes no sense at all. Far better for someone to be occasionally an asshole than consistently one. That we change and evolve our ideals is evidence that we are paying attention to the world around us, which has never stood still even once through all of time. Floating like a butterfly, stinging like a bee. Adaptation, without which we would still be swinging in the trees. Although there is an argument that the planet might have been better off if we had, but I digress…

Nonetheless, I have maintained a few lines that I feel safe in declaring unmovable. Abominable things like rape and torture, which I would truly rather die than commit.

Yet there are other bits of dodgy behavior I can't quite put the lifetime ban on. Theft, for instance. While I am not inclined to steal, I can easily see how I would, if a situation arose where that was the only way to feed my family. Likewise with murder. Depends very much on who and why, but saying it's completely out of the question doesn't feel honest. What wouldn't we do to protect those we care about? Very little, in my estimation.

But a change of heart needn't be triggered by some horrific turn of events. At age 22, I declared with great finality that I would never marry, that it didn't fit into my plans for life, and to hell with all that. A year later, I was planning my wedding, after meeting someone who I couldn't live without, a concept unthinkable to me only months prior.

Placing blanket "no" statements on situations in which we have yet to find ourselves is short-sighted. Firstly, it assumes that we will always be the same people that we are now. 43-year-old me is different in many key respects from 22-year-old me. I have no doubt that 63-year-old me will differ significantly from my present form. We are a bit like Time Lords, although our regenerations are gradual, like erosion, carving fresh channels into our psyche through which thoughts flow in novel and unpredictable ways.

When we leave home, we are the people our parents, friends, and experiences raised. As years go by, we cannot help but transform, shaped by the winds of life, an altered form mostly recognizable as its past self, but clearly distinct now from its previous iterations. Like the statues of antiquity, we lose our original coating, and show the scars of the barbarian hordes that have passed our way. But if we are lucky, we also carry lovingly applied bits of plaster, repairs and augmentations from people who treasure us and want us to adorn their gardens for many years to come.

Why do friends come and go? People with whom we once spent every free hour, now distant acquaintances. They remain a part of us, but over time, they change as we do, and sometimes those alterations are not complimentary. Is that a failure of friendship? Or is it merely honesty, the inevitable result of our personal evolution? I favor the latter.

Platitudes about standing firm in one's moral code set my teeth on edge. From whom did you get that moral code? Can you be certain it has all the answers? Without questioning and testing, it is only theory. For every wise old teacher, there is another who can provide a counter-example. Before we start laying down electrified fences around our behaviors, we'd better make damned sure the boundaries are drawn correctly.

And make no mistake, this is a lifelong endeavor. If I am not re-evaluating my opinions at age 93, then I have ceased to take in new information. I will have ossified in some past form. A being which has ceased to grow and adapt, for all intents and purposes, is dead, waiting only for its body to catch up with its mind and just stop functioning already.

We are human because we change. If we stop changing, we become monsters. Thus is fundamentalism explained. Attempting to impose permanent stasis on life and humanity is an act of unspeakable cruelty, not to mention impossibility. Human nature will prevail one way or another, and all the "no" in the world will turn to "yes" by and by. Only by accepting this can we hope to keep our humanity.

If there is one thing we can just say "no" to, it is absolutism. On the other hand…

Just Say No

by MC Dalet

NO:

It is a powerful word, and should not be used lightly.

It can warn.

It can deny.

It can bar doors, some of which ought to be secured.

It can save me from calamity.

It can rob me of experience.

It can collapse the possibilities.

It can divert a path and open new ones.

-- Sometimes simultaneously.

When I tell my five-year-old daughter "No," what does she hear?

Does she hear that she is wrong?

That she is bad?

Does it matter if that's what it takes to keep her from danger?

These are questions that I do not ask in the urgency of the moment.

No time to think;

Just say "No."

But I think about it afterward.

I think about all of the times I heard "No," or "You can't. . ." or

"How are you going to do THAT?"

and I heard

"You're wrong."

"You're bad."

"You will fail."

And in some ways I have failed. This is especially true when I listen to those voices too long.

This is the power of NO.

I said "no" once,

No to a Halloween party that I did not want to go to.

I love Halloween parties, but there were people. . .and I didn't want to feel good or have fun.

So I said "no". . .at first.

I opened the door to yes because my friends knocked loudly.

My friends wanted to go as a gang of pro wrestlers.

Fun.

But I didn't feel like fun.

"I don't have a costume. Not going."

I returned home from work to find a luchador mask on my dresser.

I took it as a sign, or at least an invitation from the Infinite, delivered by my buddies.

I went to the party.

I left the party with a woman now my wife.

This is the power of YES.

Two decades later, as I "no" our children,

I pause to wonder what I might deny them.

No can close borders and create boundaries, nationally and personally.

No can break a heart.

But some of my NOs have, undoubtedly, saved my life.

There's the rub.

I never know for sure till it's done.

I guess I have to choose –

Choose as wisely as I can

and trust the results are favorable,

as they have been so far.

Every choice is a story.

Every story, karma.

Every karmic tweak, the birth a new world.

NO:

It is a powerful word and should not be used lightly.

o

Trigger Warning

o

Trigger Warning

by Anna Bardin

I'll own it: When I was in junior high, I thought Def Leppard was the shit.

The phase didn't last long, but honestly one of the primary points of fascination for me was Rick Allen, their drummer. It was just a really compelling story, him losing his arm and the band rallying around him to go on and keep playing.

I remember reading an article about how he employed electronic foot triggers to play all the parts his left arm used to cover. The process of re-learning how to play was difficult, but he persevered. I mean, damn, to hell with you if you don't wanna cheer when you see a one-armed drummer rocking out despite the odds.

When I see people talk about triggers, it's almost always negative. But I like to think about the positive triggers that we carry inside of us. Humans are these dense Rube Goldberg machines full of switches and levers that, when triggered, activate yet more buttons and knobs, ad infinitum. I really don't know how we walk around all day with all that clockwork clanging around inside of us, triggered by a million different stimuli from all five senses and beyond.

When I smell freshly mown grass, I am immediately seven years old again, sitting in my grandfather's lap as he lets me steer the mower. It doesn't matter where I am when I smell it, that's where my brain goes. Sometimes I've been on my way to the office, and upon getting a whiff from a median or passing lawn, I have to somehow wrench my head out of the reverie and re-enter the moment of time and space I am actually supposed to be occupying to get my job done.

I dated a guy once who hit all my good triggers, and it was getting pretty serious until one day he showed up wearing Old Spice. Suddenly all of my romantic instincts rebelled, because a male presence imbued with that scent is a paternal trigger for me, not an amorous one. I'm not sure I ever quite got over the shock, frankly, and although it wasn't the main reason the relationship got terminated, I can't say it wasn't a factor. But if an older gentleman is wearing it, I have to say, I tend to get a twinge of longing for my departed dad, and might spend more time talking to the fragrant individual than I might otherwise.

I am sensitive to sun angles, because of the various cities I grew up in. Low summer sun is Omaha. Bright winter sun is Shreveport. Traveling for me is not just physical, it's mental transportation to times and places often unconnected with the actual location.

There are colors that they don't make anymore, but that were everywhere in the

1970s. Bright greens and loud oranges, plaids that defy geometric description. When on occasion I see one of these colors or patterns, generally in thrift stores, I'm suddenly sitting on a chocolate brown shag carpet watching H.R. Pufnstuf, hands wrapped around a cup of kool-aid. Or riding in the back of a Pacer, puke green vinyl upholstery sticking to the backs of my legs. It's a head trip and a half.

Likewise, words can trigger. When I hear someone say "expecially," I picture it coming out of the orthodontically adorned mouth of my neighbor Trudy, who said it all the time when we were kids. Or "cool beans," which when intoned immediately draws forth the smell of stale pizza and cheap cosmetics from my college roommate's half of our cramped apartment.

The truth is, all words are triggers. They're meant to be. Language doesn't work if a set of sounds doesn't conjure up corresponding thoughts. Otherwise we could not communicate. But since all of us have different histories, not all of our triggers run through the same bits of machinery. A friend of mine uses the term "god" in a very nebulous spiritual way that does not in any way refer to an anthropomorphic deity. But having been raised to understand that term very specifically, it always throws me off a bit, and I have to re-explain to myself what he means. It's no one's fault, but it is a consideration in conversation.

With so many triggers clicking in constant motion all around us, it's no wonder that some people get overwhelmed. Frankly, it's a miracle we're all more or less sane (although one could argue that). One of the items on my bucket list is immersion in a sensory deprivation tank. To experience even a few moments without triggers of any sort seems like something we probably all need from time to time.

And just like Rick Allen had to learn to play drum parts with different limbs, so too do we need to occasionally reassess the way we interact with people. If my perfume or choice of plaid pattern or vocabulary is having an effect on someone, positive or negative, I would like to know about it. Whether that knowledge will ultimately change my behaviors is hard to say, but I can't imagine not caring either way.

For if we are to live together, we must communicate, and we do so every moment in ways we aren't even aware of. I'm going to trigger people no matter what I do. But I can at least strive to make those triggers good ones.

Trigger Warning

by Marged Howley Dudek

Part I:

Fight is the response my body goes to, except when Dr. Freeze-Flight intervenes—ultraviolet-lit teeth and Schwarzenegger sneer—to ensure that I scream at inappropriate times and try to stay as still as possible while also wishing I had mole teeth with which to disappear. And all because a pilot-in-training at Camp Bowie is having an afternoon lesson. Poor guy (chances are nil it's a chick amirite?) has no idea. Nor should he.

Whatever. You get used to it. Except when it starts fraying and then destroying the lives of your loved ones. Then you drag your sorry ass to AA and to therapy, and to whatever else you need to, because every time a news rag salaciously drips child rape-this and daddy murder-that all over the front page you can't lose your shit. You just can't.

It sure doesn't make one like other people, though. I used to like other people. In the years when I was dissociative, before emotions had to be had, I really got along well with people. Now that I am having to relate to myself, I loathe others. There are six people I like. Everyone else—including many family members—are regarded with antipathy or (at best) a sort of distant fondness which I fear direct engagement would dissolve.

Part II:

Filtering your feed is everything when anxiety and PTSD are your companions, and that refers not only to Facebook but to internal attitudes and self-talk. Allowing bald bitterness such as the ruckus above is fine in small doses, but too much of it, and it becomes its own trigger, leading inevitably to another episode of "making mischief of one kind or another," with consequences not nearly adorable as becoming King of the Wild Things. Filter your Internal Feed; Be Ye Men of Even Temper. Synapses and hormones have been permanently set to 11, and you are your own vigilant amp-keeper. When you hate, you must consciously turn up the joy channel in response. When you worry into the 3ams with your fingers bloody stumps, you must take a bath and a nap somewhere in the 1pms. If you do not do this management, your husband may suffer a bruised eye. Your mother may suffer your funeral. When you get triggered you must learn to walk, and walking is the hardest thing to do. I am good at beating people up, and running, and hiding in closets, and so bad at a steady, upright walk. Now I am old, it's time to do that. "These orthopedic shoes were made for walking, and that's just what they'll do; one of these days they're going to support another poor soul struggling the way I do."

Part III:

It's all very Dylan-Thomas-meets-the-Tao: "gently-not-gently go: that is the Way." For, if you don't acknowledge the depth of your ocean, you will always fight it. Every time you fight your pain, you will drown, and every time luck lets you be reborn you will know as little as you did before. But if you both feel what you are feeling and reign it in, you learn to swim. It's a theory. Right now I'm in the thick of swimming lessons. Each day in the water is a cut, though. I don't know how to explain it. Healing is sorrow. One day may I no longer remember to be grateful (healing and forgetting seem to coincide?) to those considerate enough to write:

TW

.

.

.

.

.,

but until then, please know how much it means that you'd help a stranger regain her sea legs.

Thank you.

Trigger Warning

by Matthew Broyles

It always sneaks up on me.

Last year, I was reading David Mitchell's *The Bone Clocks*, a perfectly speculative novel about all the things his novels tend to be about. All was going well until I got to the chapter about the war correspondent in Baghdad circa 2003. Though the story was fictional, and the point was not the war, but the inner lives of the characters, I found myself getting angrier and angrier the longer I read, until finally I had to put the book down. I couldn't make myself open it again for a week. The references therein had transported my mind to a very dark place that it had occupied during those years, and I was re-living that time in my head, in a very disorienting and disturbing way. It was a trigger.

To be clear, I did not serve in Iraq or Afghanistan. The biggest fights I've ever been in were while I was wearing pads and overseen by a karate instructor. But the political awakening I experienced in the run-up to the Iraq War shook up my psyche from the roots, turning me into a voracious consumer of news and historical research. In those dark days when speaking against the war was considered tantamount to offering the 9/11 hijackers a medal, I dove deep into the dark underbelly of our national neuroses, and became inflamed with rage at the prospect of entering another Vietnam, or worse.

Losing that fight, protest marches and calls to congresscritters all in vain, sent me into a deep funk, solidified by the re-election of Incurious George the following year. I gave up on humanity, at a time when I was having a lot of trouble even believing in myself.

I certainly remember feeling bad at the time, but I suppose I did not realize quite how traumatic it was until I read Mitchell's book so many years later. A few chapters into William Gibson's *Pattern Recognition* a few months ago, I had the same experience as he went off on a tear about the then-fresh ascendancy of the neocons. Trembling, I had to put the book down.

Even writing this, it sounds silly to me. I had no close friends or family who died in that conflict. I certainly wasn't anywhere near it. But as I am often reminded, I'm a bit of a canary in a coalmine when it comes to disasters. My empathy nodes are overactive, and I'm prone to flinching even when the punch is being thrown at someone else.

Although…

I may make someone uncomfortable here, and certainly don't mean to, but I won't use names. A friend of mine who I follow on Facebook is married to person whose name and countenance makes my fists clench involuntarily. Someone who made my life hell on the school bus from 4th grade through early high school. It's a trigger, seeing him smiling in her pics, though I'm certain both he and I have changed significantly enough in the intervening years that such a grudge makes no sense.

Except it's not really a grudge. There's a little switch, set decades ago, that pops whenever that name and face come up. It's a defense mechanism set up for very good reason, and which doesn't realize its usefulness has come to an end. Veterans and other friends with PTSD report similar experiences; a disconnect between their instinctive responses and the actual severity of the situation in front of them, which they know logically is perfectly harmless. But that trigger gets activated regardless.

I won't go as far as saying I have PTSD, because what I experience with these triggers has not even come close to having destructive effects on my life, as actual PTSD symptoms have for so many. But I do feel like I understand the phenomenon at least a little.

So when I hear people berating calls for trigger warnings, it rubs me the wrong way. It is the epitome of the "it didn't happen to me, so it's not real" delusion that so many of us carry. A good friend of mine used to get triggered when she saw police lights, for reasons that would break your heart if you knew them. After years of intensive therapy, that trigger lost its sting, but for a lot of people, that sort of problem doesn't get addressed the way it should.

We know that stress kills. When the human body operates with even a low level of stress and anxiety consistently humming in the background, normal functions are disrupted, and resources are expended to deal with it that could have been spent on pursuing that which makes life livable. It's one more thing on the pile, and the burden is not distributed evenly amongst the population, despite the insistence I hear from libertarians and other bootstrap-humpers.

Would it really hurt us to take claims of triggers at face value? What do we lose by being considerate to the sensitivities of others? The ability to say whatever we damn well want to, perhaps. But surely we already know that words are situational. You don't give a hearty "Good morning, schmuck," to your grandmother like you might to, let's say, your drummer. We alter our behaviors based on the audience, and that is totally appropriate.

Having a trigger doesn't make you a weak person. It means you've seen some shit. And adding the fear of being considered freakish on top of that shit just makes it that much heavier.

Don't pull the trigger unless you mean to shoot.

o

Fight or Flight

o

Fight or Flight

by Anna Bardin

Despite the fact that most of my heroines are brave warrior women, the truth is that in a lot of ways, I'm kind of a chicken.

If a choice arises between an arduous fight and a workaround, I'll most often take the workaround. I like to think that's because I work smart rather than hard, but if I'm honest, it's also because I really, really hate conflict.

I'm not really sure why. I wasn't beaten or psychologically abused as a child, at least not any more than your average '70s-'80s kid. I suppose I just see fighting as something that gets in between me and my interests, so when I encounter a fracas, I just take the long way around.

Obviously, this doesn't always work. There are times when, in order to reach a particular goal, one must confront those who actively block access to that destination. When that happens, I am perfectly capable of rising to the occasion and kicking the shins of the obstacles until they're sorry they ever thought getting in my way was a good idea. But I don't like doing it.

As discussed here before, this is why the current political climate distresses me. I don't want to have to fight. I just want to sit in my comfy chair and write my little stories. But I also understand that this is a privilege, one that I have done nothing to earn, other than being born white and middle class. Though it goes against my instincts, I am fighting wherever I can.

Resenting the need to fight is indicative of my raising, though. Most people throughout history have accepted fighting as a part of life, many going so far as to actively pursue proficiency at it as a basic survival skill. Coming of age in the arms of empire, and with maybe a little too much time spent watching Woodstock, Sesame Street, and other sorts of hippie propaganda, I thought the world was moving into the post-conflict age, where we would solve our differences in civilized ways.

I wasn't prepared for the sheer amount of meanness in the world. Everyday, common malice, much more destructive cumulatively than capital-e Evil, which is more easily identifiable and therefore simpler to target. Even now, when someone at the grocery store is casually cruel to a clerk, I stand there dumbfounded, as if they were a three-headed alien. What makes a person crave the humiliation of another? Someone they don't even know?

But then, I remember stories friends have told of arbitrarily callous parents, malevolent older siblings, and bullies that bestrode their young world like bogeymen, lurking around every corner to dismantle whatever remnants of self-esteem the poor kids had left. I mean, I knew those people, but I could almost always get away from them. Imagining a life where I couldn't…I shudder to think what a different person I would be now.

It's alarming, that this is apparently the world I've been living in all this time, taking place outside the little broom closet where I whistle contentedly to myself, blissful in my ignorance of so much suffering just beyond my door. It makes me angry at myself for letting it all happen. For not fighting.

Yet I do fight. The lengths I have gone to in order to remain a part of my niece and nephew's life are not insubstantial. Giving a leg up to friends and family, comforting distressed loved ones, being there when no one else can be…these are ways to fight the darkness, to make a world where meanness and indifference do not take over completely. As long as I live, the ones I care about will have an advocate. The fact that I can't be there for absolutely everyone is simple math, and berating myself for that makes no sense.

Still, as we stride forward into this combative era, I'm making a vow to question my flight instinct more often. I can see that there will be more and more times when my default inclination to hide in my garret will be the wrong choice for the situation. I would like to think that one day, we will emerge out of the rubble and be able to pick up where we left off, going about our various interests without the need for protests and vigilant watchdogging as the foxes loot the henhouse.

I don't know if I believe it. But I would like to think it.

Fight or Flight

by Eva Moon

Immigration Lottery to be Replaced by Gladiatorial Games

by Eva Moon, AP - February 24, 2017: 2:16 PM ET

After a twenty-seven year history, the Diversity Visa Program (commonly known as the Immigration Lottery) is drawing to a close. Originally intended to promote diversity by making available 50,000 permanent resident visas annually to natives of countries deemed to have low rates of immigration to the United States, the program has been determined to be a security risk. At a press conference today, the President announced that he would clean up the mess created by Obama in 1990 which is allowing "millions of very bad hombres" into the country. "Literally millions," he stated. "I've heard that from a lot of people."

In an unprecedented move, the President issued an Executive Order for what is being called the "Fight or Flight" program that finally lays out the long-awaited details of "Extreme Vetting." According to the EO, a new department of "Bread and Security" (BS) will be created and empowered to process refugees and others hoping to immigrate to the U.S. All applicants will be transported to a secure island in an undisclosed location where they will be housed and fed, at their own expense, until each can be individually "vetted" in hand-to-hand combat against a Navy Seal in a newly constructed "Vetting Arena." The vetting will be monitored by observers who pay $200,000 each for the privilege of watching Democracy in action.

Applicants who survive the vetting ordeal will be deemed dangerous undesirables and immediately put on a flight back to their country of origin. The rest will be provisionally admitted to the U.S. for interment or cremation. When fake journalists from failing news outlets questioned the high expected cost of the new program, the White House promised that construction of the Arena and adjacent facilities would be paid for in full by the immigration applicants, themselves.

Opponents of the new program are calling it an "appalling circus." When they likened it to the gladiatorial games of Ancient Rome, the President welcomed the comparison. "Ancient Rome was the birthplace of Democracy. It's true. The birthplace. Anyone who is against my great plan is against Democracy. Maybe even a terrorist. Honestly, you have to wonder about their loyalty. Maybe we ought to vet them. Just saying!"

When it was pointed out that Athens, Greece was the birthplace of Democracy, the president was unfazed. "More lies by the corrupt media."

In an effort to quell rising outrage from relatives of hopeful immigrants, the Administration will offer bread vouchers and a limited number of free tickets to the games.

Following the press conference, the President embarked on a triumphant motorcade parade through the streets of Washington DC accompanied by legions of supporters, trucks displaying gold, priceless artworks looted from the White House and a replica of the Manhattan Trump Tower built entirely out of boxes Ivanka Trump Eau de Cologne(™).

Fight or Flight

by Matthew Broyles

I hate when I get that feeling. Where I know I've just made a critical error, whether in navigation or judgment, and I find myself in a place where I am not at all safe. It's unnerving in a very peculiar way, because I tend to live my life in such a fashion as to avoid threats to my personal safety.

Obviously that's never foolproof, but in the moment when I realize that the scale has definitely tipped into danger, my guts seize up and suddenly all of my senses become fantastically acute. I hear every creak, see every shadow, and my awareness of the disposition of all my limbs snaps into tight focus. I am ready to do one of two things, should a threat materialize.

I have been fortunate enough that none of those situations has ever resulted in grievous bodily harm, but I know that's not because of anything but dumb luck. I hate that feeling so much that I spend a possibly inordinate amount of time making sure I don't have to feel it.

Still, life is not a bounce house, and danger arises from unexpected vectors. Once, on a walk through Central Park, I found myself in need of a restroom. Serious business, not something to be managed by simply ducking behind a bush. Finding one of the park's rare bathroom facilities, I set about my task, not thinking about the fact that it was dusk outside and there were no other patrons around.

Thus, when the bathroom door opened, I didn't register it at first. Only upon noting the slow, deliberate tread of the beat-up sneakers on the tile did I observe that something might be amiss. Especially when I realized that they were headed straight to my stall.

My heart pounded in my ears as the man—I could tell from the heavy breathing that it was a man—came to a stop right in front of the closed stall door. I cast my gaze around under the walls, confirming that I was indeed alone. Oh shit, I thought, this is how it ends. Alone in a New York crapper, with my pants down. Pat Robertson will love it.

The survival instincts I normally shove to the bottom of the pile suddenly sprang forth. DO SOMETHING, they shouted. WHAT? I yelled back. Looking around, I could find no weapons. Breath damn near stopped, I thought desperately that maybe if he burst through the door, I could grab one of the products of my emptied bowels and hurl it in his face while I made my getaway. It was not the proudest moment of my life, but at the time, I wasn't entirely sure I had much life left.

Finally, bubbling up from the depths of my subconscious, the voice of my father surged forth. Channeling the memories of countless showdowns, ire brandished like Excalibur, I let the old man take over my vocal chords.

"Can I HELP YOU?????" I barked, with a bite that surprised even me.

The interloper stumbled backwards at least two feet, taken aback by the sudden outburst, a challenge to whatever scenario his probably addled mind was playing out.

"What the FUCK do you WANT???" I bit out, pulse pounding, righteous rage taking the place of the immobilizing fear that had held me hostage seconds before.

Turning on his heel, the unknown adversary made for the door, which clanged shut behind him, leaving me once again all alone.

The story is funny to me now, but at the time, it took me quite a while to quell the adrenaline rush that had overtaken my shuddering body.

Years later, back in Texas, I took a rare night off of kidwatching to go have an adult beverage at a local watering hole. I'd never been there, didn't know anyone, just wanted to be surrounded by sights and sounds that didn't originate from PBS Kids. Snorfling down a bourbon on the rocks, I took note of the shot that had sat in front of the adjacent barstool since I'd gotten there.

"Does that belong to someone?" I asked the bartender.

He shook his head.

"Guy left," he said. "Didn't pay his tab, either. You might as well drink it."

Sounded like a good idea to me, so I downed the glass, smacking it back down on the bar...

...just in time to see the shot's owner come striding up.

Thick neck, dull eyes, sportsball jersey, exactly the type of guy I avoid at all costs. And here I had just stolen his shot.

"Hey, man," I offered, gamely. "The bartender said you'd left, I didn't know..."

"Really?" he said, unimpressed.

"Here, let me buy you another one," I said, waving over the idiot bartender—who by the way made no move to corroborate my story.

The guy stood there for a minute, sizing me up. I hate being sized up. I know what size I am, and it's highly breakable. The shot was delivered, and I placed it right where the former one had been. After a long moment, the dude seized the drink, downed it, and plunked it back down on the wood with a rather deliberate thud. To my relief, he ambled over to the pool tables.

My blood pressure lowered, at least until I got into the car. Upon pulling out of the parking lot, I saw a white Mustang hot on my tail, the familiar face of the mook sitting in the passenger seat, pointing at me while his buddy drove right up on my arse as I roared up onto the access ramp. Blurry with drink and fear, I hit the gas, but the dudebros stayed fast on my bumper as we barreled down the highway. Blessedly, I had a full tank of gas, and was prepared to drive all the way to Shreveport without stopping if necessary.

A few miles in, my erstwhile assailants got bored of the chase, and peeled off to seek hijinks elsewhere. I really don't know how much danger I was actually in, but my imagination filled in all the worst-case scenarios for me, denying a single shred of sleep that night.

It all sounds rather pitiful in hindsight. But for someone who lives in their own head most of the time, the intrusion of real-world threats to life and limb is cacophonous. It's one of the reasons I do not welcome our new state of political affairs, living as I do down the street from the brownshirt recruitment office (otherwise known as a Baptist church). I know good and well that I'm fooked if the shit goes down on a combat level.

Yet part of me remembers that day in the Central Park restroom. If pressed, monkeys will fling poo at anyone who attacks them. I'd like to think that if I do get taken down, the other guy will at least have some serious cleaning up to do.

o

Us and Them

o

Us and Them

by Anna Bardin

I remember it too clearly.

The moment when the walls shifted, instantly, and to my surprise, I found myself standing outside their protective embrace, not within, from where the stones were being hurled.

It was 7th grade, and I had defended the wrong person.

No greater crime existed, I knew that. But in a moment of unthinking compassion, I told Emily, the head mean girl, to leave Lucy alone. Lucy, the orphan with the big braces and the nasally voice, who had enough problems without the taunts from the high priestesses of popularity.

I had only barely slipped in behind those walls myself, quiet and bookish as I was. The absence of any prominent disfigurement or speech impediment had kept me under their radar, and via a casual friendship with Janee, a lower lieutenant, I had smuggled myself behind enemy lines, safe from the neverending barrage of bile poured from their battlements.

But no longer. For defending Lucy, I was stripped of my credentials and tossed out like the social leper I dared to empathize with. Who didn't even rise to my defense as Emily berated me in front of the whole cafeteria, branding me unworthy and disgusting in no uncertain terms. My cheeks burned as the reality sank in that no cavalry was coming.

No knights appeared in the crowd, not even Billy, who up until that moment had been angling hard for my attentions. He turned his face away, unwilling to witness my humiliation, and certainly not anxious to share my fall from grace.

I would like to say that it was like the movies. That I pulled myself up straight and delivered the killer line that put Emily and her coven of cackling bitchwitches in their place. Or at least threw a milk carton at her evil, pretty face, ruining her carefully coiffed perm.

I would really like to say that. But I can't.

What I can say is that I did not speak to anyone for a good solid week after my public dressing-down. Not my parents, not the neighbor kids, no one. I was done with the real world, and lived in my journals, writing terrible rip-off fantasy tales where the heroine kept killing the dragon that would not die. I'm not even sure I knew it was an allegory. Mostly it was a place where I was in charge of reality. For in real life, where sticking up for the little people got you nothing but punishment, there was nothing I wanted anymore. Nothing the world could do for me that I couldn't do for myself, in my own head.

A week to the day after the incident, I came home to find a package addressed to me. This was unusual, and I had to scupper off to my room to dodge my mom's nosy glare before I opened it. Unsealing the roughly taped package, my eyes popped to see a not-inexpensive assortment of chocolates inside. A note affixed to the bottom of the chocolate container read, in feminine hand, "Thanks."

I knew it had to be from Lucy, and that she didn't have much disposable cash from whatever funds the orphanage gave her. I was simultaneously touched and mortified that this was the only way she felt she could express her gratitude. Clearly she didn't want to risk soiling my reputation even more by talking with me in front of people. The thought sank my heart, and I resolved to talk to her the next day, consequences be damned.

It turned out I was bracing for the wrong consequences. If Lucy (whose name is not Lucy) ever recognizes herself in this essay, I would like to offer her an apology. Adolescence in the Reagan era had not prepared me for the possibility of a girl-on-girl crush, and I'm afraid I reacted with a great deal more shock and alarm than I would now. Ahem.

Now fully alienated from everyone, I watched as what had once been Us spent the rest of the school year treating me like Them, and I retreated into the alternate realities within whose walls I still largely reside.

I don't fear the other, necessarily. But even in adult life, I am acutely aware of how quickly and often arbitrarily alliances can shift. I'm not willing to join any teams. Not that much has changed in human behavior since junior high, so far as I can tell. *looks pointedly at the White House*

Us is me. The rest of you will always, on some level, be Them. It's not personal. Just real. It's much easier for me to love humanity at a distance. Doesn't mean we can't have some damn good times together, so long as I keep my ejection seat handy. Let's party.

Us and Them

by Cristee Cook

I should say upfront that I'm one of *those* people. I believe in and seek out spirituality. This takes the form of Astrology, Angels, Earth energy, ancient religious/spiritual texts, and energy healing. I don't just believe in them, I use many of these tools to navigate my life. I've tried some crazy things on the path to self-improvement. I've had some incredible experiences, and some that while well meaning, resulted in additional chaos. Still, I was created with this chip. It's in my DNA. Some of my earliest memories confirm that I look to something bigger to explain my existence. I have a difficult time accepting things at face value.

Therefore, the concept of "Us and Them" is one I'm hoping we can eradicate. Unity sounds like a great idea. It's a beautiful word and a powerful consciousness to work toward. But at times, I feel the "Us and Them" mentality is impermeable*.

*Here I want to change the word *and* to *versus* – no – *vs.* I think the abbreviated version of the word indicates a battle. Both sides have something to prove. Both push and fight for rightness and vindication.

Let's make a list:

Rich vs. Poor

Race vs. Race

Religion vs. Religion

Truth vs. Lies

North vs. South

East vs. West

STEM vs. Fine Arts

I imagine you'll add a few. Separation is afoot.

I was watching a class last week, and the teacher described living a spiritual life as watching life with subtitles. The image landed. I'll experience a day designed solely to piss me off: crazy, life-threatening drivers, an unexpected bill, an argument with a loved one, and long wait times or numerous, annoying obstacles. On good days, my thoughts run something like: *Well, it's the first day of Cancer*, or *there were 3 earthquakes last week*, or *it's a Full Moon and last night we had an Eclipse*. I seek the bigger picture. Sometimes I feel it comes with a price. The battle rages with knowing there is an explanation for chaos around you, vs. not having a negative reaction to the chaos around you.

Things happen in life that are incomprehensible. Trying to look at a situation based on facts, always looking for the truth, means relinquishing judgements that I'm quite comfortable with. A contemporary example is it's easier to view a Republican Senator as a misogynist based on an internet meme versus researching the claims from numerous sources, and then making a personal conclusion. On bad days, this is the tape: *Well, I've seen this like 5 times today, this must be true. That's the whole story, I'm sure of it. It must be true if this person is posting it. I can't believe this guy would do that…*before long I'm anxious, angry, and disenfranchised. Separate. I begin to see nothing but the flaws around me. Things start to piss me off.

I had a friend tell me once that there is no "Us vs. Them." He was responding to my frustrations about communication in my workplace. I was up in arms. *Why doesn't this person take responsibility instead of running every decision through the higher-ups? Why aren't our ideas being utilized? Why all this change?* My friend's demeanor remained calm as he reminded me that while we are based in different geographical locations, we are a part of one organization working toward the same goals. "There is no Us vs. Them."

My perspective expanded in that moment. I got a widescreen slow pan of my current movie, and saw how through my own ignorance and resistance to change, I had created unnecessary separation. I had created pain for myself. I was upset, and committed to remaining so. The truth? Half of the things I was pissed off about weren't even true.

I want to say that I am far from enlightened. I am self-aware, and I have a desire to be a positive force in the world. I hope that after I finish writing this, I'll be able to cross one line from the list of "Us vs. Them" that I've acquired. But I don't think it will be easy.

Us and Them

by Matthew Broyles

It's one of the first things we learn. This is your mom, this is your dad, these are your grandparents, and so on. This is your family.

So who are all these other people? Well, they're not our family. Don't talk to them unless we say it's okay. They might be dangerous.

These boundaries are set up for good reasons. As a parent, I understand the necessity of categorizing people into simplistically defined groups to ease a child's navigation of the complex world they live in. They're the training wheels of socialization.

The problem is that as childhood gives way to adolescence, and thence to young adulthood, too often we do not take the training wheels off. A teenager, and certainly a young adult, can make more subtle assessments of humans beyond family and strangers. Beyond us and them.

But of course by that point, parents are not the only influences defining the categories. Peers carry their own internal charts and graphs as to who belongs to what group and why. These assumptions are reinforced by de facto geographic and economic environments that keep the strangers even more strange, because we seldom actually meet them.

I do it myself. I walk into a room, and my mind makes a broad array of judgments, all instinctive and involuntary:

* Older white guy in camo – Republican, avoid.
* Woman with big eyes and flowing floral blouse – Overtalker, avoid.
* Young guy in sports jersey – Dudebro, avoid.
On and on.

Yet I have friends—some very good ones—who, by those visual gauges, fit easily into those categories. But because I have spent time getting to know all the various facets of these friends, I see that they are more than what they project externally. As are many of us.

I would say "as are all of us," except that I know so many people who present themselves in such a way as to broadcast the personality they have selected from the catalog our society offers. This is yet another obstacle to cross-pollination between social groups— the fact that many of us have elected to take on a preset cultural identity, with all the do's and don'ts inherent therein. When we think as a group, we assume everyone else does, too. And sadly, we are usually right.

We have a culture that talks a lot about individuality, but in practice, humans still tend to herd. We see someone we aspire to be, and array our lives with the accoutrements that we believe might make us be more like that person.

When I walk through my house, the full bookshelves and eclectic assortment of artwork reinforces my sense that I am the sort of person who has these things. Which is who? An intellectual, a creative thinker, a learned man. To someone whose aspirations differ from those, that environment signals something very different. Snobbery, pretention, soft city folk. Someone they'd rather not be.

I can relate. When I enter a home with no books, I feel as if I've wandered into an alternate universe. The Spock Goatee timeline, or worse. How can someone with no books in their house have anything in common with me? And yet, I have had some very engaging conversations with people whose particular areas of wisdom do not lend themselves to transmission via the written word. But to discover that, I first had to defeat the guardian at my own gate.

We're all prone to searching for the enemy outside the walls. We were raised to keep an eye out for them. The people who aren't us. How strange it is when we find, to our astonishment, that our greatest adversary might lie within ourselves. And that in order to see others as they truly are, we have to short-circuit our own inbuilt defense mechanisms, which show us what we expect, rather than what is.

It's one of the hardest things any of us can do. But in the end, it may be the only thing that can save us all.

○

Cage Match: Information vs. Knowledge

○

Cage Match: Information vs. Knowledge

by Dr. Adrian L. Cook

The cage match is a specific kind of drama. It is heightened drama. Whether one is watching Tina Turner preside over post-apocalyptic fights to the death in the fictional Thunderdome, chilling with the "bros" to watch UFC, or taking in the masculine soap opera of professional wrestling, the cage match presents what one of my writing mentors described as the perfect formula for exploring conflict between characters: place two or more characters with irreconcilable motives into a space from which they cannot escape, turn up the heat, and watch it cook. In the typical cage match, this formula is applied to a physical context, reducing (and simultaneously elevating?) the drama to its purest primal form. Beat or be beaten, kill or be killed. Is this really the relationship we have established between information and knowledge? Perhaps it is. In all branches of learning, from the sciences to the humanities, the former is the precursor, the raw materials for the latter. Ironically, the overabundance of information has, in the digital age, seemingly obscured rather than enhanced knowledge.

As a scholar of the humanities, I think I have a bit of ethos going for me here, so I'll dive right in. Information is descriptive. Information includes facts, processes, and measurements -- quantifiable information. Information provides facts but not meaning. Knowledge includes meaning and context. It is interpretive. I cannot know what the information MEANS until I process it through my experience AND view it in context with other bits of information. If I have KNOWLEDGE of something (like American literature, say), it means that I am well-read in the subject, and what is more, I have an awareness of trends, historical precedents, and patterns attendant to this subject. KNOWING something goes beyond having bits of information; it involves organizing and contextualizing that information. In my example here, it is one thing to have read Frederick Douglass' *Narrative of the Life of an American Slave*, it is another to understand how Douglass' narrative charged the abolitionist movement (particularly as it was "written by Himself," thus humanizing the slave); it is quite another to KNOW how Douglass' *Narrative* synthesizes the genres of eighteenth and nineteenth-century American literature and sets a future trajectory for the American literary ethos. In short, it is context and comparison only that transforms information into knowledge.

In the beginning of our pursuit of the Truth, information and knowledge were synonymous. As a species, humans are endowed with metacognition, so we want to know how things work. When we set out on the road of discovery -- making observations, asking questions like "what?," "when?," "where?," "how many?" "in what order?" – we began to gather information, which, if you know nothing about a subject or phenomenon, also represents knowledge because the information about a phenomenon (like how the moon changes its look more frequently than Madonna) provides one with some context around the event. Ergo, the more information we have, the greater degree to which knowledge becomes a separate thing. This is why the history of academia is the story of several separate disciplines emerging from the singularity of the "liberal arts," the pursuit of liberation through accessing bit of information to form knowledge. This singularity, within which, for example, the search for theological truth was synonymous with scientific inquiry, gave rise to several different fields of study and mastery because the more we learned, the greater DEPTH of KNOWLEDGE each branch held.

Diving into a specific knowledge requires one to gather as much information about a single phenomenon or subject as possible, especially – and this is the kicker – if there is contradictory or competing information. If one desires knowledge, one goes looking for contradictory information. In fact, the space of disagreement is often the womb from which knowledge is born. It is certainly the space from which advancements in knowledge emanate. When we know what we don't know. . .or don't know for sure. . .it is then that we are hot on the trail of gaining the knowledge we seek. For instance, many principles of quantum physics were established because scientists and mathematicians understood that conventional models (even many of Einstein's revolutionary ones) simply could not account for all the variables at play in our physical universe. Spiritual masters often find their connection to the infinite by first rejecting conventional knowledge or values and then embracing the space between – the central, or middle, way – one foot in the physical, one foot in the spiritual.

If pieces of information are the building blocks of knowledge, what's the problem? We need both, right? Yes. But confuse the two, and you've got a fight on your hands. Place the confusion in cyberspace, where millions of users mistake information for knowledge, and internalize small bits of the picture as a complete truth, and use these finite pictures as strongholds; things start ricocheting around in the digital sphere, and you've got a cage match on your hands. The rise of the Internet signaled the culmination, the final stage of the Information Age. It's great. But pay attention to the name. Names are important. Nobody ever called it the Age of Knowledge. Information masquerades as knowledge here, and we claim to know what we don't know and go after each other for not seeing sense. The conflict redoubles, and it's straight-up Wrestlemania.

Speaking of Wrestlemania. . .there was a cage match, back in the 90s...This may be standard (I've since lost track of WWE), but in one of those Golden Era cage matches, the cage was a giant dome. At the top there was a door. The goal: get to the door; keep everyone else down. Make no mistake: right now information is beating the shit out of knowledge in the cyber-cage and in the Fleshworld. But information and knowledge are tools of humanity. WE are the ones throwing the punches. It is easy, even for the seasoned scholar, to drown in the deluge of information. I'm having trouble sorting through it all. The only way I can keep my head in the game is by remembering that I'm looking for knowledge. And that takes time.

It is a slow climb to the top of the cage, to reach the door; but once you are there, you are looking at the whole bloody mess from the outside. From there you can observe the PATTERNS of information bouncing around and begin to build knowledge. . .and perspective.

Another thing: it is very, very difficult to get out of the cage by yourself. Standing on each others' shoulders -- that gets us to the top pretty quick. Then we can lift each other through the hole in the top. To do this, we have to work together, and we have to listen. And we have to know that there is so much information to be had that each of us can grab a different handful. When combined, each person's collection builds another rung of the ladder that gets us to the top. So help me out of the cage. Then go to your corner. Gather more of the information that is important to you. Then, when we've finished creating our knowledge, we can share it. Standing with our feet on the ground. Outside the cage. And let's not tweet our understandings to each other. Let's meet for coffee, so we can look each other in the face. Information is static. Human knowledge is dynamic. It shines through the eyes.

Cage Match: Information vs. Knowledge

by Anna Bardin

I am of two minds. We all are.

They intersect and communicate all the time, but because of their functions, they remain separate. Handily, our explorations into machine minds have given us an easily understood designation for these discrete realms: RAM and ROM.

Whether by necessity or unconscious design, our mechanical computers divide their capacities between the data they are currently processing and that which they have stored for future use. One could easily label these two classifications "information" and "knowledge."

Everything we have ever seen, heard, smelled, or felt is information. But only a certain subsection of that information is stored in any kind of retrievable form, becoming knowledge. Often we don't make the conscious choice of which items will be tucked away in the ROM, but sometimes we do. Percentages are difficult to divine with any accuracy, but I would say that the vast majority of the information that has ever passed through my RAM got tossed out within weeks or months of its insertion. We don't need to remember twenty years' worth of tire maintenance details, or haircut appointments, or even Law & Order episodes.

The things we keep as knowledge can be telling. Think of all the compliments you have ever received. Now think of all the criticisms. Is one or the other of those more distinct, more easily accessed? Consider all the things you get right every day. Then recall something you did wrong this week. Which one pops more readily to mind?

Sometimes information becomes knowledge due to repetition. If you are told you have pretty eyes enough times, it becomes knowledge, and perhaps blasé by its common mention. But then someone says you remind them of their beloved late sister, and that statement becomes instant knowledge because of its unique character. We remember both the monotonous and the singular.

If we had complete control over what we stored in ROM and what we didn't, how many important bits of knowledge would never get saved? The other day I made a valuable contribution to a troubled friend's deliberations because of something I learned in Sunday school, a fair amount of which I have deliberately tried to excise from my data banks.

We don't always know what we need. But does our brain? Why do I need to recall the Southtown Ford jingle from three decades ago? Or my home phone number from third grade? It would seem far more important to remember what size my air conditioner filter is, or when exactly that big project at work is due, Tuesday or Thursday, I know it's one of those…or the name of the lady I keep running into in the bathroom, Elaine, Emily, something with an E…

Half the reason why we have not yet engineered a fully sentient machine brain is because we're still struggling to understand the organic one we already have. What if we build in the same sort of nonsensical categorization of essential and disposable information that our own minds employ? What kind of memory salad might we inadvertently create in our mechanical proteges?

I believe that we fear artificial intelligence because deep down, we know that we are crazy. And that if something outside of our control is just as crazy as we are, then we are truly screwed. In fact, I believe that's why we fear other people. Namaste. The crazy is me recognizes the crazy in you. Now get the hell away from me.

So we have information and knowledge. Wherefore wisdom? Here, possibly, is the key to taming the madness of the human mind. As we sift knowledge from information, so too can we sift wisdom from knowledge. And if we are one of those lucky individuals who can front-load wisdom as a filter for information, then we stand a chance at being more than the sum of our neuroses. Most of us never reach that goal, but those who do are the ones upon which the hopes of our civilization must be pinned.

Our brain is the cage. In the war between information and knowledge, the only reliable referee is wisdom. Ready, set, fight.

Cage Match: Information vs. Knowledge

by Ashley Van Arsdel

It is difficult to separate information and knowledge, because the two feed into each other, like rivers into the ocean. Yet, they are two very separate rivers, among the many which flow in our minds.

Information is fact that we acquire from various sources. We can choose to absorb information from sources we know are blatantly false, such as Breitbart, and then we are full of misinformation. The best way to make a decision is based on reliable information from a reputable source. Otherwise, bad information, or misinformation, is akin to an opinion – more than likely, one that would confirm a bias we already held. A reputable source, like a work of literature, scientific findings, something verifiable, can help us weed out the misinformation and prevent it from poisoning us.

It is easy for this to happen in the internet age of click-bait and fake news. We have to be all the more diligent to keep pollution from poisoning our streams. In George Orwell's 1984, they would rip pieces of paper out of the books and replace them with the new, government-approved information. Today, we do not have to go to such lengths. It is very easy to manipulate information now, simply with the click of a button. He who controls the past, controls the present; he who controls the present, controls the future.

Knowledge is simply information we already have, acquired through the years. I like to think it is verified and supported, but in some cases not necessarily. Knowledge also differs from intelligence. If our current knowledge changes due to some new information we are presented, do we change our outlook? Or does that require intelligence to make the distinction?

A truly smart person is capable of changing their belief on a subject when presented with irrefutable information. Those who are not-so-smart, to put it nicely, are willing to hold onto their misinformation as long as it suits their confirmation bias. There are some facts we have grown up with, i.e. Pluto being a planet and then suddenly not a planet, that have changed on us. Information is subject to change. So should knowledge be, in an ideal world.

While the two are immensely connected, their rivers flow differently to the ocean. We also see rivers like opinion and feeling flowing into that same ocean of our mind, and it can be difficult to discern fact from fiction. This is the very reason we should be careful what food we feed to our brain, and use the other river, intelligence, to sift through it all.

Cage Match: Information vs. Knowledge

by Doremus Jessup

Information is, ultimately, pretty boring when you step back from it. Information is facts. The individual facts may be fascinating, but as a whole, it's dreadfully boring. No drama, just a whole lot of isolating the confounding variables. That is what you need to know about information. There is a lot of it. Most of it is boring. All of it is disjointed. It takes a lot of work to sift through it all. It takes work and skill to sift through it well.

Knowledge is the interesting cousin to information. Knowledge is what you gain when you've learned some basic critical thinking, research, and theoretical foundations; and then begin sifting through the dull sea of information.

The 'traditional' ways of gaining knowledge are fairly well established. It involves rigorous methodology based on a solid foundation of skills. It involves, when applicable, the scientific method. It involves the application of logic to the information. It takes a long time. It is hard work. It works.

Then we have the 'non-traditional' or 'other ways of knowing.' This is short hand for non-scientific/non-rational/non-logical ways of gaining knowledge. There is some validity to this. The arts, fiction, movies, poetry, philosophy. These are other ways of knowing how others think and feel, and it are as valid as any rigorously controlled research.

Aaaaand we have the bastard step-brother: 'other ways of knowing (woo).' To know me is to know of my deep seated antipathy towards woo. Give me half a drunken rationalization and I will attack woo. OWoK*, as we will call it from here, when of the woo variety takes many shapes.

Here is a not at all authoritative list of OWoK from the school of woo.

Studying religious books of bronze/iron age myths for greater truths about the modern world. These books are great if you are such a broken person you need a book to tell you that murder, lying, stealing, and rape aren't acceptable, I guess these are decent enough, if you don't read the whole book. Get the reader's digest version. When it comes to understanding, oh, basic fucking science, these are not the books you want.

Reading inspirational books, such as anything by Deepak Chopra, or that includes the words "chicken soup" in the title. Just no.

Contemplating one's inner state. That is great for figuring out that jerking off to Men's Fitness World and crying, while your girlfriend is in the next room, might mean you need to come out of the closet. It isn't known for its reliability in understanding complex cultural behaviors.

Cultural appropriation from indigenous cultures. Guess what? Their cultural woo is just as bullshit as anyone else's woo. There are some nuggets of gold in there, but it is worth the effort of sifting through the shit?

Astrology. My sign is neon.

Palmistry. enough said.

Divine Revelation. If God, Allah, YHWH, an angel, a demon, Satan, or any other supernatural being commands you to do something…talk to a shrink first.

Guessing.

Common sense. This one is an essay in and of itself. Common sense never gets out of the shallow end of the knowledge pool.

Intuition. No one yet has been able to define 'intuition' in such a way as to allow for repeatable, rigorously controlled testing. For every case of 'intuition' there are other, equally valid explanations. The definition of 'intuition' is that damned vague.

Gut feeling. Unless the gut feeling is "I probably shouldn't have eaten at Chili's," you have a 50/50 chance of being right.

Shamanic journeying. Speaking of cultural appropriation, calm down Castanedas.

Anything "alternative". If it works, it is no longer alternative (unless you are eventually becoming intentionally ironic, see also: alternative music,) now, is it? If it demonstrably and repeatedly works, people tend to use it, research it, write journal papers about it, and patent it.

Noetic science. We aren't talking about the classic Greek philosophy concepts of the 'Divine mind.' No, we are talking about thinking bad thoughts at water, freezing it, and looking at the shape of the ice crystals under a microscope.

Meditation. Great for calming down. Good for you even. Not the best way of understanding Hmong immigrant/refugee communities in Minneapolis, Minnesota.

Epiphany. Great for realizing you might have an abusive partner who you need to leave. Not so great for analyzing data at CERN.

The 'eureka effect'. Psychologists can't even agree on what 'insight' is. If they can't define it, it can't be tested well.

YouTube videos with shockingly low production value and fucked sound editing.

Clickbait. I shouldn't have to list this as an invalid OWoK, but here we are. Obviously I need to tell people that "if you won't believe what happens next..." you probably shouldn't.

As you float through the shallows of information, trying to find your deep trench of knowledge, stick with what works. Ask yourself: does this make any sense? Can I find other sources confirming this with strong evidence? Learn some critical thinking, and the basics of the scientific method. Just don't fall for the siren call of feel good woo drawing you onto the rocks.

*yes. the OWoK acronym is a convenient play on 'woke'

Cage Match: Information vs. Knowledge

by Matthew Broyles

Let me start by admitting something big: I was wrong.

At the dawn of the internet age, and through its heady adolescence, I was one of the loudest pitchmen for the revolution in human cognition that instant access to information would usher in. Images of enlightened citizens sifting through the data of the present and wisdom of the past, unhampered by geography and income, filled my mind with wonder and hope for the future of the pig-ignorant society in which I was raised.

I should have known someone would come and screw it all up.

A whole lot of someones, in fact. A veritable army of P.T. Barnum acolytes, exploiting the built-in weaknesses of our frail wits, tapping into our lizard brains with pinpoint accuracy, to make us click on endless streams of outright balderdash, stoking both our prejudices and desire to be informed.

One can spend hours rifling through articles on the internet and never learn a single thing that is true. Witness the hall of mirrors that is Pizzagate, or the mountains of "studies" that confirm whatever it is that we already believe. We have created entire universes of information that contain no information. We have outsmarted ourselves good and proper. And we may never quite recover from it.

When two people point at a rock, and say, "rock," then they have established a common language to communicate facts. But when they have two different words for rock, and one of them assigns it a seemingly arbitrary designation of eldritch evil, then communication breaks down. If we cannot speak to each other coherently, we cannot speak at all.

One cannot help but be reminded of the Tower of Babel. Is that what we tried to do? Build a tower of knowledge so high that we might become gods? I admit aspirations of joining the Overmind, as in *Childhood's End*. I once thought it possible that humans might transcend our monkey bodies and become beings of pure intellect, spreading wisdom and ingenuity throughout the stars.

Nope. Turns out we're just monkeys after all.

We didn't even need a god to come down and twist our tongues. We did it ourselves, out of greed and short-sighted opportunism. We're like crabs in a bucket, pulling those who want to see life outside its confines back into the bottom, to thrash against one another in blind futility until death reaches in and tosses us onto the cooker.

The reason history is cyclical is because we don't change. Not really. Our daily activities and certain of our social mores shift a bit here and there, but at the end of the day, the monkey brain will still rise to the same bait that it always has.

Your children aren't safe! People different than you are dangerous! That guy doesn't deserve what he's got! Don't trust anyone who seems smarter than you!

The triggers keep getting pulled, and the guns keep going off, blasting into our society's abdomen from millions of individual angles, shooting holes in the fabric of our hard-wrought civilization, weakening the structures that the best of us try to lay down in a vain attempt to keep our chimpery at bay.

What is knowledge? To my mind, it is effective synthesis of information, allowing one to make informed conclusions about the world. The brain-poisoners know this, too, and do all the work for us, coming up with pre-synthesized theories that serve whichever interest is convenient to their bottom line. And if someone else has reached a different conclusion, then they have been brainwashed by erroneous knowledge, pre-synthesized by yet another set of interests.

How, then, can we have actual knowledge, when so many of its sources are suspect? Who has time to pore over primary sources, constructing their own knowledge untainted by the prefab information-wranglers? We have access to information by the metric buttload, but without the ability to process it into accurate knowledge, we might as well have none at all. It's as if someone drove a truck full of Scrabble pieces up to our house, and said here, put these together in the right way, and you'll have the answer to life, the universe, and everything. We could work at it for centuries and never solve the puzzle.

I wish this were an academic argument, but as the growth of the intertubes has unfolded over the past couple of decades, the effects of drinking from that spurting fire hose have wreaked irrevocable havoc upon our culture, government, and sanity.

But like nuclear fission, information overload is not a thing our society can or will unmake. And maybe we shouldn't, even if we could. You're reading this now because of that selfsame technology. Some of it might become a piece of your own knowledge, built from a chain of secondhand wisdom, seven billion souls playing the telephone game until we have not a clue what is up and what is down. *Mr. Robot* is right: We live in a kingdom of bullshit.

And yet we live. Like the animals we are, we want to survive. But if we are going to continue surviving, we have to at least be aware that much of the knowledge we possess is at best shaky and at worst utter bollocks. How we deal with that bit of information will determine how long the Anthropocene lasts. At this point, I'm not sure whether to root for us or not.

○

Like and Share if You Agree

○

Like and Share if You Agree

by Anna Bardin

It was a dad joke that did it.

One of those hoary old bits of received wisdom that pass for common sense, transmitted through the generations by men for whom tonedeafness somehow has evaded consequence, surrounded as they are by like-minded buddies at the sports bar and church. It wasn't unusually offensive, but as it stared at me in meme form there on my timeline, I began to feel suddenly powerful.

When cajoled to Like and Share if I agreed with it, I chose not to.

Any writer will tell you that as bad as rejection is, no feeling in the world is quite as painful as indifference. To put something into the world that expresses a truth that you believe in, only to watch it wither and shrivel, ignored to death by an uncaring world.

All ideas are subject to this power. On nights when I feel like scaring myself, I browse through petition sites, eyebrows raising up the entire height of my forehead as I see the outrageous and frankly terrifying proposals put forth by people who felt so moved by their ignominious ideologies that they bothered to put them up for the world to see. The only thing that brings my blood pressure down is seeing the flaccid response rates to these idiotic notions. They are not Liked and Shared. They are ignored to death as they should be.

I used to read local music press, back when such a beast had power, and was often as amused by the bad reviews as by the good. I remember bands who proudly displayed their detractors' words on their flyers, and I liked them all the more for it. Far better to be hated than ignored.

Sometimes this does not work. John Oliver famously made a point of ignoring a certain orange orangutan during his run for the GOP nomination, and ended up being unable to do so as the horror unfolded, the crazily hypothetical made shockingly real. Just because you are not giving oxygen to some slavering beast doesn't mean others won't flock to fill its O2 tank fund on GoFundMe.

In social media terms, this principle can be tricky. Too often I have seen a thread of such unbelievable fascistic, racist, misogynistic ripeness that I freeze up with indecision. To comment is to embroil myself for untold hours into a mire of ignorance that sticks like tar, from which escape with sanity intact is damn near impossible. It is at times like this that I wish there were a Dislike button, the digital equivalent of a rotten tomato, thrown in disgust at troglodytes who pollute cyberspace with their noxious ideological fumes, poisoning us all.

Martin Luther King, Jr.'s words come to mind: "In the end, we will remember not the words of our enemies, but the silence of our friends." Is ignoring a foul post a form of moral cowardice? Letting horrific ideas stand unchallenged, to mutate unchallenged until they reach the ears of the next mentally vulnerable man with a shotgun and nothing left to lose? My GenX tendencies speak up in this argument, telling me it doesn't matter, you can't fix stupid. But can you ignore it to death? The past few months do not bode well for that theory.

So what, then? Engage every crank on the net? How quickly that would take over my life, responding to pasted paragraphs of invented "facts," refuting them point by point, only to be called a libtard cunt. Surely this is not the best use of my time. Sometimes the only power I possess is not to Like or Share, in hopes that this little gobbet of cultural phlegm will drip down the drain, to be swiftly forgotten in our mercilessly ephemeral age. And often, it does.

Some of the problem, of course, is the shield of the screen. The number of times I have been called a bitch to my face pales in comparison to the innumerable utterances of that epithet online. It's far easier to flame your enemies when they aren't close enough to slap you upside the head for it. The abuse feels less important for the deliverer as well as for the victim, and so sometimes indifference is the best choice.

Where does the dividing line rest, between that which should be challenged and that which cannot be allowed to stand? In a nation of 300 million, how much power does silence truly hold? One might say quite a bit, given the number of people who routinely sit out the electoral process, leaving the nation's fate up to the true believers. That is not a cohort I have any interest in joining, though I understand the impulse. Let entropy do its work, and party as much as possible before the ship sinks.

But such an ethos does not a meaningful life make. Those of us who want to stand for something other than our own hedonistic pleasures cannot gain much satisfaction from letting the world have its way with us. This may be an odd argument coming from an erotica writer, but then, I think it's self-evident how much sex drives our national conversation, for good or ill.

What am I trying to say here? I'm honestly not sure. But I would encourage you to think a bit the next time someone invites you to click that Like or Share button. It's a bit like the old telephone game. The message that you send down the line stands an ever-increasing chance of morphing into something you might not want to exist in the world. Ripples, echoes, butterfly wings…we are the makers of tomorrow's "common sense," whether we want to be or not. Like and Share wisely.

Like and Share if You Agree

by Chris Dashiell

Sometimes I feel like I never want to read another "think piece" about social media. I don't need any more analysis of how it's destroying society. Yes, I suppose it is having a negative impact in some ways. But neither do I feel nostalgic for the way things were before the internet. To tell the truth, I felt much more isolated then.

In the 1980s, for instance, I hated Reagan and his movement, but aside from reading journalism that was critical of the administration, and aside from meeting an occasional person who agreed with me, I felt very alone. The media gave the impression that the vast majority of Americans loved Reagan, an impression reinforced by the two elections he won, the second by a landslide. More importantly, the people who happened to be in my social circle weren't that interested in politics, and more than a few of them actually liked Reagan.

After the triumph of the internet, and especially with the advent of blogs, followed by social media, I discovered that there were a large number of people "out there" who shared my political views. And among those people, there were more than a few who were witty, articulate, and engaging. I now had the opportunity of interacting with them, and not just about politics. I found people who had similar interests in literature, philosophy, history, and film, just to name a few. This network of shared interests was far broader and more diverse than what was available to me in my immediate circle. I don't fault my family, friends, or acquaintances for this. I think it's an inherent feature of society, and indeed, geography. Even if I were in an academic environment, which I'm not, the culture in a university is still limited by elements of chance and lack of sufficient time to develop friendships.

Let's be clear. The relationships on social media are not, at least in the majority of cases, friendships. That's why the notion of "Facebook friends" is trivial. They are opportunities for engagement around shared interests, not friendships. The deeper level, the emotional intimacy of a friendship, can only happen (again, with rare exceptions) through personal contact. In this respect, the think pieces are right: we still need "real world," non-virtual relationships in order to experience life fully. It is possible to get sucked into the online social network to the detriment of our active life in the world.

Nevertheless, being connected to like-minded people has been a positive experience for me. After plunging into the experience of Twitter, which for me mainly consisted of talking about politics, I often thought about my experience during the 1980s. My feeling of being isolated was probably an illusion. The fact that I had no method of accessing the minds and sensibilities of others who thought like I did, gave me the false impression that I was part of a very small and powerless minority. If social media had existed at that time, I would have realized that I was not alone.

When we say "like minded," there is often a concern that this means agreeing with one another about everything, which can create a kind of belief bubble or echo chamber that excludes alternative views, and thereby works against an open-minded exchange of ideas. I understand this, and I know it exists, but my experience has been that social media does not create this behavior—it only intensifies something that's always been a problem in society, unless we take care to pay special attention to not fall into this trap. Within the range of shared interests of the people I follow on Twitter, for instance, there is wide variety of emphasis, method, personality, and opinion. I've had my share of arguments, or spirited discussions if you will. As long as we stick to the matter at hand, and present evidence, it doesn't have to cause a split. I've had my mind changed more than one might expect. But when it devolves into name-calling, abuse, or just nonsense, there is no point in continuing. These things have occurred more and more frequently over the years, and I think perhaps it is inevitable that they would, given the huge numbers of people using social media.

The internet is of course a very new development in history, and there is a lot to be said about numerous aspects of it, positive and negative. But with all the hand wringing that goes on about the negative aspects, I think it's important to recognize that its popularity, and particularly the explosion of social media, signifies more than just distraction or hedonism. Being connected to a wider community with shared interests creates a greater sense of power, purpose and validation. People aren't going to give that up. The question becomes how we channel it.

Like and Share if You Agree

by Doremus Jessup

Maybe I was born with it, maybe it's misanthropy. I don't know what it is, but, to me, "like and share if you agree" is one of the more abhorrent sentences in the English language. It displays a pathological need for external validation I can't identify with.

I think my first, and most base, complaint against LASIYA is that it's fucking stupid. Please tell me; when was the last time you LIKED and SHARED something you didn't agree with? I'll share things I don't agree with, usually with the express intent of starting an excoriating and sarcastic diatribe. I don't like those things though. Also, what kind of low grade mental defective can get on Facebook, can find a post they like and agree with, but can't figure out hitting the "like" and "share" buttons. Not only is the concept fucking stupid, it treats the target audience like a pack of drooling morons. Not to say they aren't, but I'm trying to be nice.

My deeper complaint about LASIYA is what it says about the people who use that benighted sentence. I write, a lot. While not ever satisfied with anything I've written, I still love everything I write. I've been told I'm good at writing, and people have commented to me on how they enjoy reading what I have to write. As much as I enjoy and value reader feedback, and enjoy the thought of readers consuming and enjoying the fruits of my labors, the only validation I need for anything I choose to post or write is my own.

When you get right to the heart of the matter, LASIYA is a passive-aggressive manifestation of a pathological need for external validation. It is a sign of weakness. Yes, we live in a society, and the recognition of our thoughts from our peers does have a certain amount of influence in social groups. Needing people to value your thoughts is understandable, and can be healthy. Can be. Not is.

That is why most people have a confidant. Be it a best friend, a spouse, a parent, a sibling, or Bob the homeless meth junky, we all need that one other person we trust and respect to provide external support, and a litmus test to our self-validation. Maybe you're lucky and you have a support network providing you with a spectrum of sources for external validation offered with no effort on your part.

LASIYA is trying to influence a herd of both relative and complete strangers into being a de facto support network providing you with masses of external validation. It seems like so many people get a high off of seeing like and share numbers in the hundreds to millions. I honestly wonder some days if there is a neurochemical response; some strange dopamine receptor channel? Is it like a so called "runner's high" - the endorphins man, the endorphins - you can get sitting on your ass with your iPad?

It cheapens validation, both internal and external. When you have a small, close group validating your self validation, it is a strong system. You know these people well enough to lend weight to their opinions. Ngdukwe in Ghana who likes and shares your story about how the HRC is trying to have trump assassinated, though, is a stranger of no great importance in your life. He is a piece of a weak system. Ngdukwe doesn't give a fuck about you, as you have no fucks to give about him. Which kind of validation do you think is more valuable? There aren't enough thumb icons and shares in the whole internet to fill the hole inside you if that is where you are seeking validation.

The last problem I'll address today is the argumentum ad populum fallacy, the argument from popularity. Look at your average LASIYA post. It's usually some trite and platitudinal fluff, or some ideologically/theologically driven crap. In either case, the proposition most LASIYA posts argue for are based on fatally flawed logic. The application of critical thinking usually invalidates the proposition in most LASIYA posts. By building a base of uninformed consensus, though, they can shrug off any criticism because all these people agree with them, and they can't all be wrong.

I know. I know. That makes no sense, but most people who engage in the sin of LASIYA think like that. They think reality is democratic. They think their 4000 likes outweighs your peer reviewed science, your evidence, and your objective facts. Remember, everyone (almost literally,) at one time in history seemed to think elemental mercury and other heavy metals were medicines.

LASIYA is the ultimate badge of weakness on the internet. Actively engaging in it shows a lack of internal strength necessary to provide even a trace of self-validation. It shows the resultant need for validation by the group, no matter how ephemeral that validation may be. It shows mental weakness and a tenuous grasp of how logic works. It is fractal weakness. At any iteration it is as weak as at any other iteration.

Like and Share if You Agree

by Matthew Broyles

Ever feel like you're part of the problem?

Increasingly, it happens to me when I click that little button. The one that says Share.

Sharing would seem to be an unambiguously good impulse. Instead of hoarding information and entertainment, I'm giving others the chance to benefit from it. Ostensibly, that's true. I've learned a lot from thoughtful articles others have shared, and had much-needed levity thrust into deep funks by well-wrought memes.

Thinkpieces abound, opining on whether or not the online sharing of thoughts is emotionally and intellectually equivalent to the analog method. Having lived through the pre-internet era, I am generally loath to recommend its return. That said, I do occasionally wonder about the trade-off between breadth and depth.

Today, I can read ten different pieces on ten totally unrelated topics, whereas two decades ago I might have only had a copy of Rolling Stone to occupy an evening. But with fewer options, there can be a commitment to spend more time with what you've got. There are facts I learned in 1997 that I still retain, even if they are somewhat trivial.

While I certainly internalize a lot of what I read online now, I suppose I'm more acutely aware of how much simply blasts right through, given the volume I inhale every day.

Nathan Hamilton's song *In All That We Might Find* speaks of a breakneck mental pace that rings strikingly true to me:

I miss the day's end, the soft embrace

The stillness of our minds

When a sense of mystery remained

In all that we might find

Yet if I'm honest, slowing down my brain for bedtime is a task that wasn't easy even in the days when the dang TV shut off late at night, the test pattern reminding me that hey, maybe you oughta go to bed, dumbass.

But I'm doing something, aren't I? Disseminating facts and thoughtful opinions on the state of the world, motivating them to do likewise? I'm helping, right?

Even a few months ago, I would have said yes, absolutely. But now, as the republic burns around us, the feeble clicking of my mouse feels ridiculously impotent and foolish. Seeing the usual suspects pass it on to their usual suspects, the circle jerk of modern liberal #resistance flogging itself endlessly, a hermetically sealed bubble of outrage raising its internal temperature until its occupants' brains melt in the pressure cooker of useless rage.

Yet the alternative does not feel useful, either. Unplugging, waving signs at indifferent politicians who know that you wouldn't be there on that street corner if your wallet was big enough to fund their campaign chest. Phone banking, annoying people into lamely promising not to be quite so indifferent next time, even though that new show just came up for streaming on Netflix.

Doing things is hard. Liking and Sharing is not.

There is a mental narrowing of my eyes when someone tells me they "don't have a Facebook." But some days I actually envy those people a bit. I start wondering how they spend their free time, what life goals they might be accomplishing, things I too much achieve if my brain weren't tied to the feed, clicking away as if that is my best chance of contributing something to the society.

I remember the days of poets' chapbooks on coffeeshop tables, practically begging for ephemeral obscurity. Of demo tapes and SASEs for unsolicited manuscripts, the frantic aspirational flailing of those who wish to own a piece of the national conversation, to add our voice in a meaningful way. To share that which only we can share.

Social media would seem to be the fulfillment of that dream. Absolute nobodies with Twitter followers in the thousands, producing real-time commentary and scintillating bon mots on the news and art of the day. A global salon, the complete democratization of critical culture.

Some days, it feels like that. Like we're all doing something. That it matters. Other days, as the forces of true power meet behind closed doors, deciding all of our fates, the constant jabber of the internet-famous seems like the ultimate embodiment of futility, a closed circuit where free thought goes to loop around itself forever and ever, safe from inflicting any real effect on the outside world.

Yet even last week, when the ACA repeal failed, I wondered: Did something I shared inspire someone to attend a town hall, write a letter, call their congresscritter, add one more voice to the chorus warning those whose re-elections are less than two years away that there might be electoral consequences for their votes? How many Shares removed am I from real action?

The act of asking that question sounds pitiful and lazy. Yes, I participate in real life activism, but owing to responsibilities at home and work, I don't throw my body upon the gears of the machine as much as I feel I ought to. I must compromise, and where physical action cannot take place, that click must suffice.

Still, I find I must ask the David Letterman question: Is it anything?

Would I be better served to cut the cord, and commit my OCD tendencies to offline activities? Could I stand a better chance of making the world a better place? Experience suggests otherwise. So here I am, inviting you to Like and Share this missive, all that I have to offer on this ordinary day of mass global communion. Is it enough? Perhaps not. But neither is anything else.

Like and Share if you agree.

o

When I Grow Up

o

When I Grow Up

by Anna Bardin

It's a paradox. The older I get, the less grown-up I feel.

When I was a teenager, my cousin Audrey seemed like the oracle of adulthood. She was in her early twenties, and preternaturally mature. Aced college, got a responsible job, respectable husband, a cute little house, and a cute little baby, all before age 25.

Her example was a little intimidating as I neared graduation. I got decent grades, but no honor rolls. I only had a rough idea of what I might do out in the big world, which I figured had to include college, though I wasn't entirely sure of my direction there, either. At family gatherings, my aunts made a point of singling out Audrey as a role model for me, as I had not made any overt declarations of life plans to them.

Such meddling irked me, but at the same time, I felt that I probably should have a more structured plan for when I grew up and became a big twentysomething.

Looking back now, 25 seems a ridiculous age for having one's shit together. While I certainly did graduate college and get a responsible job, I did so with minimal effort, and no real passion. My energies were devoted mostly to reading books and exploring my burgeoning sexuality, beside which career advancement, mortgages, and childbearing seemed entirely irrelevant and uninteresting. These things which I and others identified as grown-up activities were deferred indefinitely.

Fast forward a couple of decades, and none of that has really changed. Audrey has grandchildren now, a rite of passage I will never experience, and her house is nearly paid off. Meanwhile I've been at the same company for eons, in largely the same role, which, without children, pays for my meager apartment and play money rather well. I still haven't really grown up.

And yet I do apply what maternal instincts I have towards my niece and nephew, for whom I am the coolest aunt ever. We have a good time together, then I send them off to my brother's house and poke my nose back into a book, shutting the adult world out.

The thing is, I have no plans to change any of this. I don't want a husband, nor a kid, nor the bill when the air conditioning needs a repair. On the present trajectory, I am on course to reach retirement age without having fulfilled many of the grown-up requirements that my peers have.

Why do I feel guilt about this? I am not unhappy. The bf and other occasional dalliances take care of my carnal needs. I have plenty of food, clothes, and shelter. I won't be rich when I retire, but neither will I be penniless—providing we don't bankrupt the country in the next few years, anyway. My job isn't all that fulfilling, but I'm at a point where I can perform it with half of my brain while the other half writes.

Whence this feeling of failure? That I've somehow bailed on my responsibility to be what my aunts wanted me to be, a younger version of them, a bespectacled iteration of Audrey? It makes me mad to write that, to be even slightly beholden to their expectations of me, yet I feel a legitimate sense of loss, like I've missed out on something important, even if they are things that most of my friends complain about on a daily basis.

Maybe that's part of it. When the bitching about spouses and kids starts up at work, I have nothing to say. An anecdote about my niece and nephew can work in a pinch, but there's always this look in other adults' eyes that tells me I'm not really one of them. I'm half-assing my way through adulthood, and some part of them resents me for it.

Then I get irritated. I didn't tell them to marry that harping bitch, or pop out 3.5 younglings to pay for. I didn't tell them to ignore all those sealed cracks in the foundation of that house and buy it anyway. I didn't recommend they go for every promotion that came down the pike, to end up swimming in responsibilities, in bucks that stop here, shortening their lives with every anxiety attack.

So why do I feel like I should have followed their example? I don't, most of the time, but on occasion it niggles at the back of my head: *You're not grown up yet, Anna. When are you going to do the things, Anna?*

I feel like Luke Skywalker, only I keep putting off my confrontation with Darth Vader, only after which a Jedi will I be. It seems odd, but when I watched *The Force Awakens*, and saw Luke standing alone on that island, running away from his responsibilities, I nearly shouted "YES!! FUCK THE REPUBLIC!! YOU DO YOU!!"

Maybe that's a terrible attitude. Or maybe I've decided, quite responsibly, not to add one more overworked, miserable soul to the pile. Maybe not growing up is the best thing I can do, both for me and for the world. Perhaps that's merely rationalization for selfishness. But it's top-shelf rationalization, if I do say so myself.

What will I be when I grow up? In truth, it may never happen. Can an 80-year-old woman be considered an adolescent? Unless something dramatic happens to my brain in the next four decades, I suspect I will still be resisting adulthood's gravity. The journey will be to stop feeling guilty about it. In the end, that may be the day I finally do grow up for real.

When I Grow Up

by Bruce Payne

When I grow up. Now, there's a thought. A hundred years ago, I watched *Peter Pan* on NBC. It had a profound effect on my philosophy, especially the song *I Won't Grow Up*, sung to Wendy by Peter and the Lost Boys when the Darling children arrive in Neverland. (So much greatness in those few words.)

And, although I wanted to drive, legally drink, and have my own place, I was in hurry at all to adopt the adult world as my own. My personal nightmare would be to find out that I had somehow awake one day to find I had become my father in spite of all my struggles to avoid it.

My default career choice was none. (Rock Star and Grand Prix race car driver remained inalterably out of reach.) I tried to become a commercial photographer, but only managed to book weddings, which ruined my love of photography. Before that, I'd misadventured into bricklaying, and found to my chagrin that physical, hard labor was rewarding. A fall from a scaffold thirty feet in the air left me uninjured and convinced that there were safer ways to make a buck.

Most of the adults in my parents' generation seemed to have no true joy in life, where I felt I embraced almost every thrilling moment of it. I loved going to local bars to see local rockers and drink like I was Keith Moon. Later it was the blues joints, particularly the New Bluebird Niteclub on Horne Street. There was just enough danger in that place to give it a palpable edge. Still my favorite joint to catch a live act. The fun came to an end when I showed up late one Saturday night to find everyone standing outside the club with looks of shock on their faces. "A neighborhood lady just shot and killed another lady." I did not get out of my car and never returned.

Those were my years of driving a roach coach, peddling really shitty food to people who didn't get enough of break to actually leave for lunch. Not a career there, or an adult in sight. The money was good enough that I thought I could snort coke like Neil Young, though. I kept up that foolishness for far too long.

These days, I've settled down, but I still don't consider myself grown up in the slightest. I'm still playing guitar and thrilled to have a gig Monday night playing at a place I love for people I respect. I got back into photography a few years back and work at a local camera store, but my priorities have changed. I don't take it seriously. I'm not trying to shoot for anyone but myself, and I'm doing the best work of my life. I've got dogs, a home, the same girl (she's the grownup) for 13 years and neither one of us has a lick of sense. I'm a

Socialist in Texas, for god's sake. John Lennon's truest lyric was "Life is what happens to you when you're busy making other plans."

Growing up sounds like a huge pain in the ass.

When I Grow Up

by Matthew Broyles

I'm still deciding what I'm going to be when I grow up.

Actually, that's not true. I've decided several times. But every time I try to convince the world that I should be those things, it unceremoniously stuffs me back into my little cubicle. I come up with a different thing, bam, get the cube again, ad nauseum.

What we've got here is not so much a failure to communicate as a failure to persuade. Or more likely, an insufficient assessment of the requirements prior to application. That bit's on me.

Here are some things I already am:

* A dad.
* A husband.
* A friend.
* A musician and songwriter.
* A writer.
* A radio show host.
* A writing collaborative curator.
* An administrative assistant.

Only one of those pays anything worth mentioning, and of course it's the one I'm not terribly interested in. But money isn't everything, and I can still do those other things in and around the paycheck-giver.

Yet it often still feels like I still haven't found the thing that is me. The thing I'm going to be when I grow up. Or maybe I have, and just need to stop searching, the better to appreciate those things I've already become.

Yoda knows me: "All his life has he looked away…to the future, to the horizon. Never his mind on where he was. What he was doing."

There is always a greener pasture, a more sparkly pond, just over the next hill. Something that someone else has that could be mine if only I did x-y-z. What terribly ordinary neuroses, envy and covetousness. They're in the damn Bible, fer the Pete of sake. I would like to be more complicated than that, and for a long time convinced myself that I was. That the artistic longings weren't just regular human yearnings, but profound searches for the deeper meaning of the universe.

But maybe I just want stuff I don't have.

Seeing as how *Desperado* is a song that's already been written, there's not a whole lot more to say on the topic, except that it comes as a surprise to me that I'm not exempt from such nonsensical impulses. I mock American exceptionalism, meanwhile I've been toting my own brand of it for several decades, wearing that bubble around my punkin head, proud and delusional.

Saying all of this in public is a way to hold myself accountable. Because I don't want to be like this. I want to appreciate what I've got, and not to spend so much time moping about what I don't. There will always, always, always be things we can't have. *Gold, Guns, Girls* has also already been written, and there again, how pitifully predictable that it's talking about me.

The good part, I suppose, is that I'm not alone. Every day I see people trying to decide if what they have become is what they want to become. And some of their fates are tied in some fashion to mine. As Lyle Lovett writes: "When you find the one you might become, remember part of me is you." The restless feet keep darting this way and that, and this has consequences for everyone.

We ask why so many people are dissatisfied with their lives. Look at the glowing screens all around. Happy faces of people living lives so different to our own while we muddle in the trenches. Sure, they might be batshit insane, chronically suicidal narcissists, but they don't have to print the damn TPS report cover sheet to keep from getting fired. If I had a shot, we say, I could have a life like that.

Maybe. But statistics exist, as do happenstance, blind luck, genetic randomness, and geography. We all have a shot, and a lot of us take it. But not everyone can win. As Aimee Mann says, "A chance is all that I need, and I've had it."

For a lot of us, in truth, "when I grow up" is shorthand for "before I die." Because if you're 18 or over, you have grown up. What you want to be is simply what you want to do with however many days you have left before the reaper shows up. Some of it you've already done. But there are hours yet to fill, and how you choose to occupy those will to a large extent determine how you spend the ones to come.

So here's us, on the raggedy edge. Perhaps it's time to stop asking what we will be, and start deciding what we will do. And this starts with what we think. Which is dependent upon what we tell ourselves in those dark moments when no one's around, and we wonder how we got here, being this person who doesn't feel like the person we're supposed to be. This is not my beautiful house.

What will I be right now? After I finish this essay, that is. No, scratch that. Here I am, writing this essay to you. That is who I am. In another moment, I will be someone else, doing another thing. I contain multitudes, as do we all. Embody those selves, and be those people. For if we look only to the horizon, we lose that future as we vacate the present. I fear our culture does that too much, leaving ourselves open to exploitation by present-living opportunists, and I will fully admit to being part of that problem.

Let's be grownups together. Right now.

When I Grow Up

by MC Dalet

This week is the week of my birthday. I will be 43 on Wednesday. According to the life expectancy for a white American male – 76.71 years – I am more than halfway done. In other words, it's time to admit I am middle-aged. It's a great age. I am not experiencing the midlife crisis, not in the traditional sense. I love my wife and children. They are a sweet, supportive family. I have no desire for a muscle car or a motorcycle. I have no desire to "trade in" anything that I have. In honesty, I am happy with the shape of my life, and certainly with my co-pilots. Externally, I would like to earn, well, significantly more; then again, wouldn't we all. Am I introspective? Certainly. My midlife revolution has taken on a decidedly internal focus. Have I met my potential? No. Will I? I hope so. I'm still working on my certainty. What is that potential? What do I want to be when I grow up?

Funny, that. Child me assumed that I would be grown up at 18. By the time I was 18, I realized that I still had college, that I would be supported through that, and that I still had a way to go before launching a career. I had jobs, sure, but relatively little responsibility. 22 it is, then! Except it took my SIX years to finish college, mostly because I both exploited the "little responsibility" thing, and because I kept changing majors. Not only was I not what I would consider "grown up," at 22, I had yet to decide what I wanted to be when I was.

At 8 I decided I was going to be a paleontologist. It was not only dinosaurs that fascinated me, but the idea that there was a past life to the planet, and by extension the universe – a fantastic expanse of time, events, epochs that occurred even before humanity showed up on the scene. It blew my little mind, and I wanted to know everything I could about this immense stretch of natural history. When I reached the end of middle school and was initiated into the world of speech and policy debate, I considered a career in politics or law. I seemed to have a talent for building cases, applying research, and generally making some sort of sense out of complex social systems. I hadn't forgotten my penchant for paleontology . . .not until my late-high-school science classes went and got all math-y. Convinced I could never do math when I grew up, that was the end of that. This also threw out my fleeting flirtation with genetic engineering. Between the math and the ethical tightrope act, it seemed fascinating but exhausting. As did politics and law. Actually, those began to scare me. I was scared because, in my late teens, I had observed enough of the world that I understood there was no way to "win" those jobs. In other words, no way to do them perfectly. One would inevitably make mistakes, and the mistakes I saw in those fields cost people money, reputation, liberty, life. No. I won't be responsible for that. Next option!

Along with debate came "speech and drama." I was also in the school band. By the time I got to college, I knew that I wanted to do some kind of performance. The speaking was the thing I excelled at in debate anyway, so I set my eye on theatre. . .which turned into broadcast journalism when my father admonished me, telling me I would have to be responsible when I grew up, meaning earning a living. But I didn't like those broadcasting folks. Another obstacle. Another obstacle dodged. Damn the torpedoes and on to theatre. But in the end, I did realize that "making it" in L.A. or New York would be hard. Too hard. So I decided to teach. There. I can talk about performance, try to make others appreciate it as I do, and draw a paycheck.

What I realize now, staring down the mid-40s, is that I've been through so many aborted versions of what I want to be when I grow up...and I still don't feel grown. Maybe it's because I am still clinging to the idea that "grown up" is a perfected state, one in which the grown-up feels secure, finalized. The downside to the many iterations of me is that I realize I jumped ship too easily. Perhaps I do not feel grown because I failed to rise to enough challenges that I never had the process of failing at them, then revising my approach to feel truly accomplished. The upside is that my tour brought me into contact with my wife, with many interesting people, lifelong friends I might never have met, and that would be a shame. Maybe it has all led to the mid-life realization that if you say, "That's it. I reached my destination," that the "destination" in mortal human terms is death. That's the thing. Maybe being grown up is not an end in itself, not a destination, but a state in which you know, balls to bones, that you will never reach that destination, no matter how long you live.

When I grow up, I want to be responsible. I'm not talking about the external responsibility – paying bills, not throwing back a cold one on my lunch break, going to work in the first place, taking care of children and spouse, taking out the garbage. All of that and so much more is important, yes. But when I say responsible, I mean it in a deep, spiritual sense. I mean knowing – actually KNOWING – that the blessings and chaos I draw into my life are mine. I created them. What is more, when I grow up, I want to know, with absolute certainty, that because they are mine, I can change them. I want to be responsible enough to know that it is okay to make mistakes, because how else can you learn. That's responsibility. I tell my students all the time that it is okay to fall down on your first exam or project or paper in any given class, because when you do, the professor's feedback tells you exactly what you need to improve so that you knock it out of the park on the next one. That's learning. It can't happen without fumbling. So responsibility is listening to my own lecture or, better yet, living it.

○

My Crowdsourced Life

○

My Crowdsourced Life

by Cristee Cook

I want to talk about community.

The dictionary defines community as:

> 1. A unified body of individuals
> 2. a social state or condition

What interests me about this is the alleged consciousness behind it.

And the word togetherness:

> 1. warm fellowship, as among members of a family
> 2. the quality, state, or condition of being together

These are ideas that sound easy enough on paper, but actually creating community and togetherness takes inner transformation.

Sometimes in my enthusiasm I come on strong in relationships. I go full force, straight forward with no pause to think if the other party needs or wants that amount of energy. Sometimes I think that because we have common interests or are members of the same community there is an automatic intimacy. I forget that things take time to build. The same applies to personal interests and challenges: it's all-or-nothing.

People that I admire or look to as examples tell me to let go. Let things flow. Don't try to always have the answers. This is a challenge for me. The cycle of negative tape plays in my head, where I imagine the worst case scenarios of what will happen "if"…

My chest tightens, my energy gets small and trapped and I feel like I can't breathe. My brain plays the common trick of convincing me that if I can control everything, I won't have anything to worry about.

So my focus in the past few months has been to take the hard advice: let go, let things flow, and don't try to always have the answers. It's a tremendous effort that requires constant vigilance. It's baffling how quickly I slip back into trying to do everything myself and the chaos that often follows the decisions made in this state of mind. I have some challenges in my life that are so familiar: old patterns, old thinking, all of it the same old garbage that I can't seem to break free of. I feel broken, helpless to change myself.

This is where I think community and togetherness come in. This is the energy behind the contemporary trend of crowdsourcing: we can do it alone, but the results are often more expansive when we work together.

When we invest in something as part of a group of like-minded people, we want to contribute instead of expecting a return.

So it is accurate to say that my life is crowdsourced. People who love me more than I deserve at times contribute to my potential. They look past my flaws and over-sharing and child-like enthusiasm and see my light. My parents accept my out-of-the-box lifestyle and support me in more ways than I can write in an essay. Sometimes I'm so committed to my own point of view that I can't even receive this love. People in my life show me their heart and I reject it. Or I twist it to fit into my own understanding of what it means to share and miss an opportunity to experience the growth that can only come from admitting that I don't know.

As I write this I'm in the middle of a situation that has an open ending. I don't know how some of the challenges will resolve. But in the past few weeks I've had people step forward to offer a hand up in ways that I would have never imagined. And it seems to happen in the blink of an eye. Somehow, I'm in the right place at the right time and an opportunity is presented through people and places that surprise me. So far, the results have been far better than my original plans. I'm humbled by my small perspective. I limit my reality if left to my own devices.

My crowdsourced life is a wonder. I am in awe of what we can accomplish when we set our egos aside and commit to a common goal. My relationships are stronger when I step back a bit and let things build organically. My fears of not being loved are replaced with the knowing that sometimes love shows up in minutiae, but is no less grand. If I get out of the way, I don't miss it.

My Crowdsourced Life

by Matthew Broyles

Growing up nerdboy in the 1980s, pledge drives on PBS were a built-in part of my childhood. You like this show, send us some money and you can keep watching it. Always made sense to me, even though a lot of the other shows I watched were on commercial networks, paid for by the big corporate money.

I've often likened that split to signed vs. independent music. Major label music is going to be everywhere whether I pay for it or not, much like *Knight Rider* would be on whether I bought Fruity Pebbles or just sat patiently through the ad. Whereas if I wanted channel 13 to keep playing *Doctor Who* on Saturday nights, the sense was that I had to pony up or it would go away.

I treat artists that way based on their label situation. I know that Roger Waters isn't going to stop making records because I buy a used copy of some album or another. Whereas for Allison Weiss, signed but on a small label, I will buy as directly as possible from the source. Doubly so for artists like myself, whose label and budgets are their own. For those, I will gladly pay more than the average album price, knowing as I do how many costs go into making that little disc, and how unlikely it is that they will do much more than break even.

Likewise, I will fork over for independent authors, theater groups, and venues with no corporate support network, because if these don't receive community support, then all we're left with is the millionth James Patterson novel, endless Lloyd Webber retreads, and a Chipotle/Starbucks on every corner. Giving directly to unaffiliated ventures is the only way those things survive in an increasingly uniform cultural landscape.

Which is why I get so bent whenever I hear people bitch about artists "begging for money" on the internet. These same complainers sit through ads all the time. What is an advertisement but a plea for money? Independent artists are not asking for you to fund lavish dinners for business partners, or pay for their bonus Bahama vacation. They want to make stuff, and stuff costs money.

A few years ago, I got called a "man child" for attempting a subscription model for my music. The chief sticking point seemed to be that in the promo video, I said I would rather make art than work in an office. One wouldn't think that this is a controversial statement. But I've run into a lot of people who get pissy when someone suggests that a regular 9-to-5 is not something they'd prefer to do if they had another option. By even saying that, they are reminding everyone who has a straight job that if they had their druthers, they wouldn't be punching that clock.

We tell ourselves a lot of stories in order to justify our lives. I'm here typing this in an admin office because of the financial realities of kidcare and rising rents. That's my reason. There is no moral justification attached, having to do with the inherent goodness of hard work and loyalty. But for a lot of people, the only way they can face their jobs every day is if they tell themselves that working that job makes them a good person.

To me, attaching any personal fulfillment to most of the jobs out there is foolish. Corporate loyalty is a one-way street, and those of us employed by these faceless entities should treat them as the necessary evils they are, not as anchors for our identities. Ask most Americans if they would rather be at work today, the honest ones will say no. A fair number of the ones who say yes have bought into a delusion about their place in the world.

The benefit of crowdsourcing is that you, the potential donor, have the opportunity to help create the kind of world you want to live in. Most of the time, our world is created for us, by the aforementioned behemoths that bestride our society, sliding cut-and-paste retail and entertainment options into slots made to match those in other cities and towns. We either patronize them or don't, but we are given few options on the whole as to whether or not they exist as a force in society.

Whereas if I know that Annalise Emerick wants to put out a new record, my support might stand a chance of either making or breaking the existence of that album. It is an opportunity to shape the future in a much more direct and personal way. So many indie projects hinge on remarkably tiny numbers of people in the grand scheme, and so those people's importance is not remotely delusional, but absolutely integral to maintaining a vibrant culture that contains more voices than the Biebers and Danielle Steels.

So the next time you see a plea in your timeline from someone who wants to see if maybe, just maybe they might be able to spend their time working on a unique undertaking rather than filling a cube, don't take it as an affront. Because if they can do it, with your support, then perhaps the day may come when you can do something similar. If they fail because you did not step up, that darkens the future for all of us.

My Crowdsourced Life

by MC Dalet

This invention of the Digital Age, crowdsourcing, is a means to free the artist or inventor from forced dependence on third party support lent with the sole expectation of profiting from the effort and skill of the creative party. Crowdsourcing places the responsibility of support in the immediate sphere of the craftsperson – the audience or perspective consumer – creating a more intimate feedback loop that is communal in nature. It is a much more natural state of affairs, as human beings are by nature social beings. There is real investment. It is not just money being given, but belief, energy, and desire.

Money is itself a form of energy converted temporarily into a commonly accepted currency. When it is used to create something, say an album, a civic project, or a newer, better machine, that currency is converted into another form, one that benefits, in some way, those who supported its manifestation. This is a cyclical process. The artist/inventor can sell her wares and now has monetary resources that can support someone else's efforts. This is an exchange of energy. Interconnectedness. Individuals intertwining their efforts to create something that moves the world forward, like the gears of clockworks. Each individual gear has a unique shape and expression, but none can function without the others.

This serves as a perfect metaphor for a highly functioning community. Crowdsourced projects are the perfect metaphor, also, for an individual's life. If I think about it, my life is completely crowdsourced. Yes, sometimes this involves being lent money or offered a monetary gift, but that's the tip of the iceberg, the obvious and literal comparison. If money is simply a medium for energetic exchange, we have to consider the other media: love, concern and care given toward another's physical and emotional needs, an exchange of wisdom or kindness, collaboration. I cannot complete or even continue, from day to day, this project I call life without support. Each time I withdraw, fold into myself in an attempt to solve or complete anything by myself, the short-term project and the ongoing life project fall into chaos. They stagnate and fail to manifest their potential beauty. The same happens if the so-called support comes from a profiteer; at that point, it is not truly support because there's not real exchange. It must come from my community, from the energetic feedback loop.

This communal support manifests in several ways, but only when ask and are open to accepting support, as we do with Kickstarters. In life, though, one has to consciously relinquish control over how that support shows up. The ways are myriad. I often find that those in my immediate sphere know what I need better than I do.

The first example: hunger. Yes, physical hunger. . .at least on the surface. As I do my work, be it teaching, creating and playing music, even fathering, I sometimes straight up forget to eat. It happens more often than is healthy. Left to my own devices, I fail to provide for my physical needs, throwing my mind and spirit into chaos. In this example my wife, who knows me and my patterns because she is concerned for my wellbeing, may notice that I'm not myself. "Have you eaten?" she may ask. "Do you need some coffee? A break?" If I accept her help, she makes sure I have what I need. The apparent support is that I get fed, receive physical sustenance. Beyond that, though, I am receiving love and I know that someone cares deeply about someone outside of herself, me. There is a simultaneous investment and benefit she receives analogous to someone who funds their favorite musician. She cares about ME, and by doing so SHE gets a better partner. I am appreciative. I want to share in return. And because I'm no longer "hangry," I am more capable of looking out for her and the kids.

Speaking of kids, here's another example: personal growth. I have always struggled with the disproportionate response. It manifests as anger or frustration over just about anything that does not go as I think it should, and believe me, my expectations can be rigid. This is something I desperately want to change, but I get caught up. I can't do it alone. I was recently airing a string of grievances about everything from how slow people were driving to hard-to-open food packaging. My five-year-old daughter looked at me and in a kind but baffled tone said, "Daddy, you complain a lot." This simple statement was miraculous. I suddenly saw myself from the outside, through the eyes of innocent truth. I have since been mindful of complaining. It was just the support I needed to begin breaking down this formidable manifestation of my ego consciousness. A singular statement with potentially global effect. Let me get you there.

The great twentieth century Jewish sage, Rav Yehuda Ashlag, in his book *On World Peace* describes the Meshiach (or the perfected world) as being driven by a society that consistently crowdsources the lives of everyone in their immediate sphere. He explains that we are all interdependent cogs, each with an individual Light to share. So first, we must honor and celebrate that individuality as it is part of a greater whole. More importantly, we must work to support (or source) everyone touched by our life in whatever way benefits THEM. In so doing, we benefit ourselves. If I am constantly sourcing others, I am too concerned with their wellbeing to be self-absorbed and self-serving. But I also have given them the support they need to be fulfilled in a way that enables them to source me. The gears turn toward a better, more cohesive, high functioning world. And a peaceful one. If my needs are met and I in turn meet others, there is not space for petty conflict, theft, jealousy. That's the small community.

But that's the thing: we are a global community. Each person has an immediate sphere that includes those in our close community. But each individual has a different immediate sphere. Those spheres overlap, touch each other, touch larger spheres, and radiate out. On a long enough timeline, seven billion people are connected in one global community. Hence, once person touches everyone by proxy. One community sourcing each other can eventually have an effect on the entire world. Chaos can be eliminated. But we have to choose.

Back to the metaphor, then. What crowdsourcing can teach us is that if we want quality creativity undamaged by greed and exploitation, we can pay for it, support it, and make it thrive. If we are open, we can expect the same in return. If that loop is created, it can radiate outward, infinitely. My crowdsourced life can become our crowdsourced Meshiach.

○

Relax, You're Not in Control

○

Relax, You're Not in Control

by Anna Bardin

There is a pernicious myth that pervades our society, one that I've fought as long as I've been alive. That is the idea that we need to be in control of our actions at all times.

When I think back on the most memorable experiences of my life, almost uniformly they are ones where I was not fully in control. Obviously when I say "memorable," that does not always mean good. But even bad experiences are extremely valuable, and can help lay the groundwork for much better experiences in future.

As much as we laud the idea of self-control, we as a species spend an awful lot of time trying to throw ourselves into chaos. Alcohol, drugs, virtual and augmented reality, the various magic boxes of shadows that occupy increasing chunks of our time and attention, all of these point to a society that wants to lose control, or at the very least, wants to escape responsibility.

These are exactly the sorts of human behaviors that scared the hell out of all the preachers who did their damnedest to inoculate me against the horror of frivolity. In their admonitions, God always seemed like Graham Chapman in a military uniform, warning us all to stop being silly or else. And yet even at church, the best times that I ever had were when the adults weren't looking, and control evaporated as the kids reveled in the glory of everyday anarchy.

But of all the lawless bugaboos that threaten at the edges of our moral uprightness, none received more apoplectic scrutiny than sex. No abandonment of control was more severe and frowned upon than this grave act which humans were literally born to perform. DNA replication is the reason we exist, fantastical claims of divine destiny notwithstanding. It's no wonder that we spend so much time obsessing about it.

Obviously I'm not speaking for everyone here, but for many of us, sex can be the ultimate relinquishment of control, the one time in an average workday where we transcend the strictures placed on our behavior by the demands of late-stage capitalism and simply sink into our primal animal natures. Of all the opportunities we have to be true to ourselves, surrender to sexual urges can be the most sublime. But to experience this fully, we have to allow ourselves to lose control.

Now, let's be real. I'm not advocating utter foolishness like going unprotected or joining the Duggar brigade. Yes, there must be some prior attention paid to safety and procreative barriers, but thankfully we live in an age where such things can be easily attended to (at least until the theocrats plunge us back into the Middle Ages, but I digress). It ain't rocket science.

But still, we fret over propriety. If I want to bang that guy, and that guy, and that girl, does that mean I'm a horrible slut who should feel bad about lack of control over her body's impulses?

The answer, of course, is who's asking? Do you care more about your mother's opinion of your sex life, or your own? Is the tittering of your judgmental friends bothersome enough that you will keep shutting down your body's insistent call to do what it was designed to do, stuffing those imperatives down until they fester and mutate into neuroses you will inflict on all the people doing what you cannot? Is strict containment of erotic resources worth the horror of turning into a Republican?

We do things all the time that we do not control. Mitosis, digestion, secretion, all of these processes that keep us alive. True, sometimes we curse their judgment, as when my sinuses decide that today, we should not only make enough mucous for myself, but also for about half the building, just in case they want to borrow some. Biology is not perfect. Less so psychology, that hodgepodge of inherited and acquired assumptions so thickly twisted that the twin hacksaws of head shrinkage and pharmaceuticals struggle with unraveling it.

But how much of our addled minds are only warped because we have internalized the notion that what our bodies and minds say is bad? That we must constantly be on guard against ourselves. How schizophrenic is that? *I* want this, but *I* need to assess whether it's something *I* really should want. How many people are in there duking it out, and how will we know if the right one wins?

To be clear, we can have bad ideas, so delineated by the fact that they hurt others. *I* want to have sex with that person, but *they* don't want to, means that's a bad idea. And sure, two consenting adults can get to the end of an encounter and find that maybe it wasn't what they needed after all. But I personally would rather err on that side than to shut down possibilities for fear that it might go badly. The ultimate outcome is not something I can fully control, and that's part of why it's worth doing.

I understand that different people have different thresholds for adventure. Yet I can't help thinking that if we examine our motivations for fearing the loss of control, we might find that it's because we're afraid we might like it too much. What would happen then? To me, there is little in the world more exciting than that prospect.

Relax. You're not in control. How awesome is that?

Relax, You're Not in Control

by Bruce Payne

Do you know how upsetting this week's theme is for a control freak? I was raised to take responsibility and if something is wrong in your life, fix it. (Or turn it over to "the Lord", because Baptists are also raised to believe that God is in control.)

This theme goes against the very fiber of my magical thinking being to even consider this a real possibility, despite all the empirical evidence supporting it. Yet, try as I will, I cannot make the subject go away or change. However, I CAN stress out about it, which is also antithetical to the thesis.

A couple of prima facie examples of exactly how much I am NOT in control has disrupted my entire afternoon. Our main computer has been wonky since Windows installed a mega-update two-three months back. Our printer has been reinstalled and reconfigured in every way imaginable because Windows keeps informing me that the driver is unavailable. I have downloaded that driver more times than I can count. Today, I am running a whole computer scan and purchased a driver update program from AVG, which did much to improve the overall performance of a computer that was bogging down so badly that I was certain we'd been seriously hacked.

Not a single thing I feared was true. A whole computer scan turned out fine. A scan by ShieldsUP! showed that we are invisible to the interwebs unless we initiate the contact. And I will now be able to complete the absolute dropkick to the groin that goes with filing a tax return that sticks in my craw the way filing one before never has.

I blame Trump, that orange-skinned Hulk in a Jina Shop president that gained the office by gaming the system, and now refuses to open his tax returns to public scrutiny. I don't want my money being spent breaking up families. I don't want a wall between us and Mexico. I don't want to go to war with Syria, North Korea, or even the goddamn Russians. And I don't want my money to go to support the war machine that feeds this monster.

The longer I live, the more absurd life becomes, as if whoever IS in control is maliciously insane. Frankly, the narcissistic angry monotheistic god of the desert described in the Old Testament sounds exactly like the lunatic I envision designing the policies for the Republican Party. If that nut is in charge, we are all truly fornicated.

Anyway, happy Easter. I'm done. I'm sure the inability to resolve my conflict and accept the wisdom of this week's subject will frustrate me tonight and tomorrow. Peace y'all. Merrily, merrily, merrily, merrily, life is but a dream.

Relax, You're Not in Control

by Marged Howley Dudek

So much depends upon a reaction you have to the moment that split you.

Your dad died? Your mother cheated? At some point—usually between the ages of 0 and 7—the walls fall, and you perceive how naked and small you are, and how flawed the people who made you are, too.

How you respond to realizing you're not in control—the first time you realize you're not in control—sets up dynamics for how you do it ever after. If, like most of us, you were too young to do that thoughtfully, then therapeutic intervention will one day become necessary if you want to at least control the only thing you can: you.

At least, such is true for me. I'm not there yet. But, I want to be. I have anger problems. I think I can fix things by yelling at them. Said like that, it's easy to see that it's the logic of a 6-year-old. But not so easy to see in the moment. Not so easy to see when you can't stop screaming at your husband and your 3-year-old is hiding, terrified, between your legs.

"Relax," is not how I was raised. That is not how "things get done." People who are relaxed do not write books, or get PhD's, or clean the house to a "ten." Now I realize—that's just how it was in our world. Our family had that attitude, and so that was our world. And sometimes the weather that came with it involved awful fights, nail biting, scalp pulling: the things that leave babies bawling and scared on the floor. These things darkened our door, and now they are darkening mine.

So, here it is, you 72-days sober mess of a human: if you want a safe child and a longer life, relax. It's literally the only way to survive this.

It's impossible to change the world enough, impossible to be the good you imagine you want—or imagine is wanted from you. Neither will you be able to make up for all the wrongs you've done: these things will both always exist and inevitably—inexorably—fade. So relax. And if you live where it never rains, grab a hose and take a shower, because this is all we have in life: the ability to accept, and the ability to adapt.

I cannot riot my world into conformity with my flawed ideals without destroying the lives of those who have to trust me. It's a choice between leaving the dishes dirty, or breaking them.

I choose the former.

I love you, kiddo,

Mom

Relax, You're Not in Control

by Matthew Broyles

It's odd that the older I get, the less I feel in control. It's not that I actually had more control in the past. Far from it. I have simply become more aware of the myriad forces both human and otherwise spinning madly in every possible direction and dimension at all times. The idea of a single person having much say in the universe's trajectory with all that in mind is laughable.

Nonetheless, we are expected to manage ourselves with some measure of competency. Mostly this comes down to not impeding the lives of others. In China Mieville's novel *Perdido Street Station*, the Garuda only have one crime, and that is Choice Theft. Meaning that an individual has removed the choice of another and insinuated their own instead. In the case of the book, the particular Choice Theft committed is rape, but it could easily be a host of other denials of self-sovereignty.

I try to live my life in such a way as not to commit Choice Theft, but in our global interconnected society, it's damn near impossible to keep one's hands clean. Every time I buy a product made in China, I reward employers who overwork children in conditions I would never want my son to endure. When I drive to the comic shop, my car puffs out yet another stream of carbon monoxide to poison the planet for generations I will never meet, but who will curse my negligence.

Every choice I make affects someone else's choices. It cannot be otherwise, tied as we all are together in economic and environmental bondage. It can be tempting to see all the choices that others are making that affect my world (o hai, Trump voters) and just throw my hands up, knowing that control is an illusion.

We say that we are at least in control of our individual lives, but that's not entirely true. We live in a world made by others. If my drinking water contains antidepressants or lead, am I making clear decisions? How sturdy are my bootstraps if no one at the factory is doing quality control? Our actions are intrinsically bound to the actions of those whose activities shape our starting conditions.

It's easy to see why so many highly intelligent friends of mine who recognize this fact just end up smoking pot and waiting for the end. Flailing away at baked-in injustice creates a kind of fatigue that I must admit falling victim to more and more. I can decide the course of my life, but only within certain constraints. Some of those, obviously, are of my own making. But a fair number are not, and therein lies the old adage of the serenity to accept the things I cannot change. The courage to change the things I can is the sticky wicket, and perhaps more so the wisdom to know the difference.

Complicating matters, studies showing our motor centers choosing a course before our conscious mind is aware of it point to the difficulty in assigning agency to ourselves. The brain, like the rest of the body, is a machine, just as prone to malfunction and malformation as the rest of us. We allow other animals the grace of simply being what they are, unable to change their programming. But we hold ourselves to a higher standard, because of the rare yet compelling cases of humans rising to become more than what their flesh commands.

Of course most of us fall short. All of us, really, in one way or another. Thus the appeal of original sin, the inherent brokenness of humankind, the need for salvation from ourselves. To judge not, knowing that inside each of us lies a trove of secrets that, if revealed, would unmake the image we project to the world. No one is honest enough to be fully immune, least of all those who say they are.

But there is value in the effort to better oneself, and indeed the continued survival of our species depends upon it. How, then, to square this realization with the awareness of our own helplessness, a speck on a speck on a spiral arm?

Probably, my shrink reminds me often enough, the first step is to stop freaking out about it.

It's difficult, when raised in a culture so entrenched in the language of self-reliance, to admit you can't go it alone. Worse, to admit that what you want may not even be possible, or even desirable, come to that. To let go of those expectations has been a significant struggle in my life, and in the lives of my friends. To relax, and realize that while you can nudge bits and pieces of the riverbed here and there, the chief thing is to feel the current and navigate it as best you can. Thoughts of dams and tributaries simply muddy the water. You are in motion. What's that up ahead? Is it what it looks like? Is it in any way avoidable, or do you need to brace for impact?

This all seems intuitive enough, but it runs counter to my inbuilt understanding of a world made of clay, one which I have the power to mold. Spinning pottery while being propelled downstream is tricky business. No wonder creators go mad.

If we can accept that we are not in control, then we can focus on how best to spend the rest of our journey. If a fork in the stream presents itself, we won't be arguing over whether that was a rock or an old soda can that we bumped into a few miles back, but instead steering towards a smoother path.

Or not. I'm not in charge of these things. Apparently.

○

Get Out

○

Get Out

by Anna Bardin

It had been a wonderful two months.

So much passion, almost too much, our hormones nearly bursting out of our skin when we were together, dying to mingle, to join and become one. It was physically painful, the drive for self-immolation, to extinguish the self for the sake of union.

The truth was, it was all we had in common.

Attempts at spending time together doing something other than bashing our bodies against one another proved fruitless, each of us fumbling to figure out something to say that wasn't a come-on. Ultimately we would give up and just go at it, the animal ascendant, all higher brain functions excused for the evening.

But the next day would come, and my mind would start talking again. I didn't like what it had to say.

Get out, it told me.

I scoffed at its suggestion the first few times. Are you kidding me? Last night was the greatest thing that ever happened. Go away, brain, you're overthinking it.

Get out, it insisted.

I didn't listen. Again we coupled, again, each time better than before, and thus all the more perplexing to hear my mind's admonition the next day.

Get out.

He was over at my apartment often enough now that bits of his personal belongings started to remain after he'd left. A shirt here, a toothbrush there, a slow infiltration that rang distant alarm bells, muffled by the fog of lust.

Get out, the klaxons blared, somewhere off in the mist.

I am a solitary person, never more at home than when silence and stillness wrap their arms around me and lull my senses into creative fugue, undisturbed by the world and its madness. As our relationship drifted out of hookup territory, I felt the siren call of belonging. Of being owned by another, wholly and unreservedly.

I'd felt that desire before. It nearly entrapped me, in the dark years following my father's death, as I searched for an anchor in the murk. A male one, of course, tall and protective, a shelter from the gale. So tempting was the prospect that I drew the face I wanted onto the closest candidate, convincing myself that I wanted to fulfill his dreams of domestic bliss. To be each other's haven from uncertainty and loneliness.

Get out, my brain had screamed back then.

Fate intervened in the form of a good friend who had miscarried badly, and nearly died from the complications. With shocking clarity, I realized that I did not have any interest in placing my life on the line for some hypothetical child, and certainly not for a man. This epiphany threw light onto the other aspects of our relationship that I didn't want, and I began to panic.

I got out. It was one of the best decisions I ever made.

So when the warnings started again with my new dream lover, my attempts at pushing down the anxiety grew more ineffectual the longer it went on. But why was I so scared? We hadn't talked about kids or picket fences. We hadn't talked about anything apart from boinking each other senseless. We had hardly talked at all.

Get out, the alarms wailed.

Not wanting to act rashly, I set up a dinner date. To talk, to get to know each other beyond the bedroom. He knew something was up, and deftly evaded every direct question, steering the conversation back into adolescent prurience, our lingua franca.

I felt stupid. Grilling him about his relationship goals when I myself did not have any. I wanted what he wanted, a ready carnal buffet cart that showed up when I called. Why was I making this more complicated than it needed to be? We went back to my place, and silenced our brains for the rest of the night.

In the morning, I found a note taped to the mirror.

"I love you," it read.

Get out, my mind cried again, hoarse with the effort.

I sat at my desk that day, incapable of work, flipping through the tiny dossier of what I knew about this man. As quitting time approached, he texted me:

"I love you. See you tonight?"

Emotions fought for control of my nerves, which simultaneously exulted and threatened to rebel. We seldom did two nights in a row, and never during the work week. He was escalating whatever this was, and I wasn't sure I wanted him to. I texted back:

"Maybe Friday?"

My heart thumped in my ear as I waited for the response that some part of me knew was coming. At last, my phone dinged:

"Is something wrong?"

Like the clothes and deodorant and all the little beachheads into my home, he had snuck under my radar the one thing I feared most: Control. He wanted to own me, the way I once believed I wanted to be owned. The outline of the cage snapped into sharp focus all around me, and my blood ran cold.

GET OUT.

The dissonance between what my body and mind wanted was cacophonous and excruciating, but I knew in that moment that it could not be how it had been. My guard was up now, and would be at some level, no matter how far out of my mind his divine ministrations might drive me. I had been drugged by chemicals already extant in my own bloodstream. All he had to do was activate them. And such was his power that he could do so at any time.

I got out.

Get Out

by Matthew Broyles

Escape is a common human instinct. The realization—upon looking around and realizing that oh shit, the trash compactor walls are closing in—can happen either very suddenly or steadily over a long period of time. When at last it hits us, our senses scream to get out, and we start searching for the exits.

Lately, I've seen a lot of this in regard to the planet we all live on. As polar ice melts, rivers become contaminated, and CO_2 levels rise, we as a species are collectively experiencing a panicked rush for the doors. Except of course there are no doors. The fire is blazing and spreading, and the only path out leads to a vast chasm of airless death.

So we point our telescopes at the sky, searching for life rafts. There's one, waaaaaaaaaaaaaaaaaaaay over there. Quick, let's develop the technology to reach it before the whole damn place burns down. But constructing advanced space travel is something only a functional civilization can do, not one that's flailing about, casting blame in all directions, wondering how the hell the casually destructive things we all do every day can possibly cause such large-scale destruction.

We want to get out, but we can't. This is the ultimate human dilemma: The inescapable. The Kobyashi Maru that we can't reprogram. Up till now, we have been very good at shunting our unsightly behaviors out of view. There have always been obscure patches of land to dump our leavings into, forgetting they exist. But now we are too many, and the land groans under the weight of our boundless need, a level of dependency that we appear unable or unwilling to reduce.

It would seem at first blush that our capacity for adaptation has limits. Yet there are those among us who have offered more sustainable options for fulfilling our needs. Wind, solar, water reclamation, low-impact means of acquiring what we need to sustain our immense civilization. Certainly not panaceas, but far better than driving right off the cliff into resource depletion and a poisoned planet.

But of all the adaptations we have developed, there is one which has apparently out-clevered us: Money.

The representation of power and influence carried by these imaginary chits of purported value is proving to be the primary obstacle to any sort of reevaluation of our society's structure. The wielders of the biggest hoards scream at us from their gold-plated loudspeakers, warning of plague and famine if any pieces of the giant machine are moved in any way whatsoever. And as products of this society, we have no reliable way of knowing whether they're right, so most of the time we back off, hoping one day to have our own gold-plated loudspeakers if we just work hard enough.

Yet the cliff still looms, as clear as day to anyone who peers over the edge towards which our bulldozers career. It's not an if, but a when. And as the masters of the universe continue to deny it, the rest of us scurry around like rats on a sinking ship, wondering how the hell to get out, some mode of egress that doesn't involve drowning.

What will it take? How bad will it have to get before the overlords' assertions are challenged? Before the mechanisms upon which they raise themselves are torn down? Are we smart enough, collectively, to know when that threshold is reached? In the absence of a new world to escape to, revolution is the only alternative to catastrophe. It's no wonder the powers that be are casting those two things as identical.

We cannot get out. We must change or die. That is the choice before us. Which will it be?

○

Who Am I?

○

Who Am I?

by Dr. Adrian L. Cook

It is a fundamental question, but one that we do not often take the time to answer. The advice to "know thyself," often attributed to the ancient Greek sages – but which probably predates that period – has become a cornerstone of Western philosophy and an oft-used aphorism, but like an overplayed song, this sound piece of advice seems to have lost its power. One can see such advice ignored when people vote for candidates or support policies that clearly go against their own self-interest, or that of their communities. We can feel the absence of self-knowledge when we agonize over a life decision, or a decision as simple as what to eat for dinner. As a professor of humanities and English at a community college, I observe this glaring lack of introspection every term as I ask students to critically engage the world and its many expressions. I notice this especially in my Millennial students, whose thinking seems to be quite literal, very linear, and predicated on a precise repetition of what their view of the world and/or any singular event or expression in the world OUGHT to be. I am not criticizing this generation. I am actually criticizing the preceding ones, including my own, Gen X, because it is from us that the Millennial and the – what's the newest generation?...Alpha?...Z? – have learned to navigate this thing we call life.

Millennials are, in fact, the most tolerant and seemingly progressive generation I've met, many of them believing that humanity should be post-gender, post-racial, etc. The problem is, they have no personal connection to these belief systems because the testing ground for acquiring and internalizing KNOWLEDGE, the educational system, is primarily geared toward the retention and regurgitation of INFORMATION, and when it comes to perspective, information, while quantifiable and understandable, tells one little about one's self or how (s)he actually sees the world. As a result, a person can accumulate a set of maxims passed down by fairly forward-thinking Gen-Xers without any experiential basis and it all seems to be perfectly natural instead of the social programming it actually represents.

An exercise: At the beginning of each class, first day of the term, I send students home with the assignment to answer a seemingly simple question – Who are you? Easy enough, right? The self should be a subject about which the student has an infinite body of knowledge. It is also a necessary place to start. I make the point that humanities (the study of art, story, and human expression) is a "soft subject," it is subjective and based upon the point of view of the scholar as much as it is the quantifiable elements (word usage, color palates, medium) of the artifacts observed. So I often get the question, "HOW do you want us to answer this question?" Fair enough. Our educational culture tells us that we must do assignments CORRECTLY or face the consequences of the dreaded bad grade. These students want As. They want As because A = good. More dangerously, sometimes A = good person. Good people get their diplomas (or their acceptance into that nursing program). That leads to a job that someone told them they should get. Job leads to total life fulfilment and all your American Dreams come true.

Only it doesn't.

I mean, sometimes, I guess there can be a positive domino effect; but seriously, I have such compassion for those who think this one assignment (which, by the way, students cannot possibly get wrong) can potentially result in the total breakdown of life fulfilment. Where I do see a positive domino effect is that the humanities is the study of US and how we create our reality. But we cannot create if we cannot navigate the diverse landscape of human expression that wants to create that reality FOR us. I believe not in the information that traditional humanities courses can offer us (I can Google information about the Bronze Age or whatever) but in the skills of critical thought and the generation of KNOWLEDGE that allow us to "read" our world and then contribute to the story in a positive and meaningful way. Foundational to this: "know thyself."

I have no power, no agency without perspective. I have no clear perspective if I don't know from whence my beliefs are generated. If my experience is divergent from the "universal" master narrative – which everyone's experience is to a degree – I have no way to share my reality to you if I am merely repeating information or memes.

So I answer the question of HOW to answer my question in the most infuriating of ways: "Any way you want to." You see, the objective, the product of this first lesson in my course is not the information that is conveyed, but for the student (and me) to see WHAT KIND of information they choose and the WAY they describe their being. I suggest that if they use "driver's license stats," physical descriptors, then they are scientific, linear. That is their strength. Some define their existence almost exclusively by the roles they have – mother, student, etc. These folks, I suggest, are well suited to the social sciences. They observe themselves in relation to others. Those who are introspective and describe themselves in terms of how they feel, by their experiences, and/or through value or morally based statements are my humanitarians, my artists, seekers.

The goal would be to come to a place where a little of each is present. That is what makes a scholar, an innovator, a social creator. One who sees each side of the die and every side as part of a holistic cube. But even if they never do, it is my hope that KNOWING how they see themselves tells them everything about how they see the world. Being able to say that "I see the world in terms of _____, means that that can be heard and understood for who they ARE, not as they think they ought to be or should be.

This fulfilment that we seek in life. . .it is my job as a mentor to deliver the news that it doesn't come from following a prescribed path. I am still, at 43 learning who I am. When I pause long enough to take my own advice and step off of the path myself, smell the proverbial roses, and look inside for a moment to see who I am, and who I am becoming, the view of my own unique path gets clearer. I am able to be more productive, and perhaps less critical of others. Maybe it doesn't work for everyone, but only you can decide.

Who Am I?

by Anna Bardin

Who am I?

Who are you?

Who is asking the questions here?

Who is answering them?

Why must questions be asked?

Aren't we in the same head here?

Yes, but...

So who is this speaking right now?

Umm...

Wait, was I the one asking, or the one wondering who was asking?

I'm not sure.

Start again.

Who am I?

You are me.

So who is that?

Let me get back to you.

When?

I'm not sure. After this show?

K.

Who Am I?

by Chris Dashiell

We are never told the definition of the word "I." We don't know it. We assume we know what it means, but we don't bother to define it.

The most rational conclusion, it would seem, is that I am this body, or if you prefer, this mind-body complex. Certainly this is the vantage point from which we experience life. It is the one constant from birth to death. The complications arise when we think and talk about it.

For one thing, I can lose my limbs, and various body parts, and still retain the notion of "I." This gives rise to the idea of the essential self. If the brain could be kept alive somehow and retain consciousness, I would still be "I." Or so we imagine. The key term here is "consciousness."

For in addition to the wonder of existence, there is the further wonder of someone being aware of existence. It is the wonder of consciousness, a category unto itself, truly *sui generis*. Consciousness is like a transparent container which allows there to be experience of being, rather than just simply being. Then again, it is not really like that, because metaphors can only indicate, but not literally describe it.

With consciousness comes the notion of the inner world and the outside world. But with the mind-body complex, even though consciousness is its power or faculty, I can see my body, my arms and legs, my face in a mirror, just like I see anything else in the world. What we can't see are thoughts, feelings, memories (except in the different sense of "seeing" in imagination or dream), and all else we consider just "subjective." So is this hidden aspect of our experience the true "I"? The notion of subject-object, soul-body, mind-body, and so on, springs from that idea. And it developed into the belief that "consciousness" and "matter" are two separate things.

Now we find ourselves assuming that "I" am something inside the body. It could be an immaterial soul residing in me somewhere, or perhaps it's the brain, or mind. But if we really try to locate the self, the assumption doesn't hold up. Anything I think about it is an object of thought, and anything I perceive is an object of my awareness. To think of myself is to think of that which is thinking. To perceive myself is to perceive that which is perceiving.

The subject is the constant precondition for any experience whatsoever, so to try to experience it is like trying to bite your own teeth. The house of mirrors effect will never end.

The word "I" is like a place holder used to refer to something in general that has no specific location.

Most of us just consider it a personal thing. I am this particular existing individual, with a name and a birth date and a history, and of course, a personality. We can look at all these things, analyze them, elaborate on them, without considering that these are essentially objects of our awareness, and not awareness itself. I say, "This is what my personality is like. This is where I grew up. These are my opinions," and so on. But who is it that is saying this? A personality? Alzheimer's or a brain injury can erase all that, and yet there is someone still experiencing life.

As a species we cling to identity as if it were a life raft. Beliefs about immortality and life after death almost always involve the survival of the personal "I." The thing we have feared the most is the most obviously true. The personal "I" is exactly what dies. Awareness as individuation—this particular lifetime vantage point—why would Nature need for this to survive? Trillions more of them can be born in an instant without some clumsy system of transmigration or preservation. The recognition of limitation, of mortality, applying to us not just as bodies but as conscious beings, seems to me to be the necessary start of understanding who I am.

When you're watching a movie, you get involved in all the actions on the screen—the characters, the plot, the dialogue, the feelings. This is like the world, like life. What we don't think about is that in order for the film to be projected, there has to be that blank screen. The film can only exist in that container.

Then again, it's not really like that, because metaphors can only indicate, but not literally describe it. When you walk into the theater before the show, you can see the blank screen. But the metaphor won't translate to reality, because the screen can't be separate from the film. For the screen to be separate from the film would mean that it would have its own limited, conditioned existence. It would be a measurable thing, not reality itself.

We all have an intuition of eternity. In order to map our experience, we split it up into self and other, life and death. We need the map. But we are not the map.

Who Am I?

by Matthew Broyles

There was a time when I could have told you with great certainty and conviction who exactly I was.

We are told that youth is when you search for yourself, hopefully finding the fugitive essence of your being by the time middle age begins to pull at your sleeve. Having discovered who you are, you arrange the rest of your life as best you can to accommodate this person that is you.

The ubiquity of the midlife crisis challenges that notion. Perhaps we are not who we thought we were, and as the clock ticks down to impending dotage, we'd better get a handle on who exactly we are, so our lives aren't scattered all willy-nilly when our bodies start slowing down.

Never one to get in a hurry, I've been dragging my midlife crisis out over the past decade or so. Thoughts pop into my brain, and I eyeball them warily, wondering who the person is that they came from. Often they are not thoughts that the me that I recognize from the past would have ever had. It is as if they are emanating from another person who has slowly taken up residence in my head, who is not me, but who is using my body as a vehicle to either do or not do things that may or may not have questionable merit.

The not doing is bothersome, because sometimes when I get a block of time to myself, there is a period of tension whilst the old, hyper-productive me argues with the new, laissez-faire me about how the hell are you wasting this time, you lazy bastard. I've been getting slightly better at the self-talk thing, but it gets pretty heated during prime free time, which for a parent, comes at a premium.

This other person also seems to care less in general. Having been a Betazoid-level empath in my youth, it is rather alarming now to witness how much easier it is to emotionally detach from people in distress than it once was. Sometimes this includes family and close friends.

My paternal grandfather used to eat raw jalapenos out of a jar, because his taste buds were burnt out. I've wondered if my empathy nodes have experienced something similar, responding now only to the most extreme stimuli.

Some of that, of course, is self-defense. In the creative industries to which I have pledged myself, sensitivity can be a quick path to self-loathing and destruction, Hunter Thompson's shallow money trench and all. It's a paradox, because without that sensitivity, art is impossible. Not surprising that this conundrum often leads to narcissism, a label that, though ignominious, I have not entirely avoided. But like anything, there are levels. On the continuum of arrogance, I fall well short of, let's say, Kanye.

I often wonder how people keep up emotional stamina. My mother was a nurse in the preemie ward for years. Oddly, this is not dissimilar to the music industry. In either case, a fair number of the people that surround you are doomed. The grace to survive in such a world and still care deeply about its inhabitants is an ongoing struggle for me, in a way that it would not have been years ago. Sadness is cumulative, and the ghosts of the past join forces with those of the present, chanting their portents until I plug my ears and run for the silo, where the only voice I can hear is my own.

This is a behavior exhibited by this new person I seem to be becoming, one who seems to be okay with putting off until tomorrow what might be rather unpleasantly dealt with today. This is ironic, because it's exactly the sort of behavior I criticize modern politicians for. Perhaps it's a zeitgeist our culture has fallen victim to. The 20th century was about trying on different utopias for size. In the 21st, we appear to have sloughed them all off, save for Ayn Rand-infused corporate Darwinism, which is largely just feudalism without the fluffy pants. Back to the basics.

A wise man once told me that in most human activities, there is almost no correlation between what you know and what you do. I think of this when I watch myself do something stupid, knowing the whole time that it is stupid.

I hear myself talk about fighting the system, but then I log into Amazon to watch my stories. I bemoan our dependence on fossil fuels, but drive at least an hour and a half every day, and enjoy taking long road trips. I am acutely aware of how much sleep I need, yet when the appointed bedtime hour arrives, I sit and watch myself not go to bed, wondering the whole time why I am so intent on making my future self suffer, most of the time for no reason whatsoever.

Who the hell is this person? He looks like me, and has my memories, but increasingly, I'm not sure I recognize him. Or honestly, if I like him very much. Maybe this is how madness starts, I dunno.

But I don't think I'm alone. We as a society seem to be going through something of an identity crisis at present. It's a hell of a time for it, I'll tell you what, but sometimes the only way change happens is when we are pushed to our limits. When the other option is nonexistence.

In the meantime, perhaps the question must be rephrased. Not "who am I," but "what am I doing?" If we all asked that, I expect we might start getting somewhere.

○

Wait for It...

○

Wait for It…

by Anna Bardin

Patience, I hear, is a virtue. But it is possible to wait too long.

I remember my dad talking about his dreams of retirement. There was a house by a lake that we used to pass when I was a kid, and he would always point to it.

"That's the kind of thing I'm talking about," he'd say. "You can come by anytime when you're grown, and we can hang out on the porch and watch the sun go down over the water."

I agreed, that would be lovely. Part of me must have latched onto the idea the way my dad had, because when he lay dying my senior year of high school, I remember tearfully thinking that this couldn't be happening. How was he going to buy that lake house if he was dead?

Man plans, god laughs. Even in an era when lifespans are rising, I find myself assuming the worst. If I don't enjoy my life now, I might not get to do so at all. I'm only three years younger than my dad was when he died. I don't have his bad health habits, but I do have his genes. My mom's still around, but frankly, she's a mess. Her choices were different than mine, but I can't help wondering if I need to keep seeking out adventure as much as possible before I, too, go off the deep end in my dotage.

Some of this, of course, is because I will not have grandchildren. For me, old age will just be old age, and my body will not be able to do everything it can do now. Lord knows what my mind will get up to. I fear putting off anything, lest time pass me by, until one day I wake up and realize I can't get out of bed unassisted. That happened to my grandmother, and few thoughts scare me more.

Truthfully, though, I spend a lot more time scared than I used to. With each passing day, the future looks more and more terrifying to me. My country burns, the world runs in circles with its hair on fire, and the idea of waiting any time at all to do anything whatsoever seems like a fool's errand. The diem is here now, and only now. Carpe the shit outta that sucker.

But what if we all think that way, and clamor for the party bus all at once, leaving our posts uncrewed? Then when the worst comes, we will be the ones at fault. I will have to explain to my niece and nephew why I let everything go to hell while I blew my wad on the end-of-the-world party, leaving them to pick up the bill. That's not the legacy I want to leave. Neither, though, is a life of quiet desperation. If I wish to embody my principles, I must seize life by the goolies and enjoy the ride.

It seems to come down to what it is that constitutes life. Life's properties are manifold, and differ for each person. Survival is obviously paramount, and along with that comes health, responsibility, and of course love, in whatever form it takes. We have our lists of needs and wants, adjoined necessarily by the constant assessment of which is which.

Then there's the time factor. Each of these things takes x amount of time, out of y amount available to us. And there will always be a deficit. Cuts must be made, and therein lies the uncertainty. Did I cut the right thing? Why can't I do all of it? Maybe there's some fundamental way to rearrange my life so that I can fit the whole list in. Maybe I'm wasting what little time I do have by mucking about with hypothetical rearrangements. Just live, dammit. Quickly, before you can't anymore.

I have no idea how much more time I have on this earth. Statistically, I'm about halfway done. Stated like that, my stomach tightens. From my observations, the latter half of this journey stands as much chance of being miserable as it does of being joyous. Much of it is down to happenstance, genetics, and a host of factors beyond my control.

Yet I am not powerless. I can choose whether to pursue things I want now or later, within reason. And almost invariably, I decide on the former. Sometimes that works out, sometimes not. But I would rather know today than tomorrow. Waiting is not my strong suit. If I see an opportunity, even if it is ludicrous and ill-advised, I am apt to spring upon it, consequences be damned. I have deep scars from that sort of behavior, but apparently they're not sufficiently severe to make me change my ways. Not yet, anyway.

So, no. I will not wait for it. Whatever it is. Tomorrow may not exist. And though comeuppance may rain down like a hail of volcano ash upon my foolish head, I will nonetheless be grateful not to carry the regret of chances not taken.

Perhaps that attitude will bring about the very doom I fear. But imagine waiting, and then finding that the lake house on the horizon is only a mirage. That your chance is gone. It's a horror that chills my blood, and has since I watched my father die, his dreams lost to the winds of time.

Don't wait. Now is all we have.

Wait for It...

by Ashley Van Arsdel

"The waiting is the hardest part." - Tom Petty

In today's society, people have grown unaccustomed to waiting. Some of us old folks remember waiting on a letter or a package in the mail, which could take weeks. I used to wait in anticipation for my CDs, which I would order knowing it could take six to eight weeks for them to arrive. Now, we can order music online and have it instantly. We can message our loved ones and hear back from them immediately. Certainly a lot quicker than pacing by the mailbox or hanging around the telephone.

As a musician, and especially in my musical role, I am very acquainted with the process of waiting. Piano players do not always come in on the "one." We anticipate a classy timing, a good time to jump in, that fits and enhances the tune we are accompanying. Waiting for a piano student to figure out the note during sheet reading practice, instead of pouncing and giving them the note myself. This is an especially hard duty for me, but I also realize the importance of allowing someone to learn for themselves.

In the rest of my life, however, the impatience of having to sit and twiddle my thumbs has not always done me well. I attempted to hold out for things I thought I deserved, and wound up stupidly making the "safe choice" in my rush to deliver myself from limbo. I could cite many examples here, but out of fear of revealing my own stupidity and frustration, I won't. The more beautiful aspects of life are often found in the wait, which I am just now discovering at the ripe old age of thirty-three.

Why does waiting make us afraid? Are we afraid if we wait too long, something may not happen? If we jump the gun, we may also blow the opportunity. It's a fine line. And like a tiger primes itself to pounce on its prey at the most opportune moment, so must waiting be viewed, as taking the time to properly prepare.

There are so many things I would've done differently, or would gone differently for me, had I simply taken the time to smell the roses, and wait for it. I have never been good at sitting idle. It's actually one of those times when I tend to get in trouble, when there's nothing going on. I'm not sure if it's boredom or the unease of sitting there. Idle hands may be the devil's work.

What can we do with ourselves as we wait to make the time pass more constructively? There is always the question, too, if what we wait for will actually come to pass or not. I think it's one aspect of the whole process which makes people nervous. What if I sit here and wait and this object/person/event never comes to fruition? Then what? Have I wasted my time?

I'm at a point in my life where I'd rather waste my time waiting for something good instead of taking the first rotten egg that plops into my basked to avoid the long line.

Wait for it. It'll be here sooner than you think.

Wait for It...

by Matthew Broyles

"It hasn't happened yet..." – William Shatner

The great 'it.' The transformation of effort into achievement. A moving target, of course, shifting with the goalposts as it skitters across the field, like a butterfly in a dream that you can never quite catch.

"Every room's a waiting room..." – Nataly Dawn

Chase it long enough, and fatigue sets in. Patience is learned, the reality of the conjunction between preparation and opportunity. You prepare. You wait. You work. You wait.

"And then one day you find ten years have got behind you; no one told you when to run, you missed the starting gun..." – Pink Floyd

Did it happen already? The opportunity? Maybe you didn't spot it. Maybe it hasn't shown up yet. The fear of missing it pales beside the possibility that you have, in fact, already watched the damn thing blow past, oblivious.

"But the last of the big-time losers shouted before he drove away, 'I'll be right back as soon as I crack the one that got away...'" – Tom Waits

Backtrack. Autopsy. Was it that one? That one? None of those look quite right, but you never can tell. No, face forward or it'll pass you by. If it hasn't already.

"I guess this is our prime, like they tell us all the time; were you expecting some other kind?" – Aimee Mann

But wait. You're trying to make it a story. A pretty narrative. That's for biographers to sort out later. How does it go down in real life? Does it look like what it is? What it might be? What it would be if you could figure out how to shape it, to hack it out of the rock and make it what it could be? What if it's just a rock?

"Close doesn't count; it's too close to call; it works for horseshoes and hand grenades, but that's about all..." – Little Jack Melody

Hold on. Whose ruler are we using? The predictions of the adults from back in the day? The vow of vengeance from the junior high locker room? The fear that, after all is said and done, you're one more insignificant chunk of kindling in the big bonfire of human history?

"Oh, all the things that humans do, to leave behind a little proof…" – Marina & the Diamonds

Voltaire had it figured out hundreds of years ago, of course:

"Pangloss sometimes said to Candide:

'There is a concatenation of events in this best of all possible worlds: for if you had not been kicked out of a magnificent castle for love of Miss Cunegonde: if you had not been put into the Inquisition: if you had not walked over America: if you had not stabbed the Baron: if you had not lost all your sheep from the fine country of El Dorado: you would not be here eating preserved citrons and pistachio-nuts.'

'All that is very well,' answered Candide, 'but let us cultivate our garden.'"

We like a good story. But picture the characters in your favorite book jerking their heads up suddenly and realizing that this whole time, you've been enjoying their travails, the misery as well as the joy. What is better, to be at the center of a grand drama, or to observe it from above?

"Please don't be sad; if it was a straight mind you had, we wouldn't have known you all these years…" – Traffic

As a reader, not knowing the ending is part of what makes the journey exciting. As a writer, watching the continuous flux of possible conclusions as the narrative takes place is intoxicating. As a character, though, it is anxiety itself. Is this when the whole thing goes to hell? Am I the one who has to die that others might make it to the triumph in one piece? Do the bad guys win? Or is there a twist?

"Please tell me, when will it be over now, how soon? How far must we go to prove to you? So we wait and we wonder…" – Phil Collins

How different our lives would be if we knew the ending. For those of us with active imaginations, that unknowability runs in circles, day and night, scores of possibilities fanning out like multiverses, every outcome the right one until its time has passed. It's like barreling down a 1,000-lane expressway with exits on all sides every quarter mile. This one? That one? And where the hell is this highway going, anyway?

"Oh my god, I'm gonna die when I get old, and I'm not ready…" – Adam Holmes

Story arcs demand endings, or at least satisfying denouements. When your mind is inclined to create stories, it is difficult not to search for narrative patterns in your own life, subplots and turning points, the gun in the first act that goes off in the third. Accepting that these rules do not universally apply to human lifespans is the toughest pill to swallow.

"When you're telling a story, at some point you stop; but stories don't end..." – Dawes

So we work, and we wait, and we create, and we wait, and we seek out that which makes the passage of time most fulfilling, whether it leads to a predictable destination or not. Sometimes enjoying most the things which could go either horribly wrong or amazingly right. It's a gamble we take by continuing to live, and not just exist.

Some of us win. Some lose. Some of us don't know which one of those we have done. And like any story, much of the action is happening offscreen. We may one day learn which character we are. Or maybe that determination will be left to future readers.

"Here we are inside a novel, waiting for an end; but we don't know the authors of the book..." – Guster

Write as if your life depends on it. It does.

"Pick up here and chase the ride, the river empties to the tide; all of this is coming your way..." – R.E.M.

o

What I Did During the Revolution

o

What I Did During the Revolution

by Anna Bardin

I can't hear you.

Okay, I mean, I CAN, but I'm trying really hard not to.

You think everyone wants to hear that mad fiddling all day and night? Some of us have stories to write. And when the world is on fire, we need stories more than ever. As Blake said, this world's a fiction and made up of contradiction. Kind of sounds like a hip-hop lyric, now that I type it. Maybe I should make a William Blake rap musical…

Stop your shouting, you infernal string-scraper. Yes, I KNOW entropy is real. I KNOW there are too many of us. The hell am I gonna do, go out with a couple of Uzis and thin the herd? Is that more useful than giving people something nice to read? A way to take a break from the shitstorm outside, if only for a while? We are where we are.

Apathy, I know. It's bad. Seriously, though, I called Ted Cruz this morning, and I'm on his mailing list for life now. Does that help anyone? When the children of my niece and nephew ask what Great Aunt Anna did during the revolution, will a story about chewing out a Senate staffer impress them?

I'm not a hero. Never have been. I stand up for friends in need, though, and do what I can not to make things worse. I did no harm. Is that a good epitaph?

Maybe I am part of the problem. But you have to admit, the problem is pretty damn big. If an army of lemmings streams towards a cliff, and one decides to run the other way, will it help? That's still a lot of dead lemmings. They run off cliffs. It's what they do, everyone knows that. Wait, they don't really? Well, shit.

Can I just…I only want to write my stories. Don't look at me like that. I know people are dying. I'm a woman, and that's a pre-existing condition now, so I'll be dead sooner than later.

You want me to shout at the orange shitgibbon and his troop of red-assed baboons? This is helping whom? Far better to offer comfort to those bearing the claw marks of their atrocities. Like Mister Rogers said, look for the helpers. I'm helping. I think. Don't do the Ralph Wiggum voice, dammit.

Okay, okay…to the battlements, then. Where do they keep battlements? That's a parking lot, not a battlement. No one's here, it's a Sunday. Maybe we can yell at their window. Fuck you, Republican scum! Now the maintenance guy is staring at us. Did I help?

Monday's here, time to call my reps. I do, I really do. The admins know me by now. Yep, yep, outrage, will vote for opponent, yes, right, got it. Fries with that? I did it, I called. Stories now? Yes? I mean, I'm writing on company time. Sticking it to the man. What did you do during the revolution, old lady? I withheld a few hours of work that a trained monkey could do so that I could write stories that get people's bits excited. Kudos? Does no one use that word anymore?

There's that damned fiddle again. SHUT UP, SHUT UP. I didn't ask for you. I don't want to make America great again. I have no problem with America being bog-standard and average, just so long as I can wring stories out of my little brain and share them with people. I really don't think that's an outrageous request. I suppose I'll find out whether I'm right when they show up to decide who gets shipped to the FEMA camps. Maybe I'll get a notebook in my cell.

What did you do during the revolution, ancient crone? Mostly, I waited for it to be over. To return to a time when my greatest concern was whether I could afford to buy those kickass boots this month or next month. When this feeling of creeping dread didn't lurk around every corner, threatening to upend everything I love about the world. Can we just go ahead and have the revolution now? I'm tired of waiting, I have shit to do.

Yes, YES, I hear you. Fine. Let's do this. Whatever this is. Do I call again? I'll go to a march, maybe. Make a meme? Does tweeting count? Add my tiny voice to the digital mountain?

K, did all that. No revolution yet. Sigh. How do I fill all these hours waiting for critical mass to metastasize?

Maybe I could write a story. Maybe that's the best thing I can do. Maybe it isn't enough. But honestly, I'm not sure what is.

What I Did During the Revolution

by Matthew Broyles

Americans like to talk big.

I certainly do. 'Why, if that so-and-so does that to me, I'll [hyperbolic statement] him into next week.' But the truth is, most of us let things slide on the regular. Important things, like being shafted by corporations, government, bosses, co-workers, and pretty much everyone.

If we actually fought every instance of injustice that came our way every week, we would have time to do nothing else.

Which makes our current national predicament problematic. The wholesale dismantling of our regulatory system, coupled with the nepotistic and aristocratic seizure of state power for its own ends is nothing short of jaw-dropping. Imagine if someone walked up to you and said, "Do you mind if I use your tax dollars for weekly golf vacations and promotion of my daughter's clothing line? Oh, and can I sentence you to death if your bank account falls below a certain threshold?" That and more is precisely what is happening to all of us.

All over my social media feeds, we are exhorted to get in the streets. And then we do, but of course only on weekends and convenient times, because we still have to go to our jobs, pick up the kids, and pay our bills. We might have a couple hours on Saturday for revolution, but only after the soccer game and a haircut.

I always see images of mobs in foreign countries, crushing against barriers surrounding state houses, and I wonder how the hell any of them got all that time off work to do that. GOP toadie tweeters ask the same question, assuming that if you have time to protest, you probably don't have a job. I hate to say it, but I can't help wondering the same thing.

If I decide to go camp out in front of Kay Granger's office during a workday, my ability to keep my family housed and fed is compromised. Yet I recognize the larger issue that if I DON'T protest, that very same ability to take care of my family is undermined as we're all sold down the river.

It has to get bad enough that we have more to lose by not missing work than by missing it. And that's pretty damn bad. Perhaps we're nearly there. The unemployment rate for the under-30s is 25%, the same as it was overall during the Great Depression. My son has only five years left before he can try and find a job. If he can't, maybe he and all the jobless youngsters will take the opportunity to storm the gates and demand better.

But we are easily distracted. Hollywood keeps us entertained, Silicon Valley gives us the new and shiny, the Fed keeps the rot from showing. Outrage fatigue has already set in. There is no such thing as a slow news day anymore. Flipping open the Google News tab to see what fresh horror has transpired is a daily adrenaline rush, accompanied by hours of venting and commiseration with sympathizers both foreign and domestic.

When does that anger manifest into revolution? I saw the seeds of hope in the ranks of my Berniacs last year, people who dared to dream that we could reform the system, defy Moloch & Mammon, create a society designed for the many, not the few. But loss transformed that disillusionment into apathy, and now we all sit around planning for what we'll do when the worst finally hits. Me, asking veteran friends if I should get a gun. Contacting Canadian acquaintances to inquire about the possibility of refuge.

A good many of us have already accepted that we are screwed. Protest seems like a mug's game, standing out on the street corner, being ignored by corporate-funded empty suits who know damn well we won't actually charge in with guillotines and cut their heads off. There is no real fear of revolt. We are pacified by our opiates, our coping mechanisms, our worldly certainty that human nature and will to power is unchangeable. We wait for our demise, sleepwalking down well-trodden corridors into the valley of steel.

We live in fear of the sword's terrible blow, all the while bleeding to death by a thousand tiny razor cuts. By the time we realize it, our strength is sapped, our blows against the enemy weak and ineffectual. Our opportunity passed, all for the want of a clearer catalyst.

This is how liberty dies. Not in thunderous cataclysm, but in slow dessication, until we look around one day and find that our green grass has browned, our water rusted, our air thickened with the detritus of our excess. The equation will not square, and into the banana republic bin of history we go.

I am as much to blame as anyone. I'm typing this on my work computer, occupying a desk for these hours so that I may provide food for my child. An armchair activist, exhorting someone else to go do what I cannot bring myself to contemplate. But my fellow revolutionaries sit at their desks, each afraid of the same spectres which haunt me. Poverty, homelessness, uninsurability, death. All for what? To be mocked by pundits as the banksters do their dirty work anyway, unfazed by the threats from the proles?

So what, then? How does this whole revolution thing work? How do we discharge our domestic duties and also safeguard the foundations upon which our society is built?

No, really. I'm asking you.

Starting Over

Starting Over

by Anna Bardin

I have a funny relationship with the concept of starting over.

Because really, that's all I've ever done.

As a kid, my dad's job relocated frequently. I seldom spent more than a year in the same house, with the same neighbors, in the same city. I did not make many attachments, because I knew that my presence in these locales and in these people's lives was temporary. Eventually, they would be my memory, and I would be theirs.

For most of my adulthood, I conducted my romantic relationships similarly, never lingering long enough to get comfortable. Change was inevitable, so I kept my ties loose, the better to move on gracefully. Friendships could hang on a bit longer, more so with the advent of email and social media, but still, those digital links aren't as strong as physical proximity. Life for me has been ephemeral, made of shifting sands, and I have surfed those dunes lightly, lest I get grit stuck in my shoe and have to stop to empty it out.

It's odd, then, when I look around right now as I'm writing this. I've been in the same apartment for over a decade now, paid for by a job I've been at for longer than that. Eight years ago, I let my bf park his sundries in my closets and cabinets, and they remain there still, more permanent than his actual body, which travels nearly constantly and only graces me with its presence when schedules and planets align. A fit arrangement for a woman who resists attachment.

I have seen friends go through bouts of teeth-gnashing angst when the possibility of starting over rears its head. A relationship gone bad, a once-solid job beginning to wobble on its foundations, a house behaving likewise. The fear of losing something they have invested in haunts them relentlessly.

That fear is not altogether alien to me. The prospect of something happening to my niece and nephew, with whom I spend a fair amount of time, is chilling, even though they aren't my kids. Likewise with the bf, who went through a health scare last year that shook me more than I like to admit. And of course I don't want to lose my job, for reasons that have less to do with the work itself than with how much less wine I would be able to afford without the money.

It's not that I don't fear loss. We all do. But I guess I have lived my life in such a way where I don't have much that I couldn't do without if it went away. I can get another job, find another apartment, and yes, procure another bf if I want. Some might consider that cold, but to me, it's a continuation of the constant upheaval with which I was raised.

One might venture a psychological explanation as to why I've remained fixed in place for so long as a grown-up. Maybe I'm trying to forge roots that I could not back then. If so, I'm doing a pretty crap job at it. I have no particular bond to my geographic location, nor my cubicle, and my experience with romantic partners is wide enough that I know how many fish are in the sea. Everything is replaceable, except those kids. I suppose I've become a vicarious parent of sorts through them, but at the end of the day, I still send them back home and sit down in my replaceable office chair at my replaceable desk in my replaceable apartment in my replaceable suburb of an eminently replaceable city.

I myself am expendable. I know this. Family and friends would mourn for a time, but they would move on. I might get referenced in a conversation here and there, but their lives would continue more or less as they had when I was alive. I have created a footprint small enough that my disappearance would not require anyone to start over.

Many might be alarmed if such an assessment were put to their lives. Most people want to matter, to be missed, and I confess a bit of that yearning. I do want a few tears shed on my behalf. Yet I don't want to inconvenience anyone. I have no interest in becoming such an integral part of someone's life that they are thrown into turmoil if I step out of it. That pressure is paralyzing, and I frankly can't understand how anyone lives with it.

I'm speaking, of course, in the long term. When entangled with a lover, you'd best believe I want to be the most important thing in the world to them at that moment. But when our carnal dance has ended, I'm more than content to fade back into the ether, leaving a satisfying aftertaste. That makes me picky about who those dances are conducted with. It's no coincidence that those of us with traveling childhoods tend to flutter in the same flocks, seeking temporary landing points before we jet off to the next atoll. We know we are not built to last, and eye warily the ones who seem to be.

Starting over does not scare me. Building something solid enough that I fear to lose it…that's the real nightmare.

Starting Over

by Cristee Cook

The accident happened on a sunny morning in September of 2009. I was forced to start over. I was forced to start over on a Tuesday. I had gotten up earlier than usual that morning. I was working as a freelance costume designer, and I was feeling behind on the project. I awoke nervous and anxious. I rushed through my morning routine and out the door, barely pausing long enough to hug my husband.

In 2009, before I was forced to start over, rushing through life was the norm. My mother came to visit me that year and compared my daily schedule to a fire drill. I was a busy freelance costume designer in a small market; the flailing captain of my one-woman company. This September Tuesday was no different. My head was full of unfinished alterations, actor personalities, and budget concerns.

I want to spare the details of the accident I witnessed. It was a blur of tires screeching, loud concussions, and frantic screams. I was one of three witness cars that were not hit, but who stopped to help. The highway was eerily quiet, a disturbing stillness. My adrenaline ran towards the car that looked the worst. The driver had been ejected. Another witness came right behind me. I told her to stop. Call 911. A third witness rushed our direction, saw the scene, and panicked.

I got down on the ground with the victim and held his hand. The peripheral scene vanished. I heard my voice say, "It's ok to go."

I felt a hand on my shoulder, a strong voice asking me to step away from the scene.

Questions followed:

Did you witness this accident?
Where is the car that hit this car?
Who was driving?
Do you know this man?

I answered the questions:

Yes.
I don't know.
I don't know.

No. Yes I guess I do now. No, I don't know his name.

I sat in the back of the ambulance while they took my blood pressure and asked me if I needed anything. I answered the same questions. I signed a waiver that I did not read.

They offered me a ride home:

Can we call someone for you?

I drove myself home.

My husband was still home.

I told him: *I just can't do today. I'm staying home.*

Concerned, he asked me several times if I was alright. I lied, encouraged him to go to work, told him I would have some coffee, maybe take a bath, try to relax and reorganize. He believed me and left for work.

I sat on the couch. Everything was in slow-motion. The phone rang. Alison. I told her what had happened with almost no details. She came over. We sat on the couch. The day ended.

That was the day I was forced to start over.

After, I wasn't sleeping well because the accident showed up in my dreams. I felt withdrawn and angry. I systematically took a scorched-Earth approach to my life. I abruptly resigned from all of my creative projects. I stopped participating in my spiritual life and personal hobbies. I hurt people who depended on me.

I reluctantly sought out a professional counselor with whom I spent the next six months rehashing the details. Searching for an explanation. I worked hard to understand that I was not responsible, that I could not have changed the outcome, that I did not fail.

I learned about myself. I learned to start over.

Now, it's been almost ten years since I was forced to start over. Most days I don't think about it. My life is happy, fulfilling, and dramatically different. But early dateless Tuesdays in September hold a fog I still can't quite penetrate, and then I remember. And I start over on those days. Now, starting over is a familiar, practiced experience of acceptance, forgiveness, and the release of love sent to the man whose name I did not know. To his family. To the world.

Starting Over

by Matthew Broyles

I grew up hearing about my permanent record. A list of all my achievements and transgressions that would follow me through life.

Though I never completely believed such a thing existed as such back in the '80s, the truth is that we all probably have more of a permanent record now than we used to. How many old tweets have been dug up to prove a politician or celebrity's hypocrisy? Go back through my old song lyrics, and you will find contradictions aplenty.

In his song *Leaving Oldtown*, Glen Phillips talks about going to a place where no one's ever heard of him or his foibles. That vision is appealing some days, when the mountain of self that I've built over 43 years starts pressing down, demands of consistency clashing with new awareness. The desire to change runs headlong through halls of pre-existing decisions that circumscribe any route forward. Seeing something from a distance, and trying to work out a route that will get you there, paths seeming to lead in that direction, but doubling back inexplicably, until you're not sure if you're still headed that way or going backwards. Or worse, getting there after slogging through traffic and realizing it wasn't worth the trek.

You can always go back, but you can't go back all the way, as our observant friend Robert Zimmerman notes. There is always a permanent record of sorts, the weight of past mistakes and the consequences issuing out before you as you walk, bumping you back onto the path when you think to stray. You could break out entirely, go off the rails, but what if that exit ramp only leads to a 100-foot drop into the abyss? And then you have another regret to stack onto the pile. If you survive.

Living in the moment is all very well in theory, but not all moments are created equal. Our society is not set up for gadflies, flittering from one flower to the next in search of novel experience. Each jump creates a gap in health insurance, a setup fee for utilities, a smaller likelihood that any resources will be left when dotage creeps in and the safety net finally drops your generation into the tent city.

We choose the future over the present all the time. It makes quite a bit of sense, really. A society grows great when old men plant trees whose shade they will never sit in. Squirrels don't eat all their acorns in one sitting. If we all live for thrills now, we toss tomorrow into the bin.

Hitting the reset button comes up in our national conversation a lot. Pick a period in history we like, say we need to go back there, and start dismantling the bits of the past that have changed since then. But time does not wind itself back thus. The only way forward is forward. There is no backward, only a forward that reasonably simulates backward. An illusion. We want to be able to start afresh, to wipe our historical slate clean so that we're not weighed down with the consequences of our past behavior.

But there it is, the permanent record, in the form of ghettos, debt, environmental depletion, piles of plastic bags, maimed veterans, irate neighbors…we can't start over. The only way forward is forward, dragging our pack with us, stopping off to redress what past grievances we can en route to creating something better ahead.

We are a utopian people. I feel it every time I assess my life, and the first instinct is to try to take everything completely apart and start fresh rather than try and repair the bits that are causing me consternation. Fuck it, start over, my brain insists, impatient with incremental moves, baby steps that will take months or years to alter course, if even then. Somehow I and many of my fellow Americans have this Monopoly view of the world, where if you don't like how the game is going, you simply clear all the pieces off and start a new round.

It doesn't work that way. I know this, but it's still my first thought when things start going to hell. Just turn it off and back on again, that should fix it. Hard reboot. We do it with entertainment franchises when they've written themselves into a corner. Restart, clear the board. Just leave that other universe to wither, it wasn't interesting anymore.

Humans cannot be written off this way. We create tangles of interpersonal relationships as we go, and when one friendship fades, it does not go away. It becomes part of our fabric, informing all future friendships. It's been six years since my friend Jason died, and I probably think about him more now than I did when he was alive. Those thoughts make me cherish the friends yet living, and seek to kindle new relationships. To keep the ones who know all your old secrets, but also to seek out those who see you as you are now, not as compared to the you they met so long ago.

So maybe starting over isn't impossible. Perhaps it is a process that runs parallel to riding out the ripples from the past. Adding rather than replacing. Then when something old gives way, maybe we don't have to leap off into complete uncertainty, but rather scooch our way over onto the track we've built alongside the existing one. Maybe starting over is something we can do every day, even if it doesn't feel as dramatic as burning the whole thing down and rebuilding from the foundation up.

Future becomes present, present becomes past, but the place where they all switch over…that's the place to start.

Starting Over

by Scott R. Rey

I was 42 when I pressed reset. I didn't really know what to expect. The only thing that was driving me was weighing who I was vs the value of my past. Was there enough "me" there to warrant more? There was nothing traumatic I needed to escape, I had witnessed no murders, but I was done being me. The decision took six weeks, but in the end, I felt I could abandon everything I was to become who I wanted to be.

What they don't tell you in the movies is that today, in our modern society, you really can't do much without proper ID. I've seen dozens of movies where the handsome spy has a safe deposit box with seven passports and bundles of exotic cash. I had $1,319.53 and a driver's license for a person I wanted to escape, so how do I go about leaving four decades?

So, in week seven, I convinced a librarian three towns over that I had forgotten my card, and needed a new one. New name chosen, even if it was only in pen on a poorly laminated card. I picked a name that blended the name of my aunt and an cousin that I had visited growing up, I thought It would be nice to pay homage to those good days. On Tuesday, I used my library card to sign up for a grocery club card, and with those two pieces of "identification" I talked my way into a picture ID at Sam's Club. Who knew they had pictures on those things now. No more can the tyranny of bulk bananas be associated with a different person. My new person now had roots, even if they were firmly planted in a lie.

In week eight, I started to cut ties to my life, not that there were many to cut. I called my ex and mentioned I was moving because I had a new job offer in Cleveland. No disrespect, but I thought that no one would come looking for me. I gave my job two weeks' notice. Again the story about a job in Cleveland. I really wanted people to think I had made my choice, and that no one would file a missing person report.

In week 9, I panicked. What was I doing? Was there really nothing worth saving? I had scoured my three room apartment to see if there was anything I really wanted to keep, and had found a picture of my parents and me when I was a kid. We didn't have Disneyworld money, so we had gone to the local Six-Flags over wherever. I vaguely remembered that the original six-flags park was related to Texas. Apparently they were 6 different countries at some point. However, I knew that Georgia was not Texas, and I doubted the name held true. I loved those people. Was I going to throw this picture away? I wanted to make a clean break, and if someone found this on me, could they trace me back to my old life? I made the decision and moved on.

In week 10, I committed murder. well that sounds dramatic, but I threw away everything that had belonged to my old life. I called it "my murder" because I dragged a huge duffle bag to the dumpster after dark. I must admit I chuckled as I heaved that thing into the trash. It was almost like dumping a body. I realized that this was the first time I had laughed since I made my decision. I took that as a sign. Again, I was not interested in the police following me, so I took the time and made the effort to clean my apartment and ensure that it looked like I had left on purpose.

I was ready. I locked the door, slung my backpack over my shoulder and left.

I wanted to start over, and maybe I did. Did you know that even Greyhound requires photo ID? Maybe who I will be can be better than who I was. I bought my ticket in cash, proved my identity with Sam Walton vouching for me, and I headed west, into the sunset, because that felt like something the new me would do.

How the Other Half Lives

How the Other Half Lives

by Anna Bardin

I've been called a man before.

Not that anyone would mistake my buxom profile for a dude's. The comment was made about the state of my brain, which apparently is not wired according to the proper feminine diagram.

I pressed on this, curious as to what it is I'm supposed to want. A few themes came up: Commitment, kids, protection, color coordination…okay, that last one I can't argue with. But I take pretty serious issue with the others, and I don't think I'm alone in this.

We bifurcate our culture the way Romance languages gender nouns. Something cannot simply be, it must be designated male or female. Toy aisles, clothing sizes, bathrooms, pay grades…no matter what universe of society you inhabit, you know that there is another universe just on the other side, wherein lies the other half's version of whatever it is.

I remember going into the men's restroom with my dad when I was little. Part of me was a bit surprised at how much it looked like the girl's. Somehow I expected some dramatic difference other than the presence of urinals, which seemed fairly logical to me. That big wall of separation didn't make as much sense once I was in there. Only in the junior high locker room did I discern any reasoning behind the split. Although years later, a gay friend's recollection of her hormonal feelings in that same situation made me question the dichotomy.

Much more than physical separation, though, the messaging we receive as part of one half or another is starkly different. The incident referenced above, when I was called a man, didn't really surprise me, as I've been told all my life that I should want the picket fence and the 2.5 kids.

I took Home Ec in high school, and it was of course all girls. I thought I could pick up some tips on cooking, which I did, but it did strike me odd that so many of the chefs I saw on television were men, and yet there were no men in this class. Perhaps there was a cooking class for the other half that I just wasn't aware of. The fact is that if a man takes a cooking class, the expectation is that he is doing it for career reasons, whereas for women it's just a requirement for being marriage material. Something about that irked me, and to this day I don't put much effort into cooking, for fear that it will activate some latent wife gene that my manly behavior has kept shut off all this time.

These days, stories abound of gender confusion and identity. To be clear, I am very comfortable being a woman. I like the clothes, I like being able to come a lot during sex, I like the way I look. The parts I'm less comfortable with are the add-ons that people keep wanting to shove onto me. I feel like a yearbook photo that keeps getting scribbled on. Here, let's put a pregger belly on her. And a nurse hat. Maybe a mustache, just for fun. No one just wants to see the picture for what it is. It must conform to what they believe it should be.

This would be irritating enough on a personal level, but then we have its recurrence on the political stage. I'm told by my government representatives that birth control should not be covered by my health insurance. When I ask why, I get the distinct impression that they believe my desire to have childless sex whenever I choose makes me a whore. Whereas if some old fart wants to go get some Viagra to impregnate whoever he can cajole into conjugal communion, that's just fine and dandy. I'm supposed to be okay with this because I'm a woman and babies are magical gifts from god that I should want popping out all over the place, apart from minority neighborhoods, of course, and when are you going to settle down and start a family already, you know you need a lock a man down before everything sags too much and your usefulness as a female will be completely depleted…

I just punched a wall after typing that sentence. Sure. Fine. Maybe I'll just go ahead and be a man. I know where to buy attachments for that sort of thing. It would probably be easier than continuing to explain myself to other women, who by the way are worse than men when it comes to calling me out on my aberrant behavior. Given a choice between a mouthy dudebro and a catty church lady, I can honestly deal with the former much better. Truth be told, sometimes I understand the other half more than I understand my own.

Untangling centuries of cultural conditioning seems hopeless, for those of us caught outside its constraints. That said, I am heartened by the conversations I see flying across social media, discussing modes of gender identity that have hidden in the shadows for so long. If we have come to a place where those discussions are possible, maybe a woman who doesn't conform to standard notions of feminine desire can feel freer to express herself. Like I'm doing now.

Call me whatever you want. Just don't call me late for my period.

How the Other Half Lives

by Ashley Van Arsdel

The red nail polish oozed on the tip of the brush as she pulled it out of the bottle. Francis had red hair, and people, especially her mother, had often told her not to wear red. She was not known for listening. Absently, she popped another bubble with her pink chewing gum.

On full blast, the radio blurted the tunes of the day. It was 1977, and Francis couldn't stand disco. Rock n' roll was far more interesting. She flipped the dial in a vain attempt to find the rock station, but the reception was poor out there in the country. With a sigh, she flipped the small black-and-white TV on the kitchen. The Price is Right, again. Another sigh and then back to the task at hand.

It was a free morning for Francis. The walkie-talkie she was obligated to carry was pleasantly quiet because her boss, the head maid, Millicent, was out getting groceries with the old driver. "Do not call me 'Millie'!" The old woman had once barked. "It's Millicent!"

"More like militant." Francis said aloud, laughed to herself and painted another nail. The freedom this particular morning was nothing short of exhilarating. Gingerly, she took a slow sip of coffee, as not to upset her progress on her nails.

The McCulloughs were low-maintenance in the morning. Mr. McCullough was still in the city on Tuesdays, which was a good five hours away, and the wife, who was much younger, was usually still sleeping off a hangover this early in the morning. Little Bobby had just started boarding school this year, which made the mornings very dull lately. It was 9:00 am, and Francis wasn't actually expecting to be annoyed via walkie-talkie until 10:00 or 10:30.

$2.00 an hour was her pay, less than minimum wage, but board was included. Her room was a small, plain one upstairs in the servants' quarters, directly across the hall from Millicent. The gates to the estate closed at 9:30 pm and were locked down tight. This meant that she either had to be back in by 9:30 pm or stay out until the first delivery drivers came at eight or nine am. The closest "fun" town was 2 hours away, so by the time she got off work and got there it would be time to turn around and go back to the estate. It also meant waiting stealthily outside the gate in what she wore the night before, one of two dresses, either the lime-green tie-dress or the red one. She only had two. Ringing the doorbell and waking Mrs. McCullough or Millicent presented another huge problem and was decidedly not worth the risk. Francis had phone numbers and met plenty of guys she could crash with, but again having to be home so early meant chugging a coffee and quick peck on the cheek, then off to a busy day and a gripey old boss.

Most of the time, it felt like prison. But not today. Not yet. Another pink gum-bubble popped. Only two nails left to go.

The view outside was lush and green. The McCulloughs had an expansive country estate in upstate New York. Peaceful, quiet, and the house was huge. A lot to clean, but a beautiful garden. Mrs. McCullough slept a lot these days, but when she did need something it was extremely urgent and immediate. There was no threat of that this morning.

Francis painted another nail and gazed longingly through the window. There he was! The man she knew so little about but could not stop thinking of. Michael. The handsome, slightly-older-than-her driver. Michael haunted her dreams, and for the two years she had worked for the McCulloughs, had barely said two words to her. Pleasant as the interactions were, they were painfully short, and she had so many questions to ask. Was he married? Where did he live? How come she couldn't see him more often? Another sigh and another nail painted red.

He was here already, sitting in his car, looking around. Had someone called him this early? Unthinkable. Unless? A black limo pulled up directly next to the black towncar Michael was driving. Mr. McCullough stepped out of the back of the limo, with a blonde young lady in a low-cut black dress. Though Mr. McCullough still had his wrinkle-free black suit on, the pair looked as though they had been out all night, the woman's hair was a mess and her dress was askew. The mystery lady tugged her dress down a little in the back as she stepped out and kissed Mr. McCullough on the cheek. Mr. McCullough was not a young man anymore, but Francis knew firsthand the wonders cocaine could do for one's nightlife. Mystery lady stepped into Michael's car. McCullough gave Michael a green dollar bill (Francis couldn't see how much from the window), said something indistinct to him, and Michael started the car.

The fingernails were done now, and Francis was fanning them to dry while watching eagerly out the window. The white work truck pulled up behind Michael's black towncar. Millicent got out, huffily, and Michael's black towncar drove away hurriedly. Mr. McCullough patted Millie on the back and proceeded into the house. When he was out of view, Millicent pulled the walkie out of her apron with her free hand, heading to the house with her shopping bag. Francis anticipated and picked her's up.

"Mrs. McCullough saw the whole thing from the window." Millicent's voice, then the Chssh of the walkie. She must've seen Francis watching.

"She's going to need one of her pills then?" Francis replied back, trying not to sound to eager.

"Yes. Get going. This is going to turn ugly fast." Chssh.

"Yes, ma'am." Francis gave her nails a final wave to let the polish dry, and proceeded upstairs, The Price is Right left blaring loudly in the kitchen, and the lid left off the bottle of red nail polish.

How the Other Half Lives

by Mandy Dnah

"I'm going to bed. Love you."

It's two o'clock in the afternoon. He worked all night at the hospital, supervising the Security Division while everyone in his family slept. Every morning, he comes home and spends a few hours on the computer with a couple of beers. Everyone needs some wind down time at the end of the day, and this graveyard shifter is no exception.

Sufficiently calm enough in body and spirit, he lays down in a never-dark-enough, never-cool-enough, never-quiet-enough bedroom. The sun refracts through dingy 70s curtains to produce a gold tint in the small, sparse room. The window air conditioner tries but fails to abate the stifling late spring Texas heat. The neighbors, day shifters like his family, do the things that people do outside during the day - yard work and home repairs - which if done at night would invoke a noise complaint.

Yet, here he lies in a loud, bright, stuffy bedroom, with no recourse but earplugs and chemical induced fatigue.

It wasn't always this way. There was a time when he was a day shifter too, when sleep was at night and accompanied by his wife.

Does he wonder how he got to this point? How did his life become a game of catching up - on sleep, on time, on his relationships?

Will there come a time when he feels caught up?

These are the things I wonder and imagine when my other half says, "I'm going to sleep. Love you." at two o'clock in the afternoon.

How the Other Half Lives

by Matthew Broyles

I live in a hall of mirrors.

Each day, I communicate with my self-selected peer group, both online and off. We debate amongst ourselves the relative merits of concepts and theories which involve at least a modicum of intellectual consideration. Sources are cited, and biases examined. In the end, though we may not always agree, there is at least an understanding that our individual conclusions are coming from an honest attempt to assess facts and opinions and distill their essences for a clearer grasp of whatever truth may lie within.

What I forget, at my own peril, is that this is not normal.

I grew up in a relatively small Texas town. In that time, I learned a lot about how what would come to be called Red America makes its decisions. Gut feelings are prized far above the so-called "facts" that the pointy-heads who think they're better than you trot out from their ivory towers. They tell you to question your feelings, but those feelings were put there by god, and "facts" are meant to trick you into betraying your creator and your culture. Science, psychology, challenging tradition, all of these things are the enemy of the gut, which you must clear your mind to hear, and it will channel god's will through your heart.

Raised in that environment, even with parents who did not wholly cotton to its tenets, it's been a difficult journey for me to emerge from that state of mind. To learn about confirmation bias, and the twisted narratives of cultural history that require us to question our fundamental instincts when considering new and contradictory information. To know that just because something feels right does not mean that it is.

Having traveled that road, confronted many a misconception, and adjusted my worldview accordingly, it often escapes my notice that a lot of my fellow Americans have not done likewise. They make their decisions with many of the same gut reactions I used to have, except that in their own self-selected peer group, this behavior is socially rewarded. The blinders fit very well, and so long as they stay in their small towns and exurbs, those instincts will not be challenged.

So when my timeline explodes with OMG THIS IS BAD FOR TRUMP SURELY HE CAN'T SURVIVE THIS, I have to remember that there is a whole other world out there that either doesn't know or doesn't care about the latest outrage from Cheeto Mussolini's radioactive garden of freakshow delights. Maybe even two.

We used to talk about the three worlds: First, second, and third. The first represented western-style democracy. The second, the communist bloc. Third was initially coined to denote non-aligned states, but has come to mean anywhere that lacks Pokestops and other modern amenities.

I would venture to say that now, there are three worlds which exist inside the United States.

The first is comprised of the thinkers, the ones who read articles and books, gathering information upon which to base their opinions. Arrogant sumbitches like me.

The second is the gut-based world. As detailed above, all this newfangled stuff about gender fluidity, the unreliability of our triumphalist history, and all them other big words just don't feel right. Fossils were put there by Satan to confuse us, and oil deposits were created by Jesus, who wants us to be rich. Don't think, feel.

The third is trickier, as it tends to blow this way and that in the wind. These are the people who are poor and vulnerable enough that they really don't have a lot of time or energy to commit to solving the nation's problems, since they're mostly focused on staying clothed and fed. As the income gap grows, this world follows suit, an entire stratum of society more or less permanently locked out of the middle class.

Where this last group falls on any given topic is difficult to nail down. Some might be fiscally liberal yet socially conservative, or vice versa. But whosoever has the message that can reach down into the pit of anxiety that accompanies poverty and offer some sprig of hope will be the one to at least temporarily gain their loyalty. This time around, it was the orange orangutan, a seasoned carnival barker with no complicated policy statements, just an angry voice against the winds howling into the cracked windows from all directions. Yes, they replied. We're pissed, too.

When on occasion I blunder into one of these two other worlds, it's always jarring. The look of startled suspicion from a redhat when science is invoked. The who-gives-a-shit expression of someone who just wants to get through their workday and get off work so they can spend at least a few minutes with their kids before staring down the bills. I am forced to remember that we do not all inhabit my world, the one where policy distinctions are interesting, where questions of gender identity and transformational learning can spark an all-night gab session.

The chief difference, in both of these other worlds, is the predominance of fear.

Economic fear is no stranger to me. I've been flat busted many times, and could easily become so again. As I've written in this space before, it's an ever-present spectre in these times.

The fear that accompanies the second world, though, is the kind I have no truck with. Fear of upsetting tradition, fear of angering god, fear of people whose physiology is different…these are medieval fears, to my mind. Or at least Victorian, pre-atomic fears. We live in the age of science, which certainly does not have all the answers, but has a far better chance of providing them than the Goat Farmers Guide to the Galaxy, written when the world was flat and the sun revolved around the earth.

But even as I write that last sentence, I hear my words muffled by the membrane which separates our worlds. They do not penetrate. Their mechanics are not the mechanics of faith. In such a state of affairs, how does one world communicate with the other?

Answer: They don't. And here we are.

How the Other Half Lives

by Paul Williams

A limousine driver pulled over and parked against the curb outside the theatre. In heavy rain, he hustled around the back of the car and opened the door for his fare. Saul Cohen closed his umbrella and climbed in. A minute later the limo gingerly pulled into the slow delicate flow of traffic, the kind peculiar to patrons of the fine arts.

"How was the show mack?" asked the limo driver.

"Divine" Saul replied.

"Now there's a word…Use it daily."

"Trust me, this was truly magic sir… It could've been a rancid show, and I'd still be a silly, blissful glow."

"Not a critic, eh?"

"It was my first opera… Dream-Ful-Filled…yessir."

The driver chewed on this statement.

"Could've fooled me. You don't look like a rookie."

"I'm not usually so well-heeled."

"I bet… Boy, but would I sure love to be making that set. Gotta be good being rich… All those beautiful women, all that dough… Jesus…what I wouldn't give…"

Saul said nothing. Removed his hat. Settled into his seat. The limo driver glanced at him in the mirror.

"Where to?"

"127 Flatbush avenue."

"Brooklyn? …feeling frisky bub? It's getting late."

"I live there."

The driver turned and looked at Saul. He turned back. Shook his head.

"I'm surprised they let you in the place."

Saul said nothing. He smiled. He brushed some raindrops from the lapel of his weathered but stylish tuxedo. The limo drove across the bridge, away from Manhattan. The further it rolled, the more peculiar it appeared.

"How is it this is your first time at the Met?"

"I'm a man of modest means…grew up during the Great Depression. But I've worked for the Rich the last twenty years or so. And I'd come to adore opera, but only from afar. My last employer, upon my retirement, handed me a ticket to the show tonight…paid for your services as well."

"Poor slob finally gets a taste of the brass ring, eh?"

Saul smiled.

"Thanks to him, yes. There's always a couple good ones, even in a barrel of rot."

"You talkin' 'bout the rich?"

"Those who worked their way to wealth, I have no truck with. Those who have it given to them, and that's the vast majority friend trust me...those you can have."

The limo rolled on, down skeptical streets.

"Must've been tough growin' up back then..."

"It was cheap to be poor when I was a kid. We'd get by on eight, ten bucks a week. Bein' poor got expensive after the war. We'd stock shelves for a couple hours, throw fish on Fulton for pocket change. Fifteen cents for breakfast--three eggs, toast... Stickball in the street, real baseball on the radio. It weren't so tough... Tougher on grownups, but even they had hope. Wanna know why? Roosevelt...He told us all, every last immigrant slob come here from every place on earth, that it was our right to dream of something better. He believed it...and he made us believe him."

The driver pulled over at 127 Flatbush. He turned to Saul.

"I don't know mack...I think I'd prefer the money."

"The people in that Theatre, they could smell me a mile away. A nice suit and a straight back don't hide bloodlines. Quite a few evenings were ruined merely by my presence. What does that tell you about the rich and their money?"

The limo driver turned toward his door. Saul stopped him.

"I'll let myself out." Saul Cohen said.

"You know...for me this was...nirvana...for them? Another snooze. When you're rich, what's left? They say it's not the destination, it's the journey? For the rich, the goddam journey is over! And it weren't a long one friend, trust me...Rich people are the very definition of bored...of boRing... What good is all that dough when you look around and realize, this is IT, there's nowhere else to go. I always had somewhere else to go. And deep down that scares 'em *just* enough, 'cause they know the hunt is on... They try'n blot it out. Smash the mirror... Booze helps... Once in awhile some self-aware rich schmuck will give a big chunk away, to try and feel something... Then I walk into their bubble, a barbarian at the gate. Ha! Someone fancy once said "Half of this world has no idea how the other half lives. They only even con*sider* a runt like me in a panic to make themselves feel better by comparison. Otherwise? I don't register... What they don't realize is, the empty glass only holds so much emptiness...same with the empty stomach."

Saul opened his own door and set one foot on the street. Then he paused.

"You know, during the Depression, the divide between rich and poor got so bad, there were no customers. No one could *buy* anything. FDR saved their ass. *Socialism saved capitalism for the capitalists, only the capitalists were too goddam ignorant to know it.* Still are... Looks like we're headin' there again friend. It's almost 2000 now...there's a reckoning coming for this country. I hope I'm still alive to watch. They won't understand until it's too late, and it *will be brutal...*"

"You seem pretty ok about it mack."

"I'm light as a feather."

○

Everybody Knows

○

Everybody Knows

by Anna Bardin

One of the most persistent foes I keep encountering in my life is conventional wisdom. Those things that everybody knows, whether or not they are true. Sugar and spice and all things nice, snips and snails and puppy dog tails. Happily ever after, meant to be, all these phrases that are placeholders for concepts we as a culture have internalized.

Nothing creates more consternation and alarm than challenging a working assumption. Especially one whose very basis is keeping you in your place.

Sex policing has always been one of the chief methods of keeping people under control, both male and female. Right now I hear the women bristling, ready to tell me that the patriarchy has oppressed women far more than men, and how dare I equate the effects on both sexes?

Here's the thing, though. Patriarchy isn't good for most men, either. The toxic standards of masculinity that men are held to contribute to their outsized suicide rate compared to women, and to feelings of disconnection with their children, their friends, and yes, women. Legions of men cut off from healthy expressions of their feelings were instrumental in creating the cult of Trump. Everybody knows men can't be nurturing and vulnerable, and so they are not afforded that opportunity. This cripples them, as it did my own father, who often struggled with the expectations placed on him by his very own friends.

And as much as patriarchal influence circumscribes the behaviors of women, I'm here to tell you that no male enforcer in the world is as strict as another woman. If a boy calls you a slut, yeah, it sucks, but whatever. But if the girls take up the chant, lord help you. Fear of violating the female code of conduct rules women like a vise around the waist, which by the way should be perfectly trim.

A co-worker of mine is consistently labeled a lesbian by the other office ladies because she wears unfussy shoes and goes to Super Cuts. They would hold forth on her obvious manly disposition in my presence, until I finally had enough and told them they were full of shit. So now I'm a bitch, because everybody knows you don't question the queen bee in her hive. I haven't gotten it confirmed for sure, but I've probably been deemed a lesbian, too, which, to be fair, is about 30% right.

Here's another violation: I don't wear pink. I'm not categorically opposed to the color, I just don't look good in it. Give me black, purple, burgundy, royal blue…winter tones for the pale brunette, please. Yet when I get an invite for a girl-related event or sale, it always looks as if someone had spilled a bottle of Pepto on it. I even got the stinkeye when I bought my brother's daughter a blue onesie. It had R2-D2 on it, for pete's sake, what's not to like? But there is suggestion inherent in subverting the color coding, and I did not once see that badass onesie on my niece. Oh, weird Anna, she must have forgotten the kid was a girl.

One thing I do like about the modern age is how much more socially acceptable it has become to be a female nerd. That support network did NOT exist when I was a kid, and the threat of spinsterhood that reared its head anytime I expressed an affinity for Ford Prefect or Max Headroom was difficult to endure, even though I half suspected that I didn't want to get married anyway. Standing in line last weekend with little girls wearing Wonder Woman costumes, I damn near broke down and cried at how beautiful that freedom must be for those kids.

It's better and it's not. On the one hand, there is now a cultural conversation about gender roles and expectations that is happening on a scale undreamed of in my youth. On the other hand, this conversation has sent proponents of the patriarchy into mad panic, rushing to turn back the clock on women's freedoms, lest we all become wanton hussies who believe —gasp—that we have a right to childless sex and staying single, should we desire it. The rattle of clutching pearls and dropped monocles clatters forth from my radio during every commute. The sound of change and of backlash are seldom far apart.

The outcome of this battle rests on the shoulders of women. If our internalization of our prescribed roles is stronger than our desire to be free from them, then back into the box we go. The modern Phyllis Schaflys are everywhere, wagging their judgmental fingers at ladies whose aspirations violate the code of proper female conduct. You don't want to be one of those hairy-legged feminists, do you? Everybody knows that's for ugly girls and bulldykes. Look, there's that Tomi Lahren girl, all blonde and pretty. You want to be like her, not like that mouthy, butch Rachel Maddow.

To change what everybody knows, we must first change what we know. Which means taking a hard look at our own assumptions, and figuring out how many of them come from unreliable external sources. Speak those fears aloud, as Nora Ephron did in *I Feel Bad About My Neck*, a title more honest than most of us are willing to be in public. When we do that, we find others with the same fears, and we can talk about them. Where did they come from? Is this a thing or not a thing?

Everybody knows something's gotta give. Push on the walls a bit. We might find that they're made of wallpaper, and that the world is much bigger than we've ever imagined.

Everybody Knows

by Chris Dashiell

Between knowledge and belief falls the shadow of the social order. Many of us believe what we don't know and know what we don't believe. What we all know is that reality is eternal. This knowledge, however, is so inherent that it is practically unconscious—and the conclusions we draw reflect only our wishes and fears, not the truth.

Can knowledge that we do not claim, that we don't bring into self-awareness or avowal, be legitimately called "knowledge"? Not according to our customary definitions. If we "know" something, we must know that we know it—consciousness is our measure. Fair enough. But "intuition" has an aura of uncertainty. It is not that we do not "know" what we know—an absurd statement on its face—but that we don't *admit to ourselves* what we know.

We see *through* the social order, but then we quickly turn our mind's eyes away and erase what we saw, because who wants to question everything that sustains our living in the social world?

We believe that we are governed by ourselves, and that our common standards of behavior are determined by values of public good and reason. But everyone knows that underlying all that, the principle that prevents the violation of these standards, is *force*. If you won't stop doing something because Mom and Dad say it's bad for you, the "should" will eventually become the "must." Mom and Dad's physical superiority will force you into compliance. This basic principle is not exactly denied, but it is not overly emphasized either. If you question the seeming contradiction between love and power, it begs the question of how else to solve the problem. Religion and philosophy have struggled with this, and offered various solutions. But force has not gone away.

We believe in images and models of gender and its corresponding roles. But everyone knows that gender in the world is much more diverse than the images and models we are given. Presented with what a man or a woman is expected to look and act like, most of us make a choice between hating ourselves (and, if even remotely possible, trying to change ourselves to fit the image) or rejecting the standards we've been given. Sexual preference or orientation is even more wrenching in its consequences. You know whether or not you're attracted to the same sex, but if that's taboo, you might try not to know, or wish you didn't.

The most blatant examples have to do with religious doctrines involving miracle or mystery. Everyone knows at a deep level that people don't come back from the dead. If your religion says they do, or that a certain person did, believing it would mean recognizing the miraculous nature of this fact, in other words, that the event differs from what we know about nature. Fair enough. But if this religion has become dominant in society, a key part of the social order, and therefore this belief has become, in a sense, mandatory for social acceptance, miracle is turned on its head and becomes what you must accept about the nature of the world. If you choose not to believe in this thing that differs from what we know about nature, you are a heretic, and not just a person resisting a claim for something that is implausible by the very definition of the word "miracle."

Two of the world's most powerful religions, and some schools of thought within others, teach that we are rewarded or punished after death for how we behaved in life. This is arguably the greatest game of "make believe" in human history. If you were convinced of this, with no doubts, would you ever do anything wrong? Wouldn't the certainty of eternal punishment be enough to frighten you into moral behavior? Adherents have arguments against this, often involving struggles between "spirit" and "flesh," and so forth, but these arguments lead into even more perilous contradictions.

In fact, everyone knows that it's not true. And here, my notion of "not admitting that we know" is most pertinent, because most adherents would vehemently deny my claim. But because no one has ever "come back" to tell us about an afterlife, and all we have are ancient visions and occasional modern accounts that clearly reflect the limitations of the tellers' experiences, I maintain that we *know* at a deep level that it's false. And the proof is in the result. Despite the deep entrenchment of this belief in our culture, it has not improved the behavior of humanity. The powerful routinely ignore it. Lying, malice, and corruption are as widespread as ever, if not more so. Everyone also knows that reward and punishment do not inspire good thoughts or good behavior, but only desire and fear.

Here we come full circle to the parents who must finally resort to force in order make the child behave. That a society could function without the power principle is an impossible utopian dream. Perhaps, then, it is the denial of what we know—that love and power co-exist in this world—that is the real problem. Maybe we hide the truth about ourselves through a bad conscience, because we *know* at some level that basing our lives on narrow self-interest does not make us happy. The truth will makes us free, but we don't want to know it, because we're afraid of the responsibility.

Everybody Knows

by Matthew Broyles

(with apologies to Leonard Cohen)

Everybody knows that inside every human is an ongoing war between emotion and logic.

Everybody knows that neither side of that war is completely wrong or right.

Everybody knows that no one stays the same.

Everybody knows that change is hard.

Everybody knows that there is strength in numbers.

Everybody knows that stupidity spreads faster in a crowd.

Everybody knows that not everyone can win.

Everybody knows that they don't want to be the one to lose.

Everybody knows someone they want to be more like.

Everybody knows someone they fear becoming.

Everybody knows that someone else has something you want.

Everybody knows that someone wishes they had something you have.

Everybody knows that life is short.

Everybody knows that life is long.

Everybody knows what it is they fear to lose.

Everybody knows that one day it will be gone.

Everybody knows what feels right.

Everybody knows what feels wrong.

Everybody knows that what feels right to them feels wrong to someone else.

Everybody knows that what feels wrong to them feels right to someone else.

Everybody knows what makes sense.

Everybody knows that what makes sense isn't always what makes you happy.

Everybody knows that no one is perfect.

Everybody knows that imperfections break hearts.

Everybody knows that they don't want their heart broken.

Everybody knows that it will be.

Everybody knows that humans are animals.

Everybody knows that we want to be more.

Everybody knows how much it hurts to be alive.

Everybody knows that they don't want to die.

○

Nobody Knows

○

Nobody Knows

by Anna Bardin

You think that nobody knows. But I do.

You probably assume that since I never bring it up on the few occasions we see each other nowadays, that I don't remember. Or that I decided it was okay.

I remember. It would be impossible to forget. And it's not okay.

You didn't succeed. But you tried. Which is what matters.

That you failed was a fluke. The fact that I was as strong-willed as I was at that age surprised both of us. That I was able to tell you no, with a conviction that made you stop, afraid that I would tell everyone. Whether I would have, had you gotten your way, is uncertain. Shame is a powerful force, and has silenced many victims. I would like to say that propriety and the need for stability kept me quiet afterward, but if I'm honest, shame has always been a persistent voice in my motivations.

If I had it to do over again, would I have told someone? It's hard to say. A 13-year-old girl's word against an adult's isn't a promising scenario. The turbulence thus created may have outweighed any comfort that exposing you for what you are might have provided.

Perhaps that's selfish. I would like to think that being rebuffed means that I was your last attempt, but that's probably foolish optimism. I've never heard from anyone else that something happened with you, but then, no one's ever heard from me either. Maybe you succeeded, and someone I know is carrying the burden of that memory because I didn't blow the whistle way back when. My heart pangs at the thought, to the point that I cannot even think about it without having a panic attack. For now, let's just say it was a one-time incident.

I know what it's like to carry this weight around, and I wonder what it feels like to you. It's certainly not a daily struggle for me, three decades hence. I may go six months without it occurring to me. But it comes up more often than I'd like. When I hear a news story, watch a movie, read a book, anything that involves a young person's trust in adults being violated, a little synapse pings in the back of my head. I stiffen a little, bracing for feelings I would rather have had done with ages ago.

Then the anger kicks in. The resentment that I have to feel these things. That it's not my fault, and that you should have to be the one to feel them for the rest of your life. And maybe you do. Maybe those very same triggers awaken a deep sense of shame and regret for your actions. I would like to think so.

Sometimes I want to call you and ask. Is this hurting you as much as it hurts me? But then I stop, because what happens if it turns out that you have zero remorse, and I'm the only one who lies awake some nights, questioning the universe, questioning the judgment of every man I've decided to trust, men like you, respected and loved by friends and family? How many men like you are out there, that I see all the time, who have put some young girl through hell because of your unexamined neuroses?

So I don't call, because the fear of finding out that you are simply a monster who happens to be a really good actor, makes me doubt every hope I have for humanity. The rush of emotion threatens to turn me into Charlize Theron in *Monster*, castrating or killing any man whose behavior suggests that they might ever hurt a female, young or grown. In those moments, such an approach does not feel outrageous to me. It feels logical, a cold calculation based on immense mountains of evidence from so many women all around the world. It makes me want to live on Wonder Woman's island, free from fear of men like you.

But then I remember all the beautiful experiences of love and laughter I've shared with men. Wonderful men, tender and sweet, funny and thoughtful, amazing human beings without whom the world would be immeasurably darker. I get upset at how long it takes me to trust them, because of you. At how much some part of me still does not entirely believe they are what they seem. Because of you.

You think that nobody knows. But I know. And when I give you a thin smile at a wedding or funeral, because an outburst in those circumstances would be unfair to those for whom we are gathered, maybe you think that I've forgotten, or forgiven.

I have not. I will not. And I hope with all my heart that you haven't either.

Nobody Knows

by Matthew Broyles

You have the right to keep secrets.

While that idea is not enshrined in so many words in the Constitution, it is nonetheless one of the more important underpinnings of a free society.

I've been reading *On Tyranny* by Timothy Snyder, a concise guide to navigating our times that I heartily recommend to all Americans. In it, he makes a statement that caught my attention:

"We are free only insofar as we exercise control over what people know about us, and in what circumstances they come to know it…Tyrants seek the hook on which to hang you. Try not to have hooks."

Having lived in the internet age for nearly two decades now, it's surprisingly easy to forget that there was a time when very few companies knew your personal business. When I write an email today, I assume that at the very least, Google and my ISP are storing its contents in case future retrieval is necessary. Google's bots read my words and make ad-placement assumptions based on them.

The same happens when I post on social media or in places like Second Life. Netflix knows what I'm watching, Amazon knows what I'm reading, Apple knows what I'm listening to, Guitar Center knows how often I change my strings, Kroger knows how much toilet paper I buy…

Thinking about it, I can name very few aspects of my personal life that are not recorded and analyzed in some way by a corporation. I'm typing this on Microsoft Word to post on Facebook, on a computer monitored by antivirus and other background software. The details of my life are known to a rather astonishing degree by the powers that be, in a way that they certainly were not 20 years ago.

I had a roommate in 1996 who bought a book called *How to Disappear Completely and Never Be Found.* It contained information on changing your Social Security number and dodging various methods to track your whereabouts. Two decades on, the mind boggles to think of how one might go about disappearing today. Sure, people set up false identities online all the time, but eliminating all traces of your actual self and your financial, medical, and social activities seems a million times harder now.

The riposte that comes up every time someone frets about all of our data floating about willy nilly is that since absolutely everyone is being tracked, the likelihood of your specific info being seen by another human is next to nil. This carries a certain amount of logic, since the sheer mass of communication and economic telemetry we broadcast every day dwarfs the number of people who could possibly review every single shred of it. The trick is to stay off the radar.

But piss somebody off, and you're toast. Witness Reality Winner's quick apprehension, brought about by sifting digital tips with her own social media feed. I know local law enforcement officials who keep an eye on known offenders' Twitter accounts, where people too often tell more about their goings-on than they should if they don't want to get caught. And it doesn't even have to be criminal. Offend the wrong person, the embarrassing bits of your personal history can be plundered by the vengeful and broadcast to the world. Young candidates for political office are finding their early drunken party pictures and ill-considered naïve musings the fodder for opponents' hatchet teams with an ease that would have made Nixon's ratfucker squad salivate.

Imagine going off the grid now. I mean truly dropping out. Cash only, no internet, no phone, no GPS, no rewards memberships, your only correspondence conducted via typewriter, paper and a PO box. No car, if you don't want the DMV knowing where you are, not to mention your insurance company. To say nothing of the feats of legerdemain required to stay off the IRS rolls. Even not going to quite that extreme, simply returning to 1990s levels of personal privacy essentially sounds like becoming the Unabomber.

What does all this mean for a free, democratic society? Knowing we have to watch our backs, that we should not post or send anything that we wouldn't want plastered up on a billboard one day? To effectively keep ourselves to ourselves, we must practice a sort of mindfulness about our communication, whether online or in the retail world. It means turning down all the enticing offers of convenience presented to us every day by the data-driven culture we inhabit, whose target is the contents of our heads. To know us is to profit from us.

This has political ramifications as well. When we stand up to power, we must know that power will take every opportunity to discredit us, using our own words and deeds as ammunition. We must therefore be extra vigilant about what we put into the machine, knowing that the moment we run afoul of the system's administrators, control over our privately-shared secrets is forfeit. Exes, opportunistic acquaintances, the unblinking eye of the internet, all of these may turn on us at a moment's notice.

Check your digital history. Google yourself. Scroll through your Sent box. Scrub your social media trail. It is unfortunate that we have to consider these things, but faced with a budding authoritarian regime, it may be that reclaiming privacy is one of the most important preventative tools we have to make sure our resistance does not get lost in a sea of ad hominem backlash.

And in the process of cleaning up our act, maybe we can take the opportunity to reflect on just what it is we are putting out into the world about ourselves. In doing so, we may find a new appreciation of privacy.

Nobody Knows

by Paul Williams

Nobody, and I mean nobody, knows what happens to us after we die. There are many possibilities I suppose, although most people who are of the logical and scientific persuasion would argue, exasperatedly, that nothing happens. Nada. Zero…They may even raise their voices and use flailing hand gestures as they say this, beside themselves that any sensible person could think otherwise. But nobody knows.

Then there are those who believe that we have a soul, a spirit force, living or existing in a somewhat contained way within the physical boundaries of our bodies, of our exterior skin and hair, our fingernails and toenails, eyes and ears. In fact, the vast majority of people on planet earth believe this. Many if not most of these people feel a brotherly fraternity of scorn towards the science and logic crew… "Can you believe those atheists?…so arrogant, so sinful." But let the knife cut into the cake of belief and it will take about a nanosecond for various belief factions to turn on each other. Because some of these "spirit believers" believe that the spirit, upon death, leave the constraints of the physical body cell and travels somehow across physical distances, and perhaps time itself, to then inhabit another physical being, perhaps a human being and perhaps not. But they don't know any of this of course.

Many of the other "spirit believers" will of course sneer at these people with an extra special kind of mockery, less hateful than they have for the atheist, but a more fearful type of scorn, as if, "Well, they do believe in God and spirits, but the rest of what they believe is just strange, demonic even, … ridiculous! How could they POSSIBLY believe that is what happens to our souls after death? What nonsense!" It's enough to make a cat laugh, because, of course, nobody knows.

The vast majority of these people, Americans mostly, believe that they really have the answers dialed in. They know the truth for sure, and if you don't agree with them, guess what? You are fucked eternally. This notion tends to cause them little distress, quite the contrary in my experience, actually. They take a certain joy in the feeling that they are on the lifeboat and those that don't harbor the same belief system will drown. It's like an existential sporting competition for them. They believe in a spiritual city with spiritual streets, spiritually paved with spiritual gold, where they will sing praises to God for all of eternity. But they don't know of course.

The degree to which so many people's happiness, contentment, and self-image is derived by their confidence in knowing what happens after we die is really astounding. Families are reduced to rubble over disagreements concerning what happens after our hearts stop beating, our lungs stop drawing in oxygen, blood stops flowing through our veins, our brains shut down, and then permanent unconsciousness and physical decay set in. I personally have experienced this phenomena in my own family, and have seen it in many other families. It is the deepest kind of cruelty, deeper than infidelity, deeper than physical harm, deeper than social mockery. It is a primal kind of cruelty, born of fear and embarrassment. Oh humanity, …we constantly fail to recognize the true measure and potential of our greatness. Instead, we reduce ourselves to barely more than animals, because we act with such fierce certainty and loathing toward each other concerning matters where it is beyond our abilities currently to know what is true and what is not. Is our species en masse capable of anything better? Not in the past. Not in the present. How about in the future? Nobody knows…

○

Words Matter

○

Words Matter

by Anna Bardin

As a familiar name popped up on my newsfeed this weekend, I was shaken out of the fog that has descended over my awareness of current events, now too briny and overchurned for individual horrors to make much of a dent in and of themselves.

The name was Philando Castile, and just like the first time I heard his story, what seems like ages ago, my heart broke.

I have relatives who are police officers, and they often warn me against trying cases in the court of public opinion. I've sat on juries several times, and I know that what that small group of people hear in the confines of a court room can differ from what will fit into a news story.

But for the life of me, I can't imagine how the hell that cop got acquitted.

Despite the pain in my chest, I did review the video again, replaying those last awful moments of his life, the terror that will forever scar that woman and child who were in the car with him. And through my tears, I remembered three words that I haven't heard in a long time: Black Lives Matter.

Just months ago, absolutely everyone was arguing vociferously about what lives matter. Maybe the election of a certain orange demagogue settled that question in our minds somewhat. Clearly, in America, some lives matter more than others. Arguing the opposite only motivates Middle America to turn out in larger numbers to beat that contention down. And in the ensuing chaos, reasonable debate has been tossed out in favor of rage and resistance.

It shouldn't surprise me that a lot of white people don't understand what is being said by the BLM movement. I still overhear them asking why they can't use the "n-word," since it's all over the music their kids listen to. My fists ball up in the face of such clueless entitlement. I can't imagine why a white person would be itching so bad to use a word that carries the burdensome weight of our ugly history. That it still gets used by those against whom it was originally directed is an indication of how little has changed, if appropriating and repurposing it is still necessary. Think, McFly.

I'm reminded of a friend who used to wear a t-shirt which proudly featured the word "Cunt" across the front. She had been called that so often by misogynist assholes that she just decided to go with it. If that's what someone who stands up for themselves is called, she reasoned, then why not be proud to be one?

By now we know that the old sticks-and-stones chant isn't true. Words do hurt, often more than physical violence. Because they are insidious, and sneak into cracks in our consciousness in a way that a fist to the face doesn't. Words and their perceived meanings lodge there, and only the most comprehensive flush of the psyche stands any chance of removing them. Call a girl fat once, and she may spend the rest of her life analyzing every shift in the scale's report, searching her body for imperfections, certain that she is undesirable to the men whose love she seeks. Give me a broken bone any day.

The same goes for words that should be said, but aren't. I remember when a woman I admired very much called me her friend. My heart leapt, because while I had hoped that we were becoming friends, I couldn't be sure that she saw it that way. Absent that acknowledgement, I might have kept my distance a bit more. Such a tiny word, but with a world of meaning.

Show your gratitude. With actions, certainly, but also with words. Inferring is not the same as knowing, in a voice that isn't the same one where your doubts live. I refer you to Mr. Paul Simon…

Some people never say the words 'I love you'

It's not their style to be so bold

Some people never say those words, 'I love you'

But like a child, they're longing to be told…

We all need confirmation of our feelings and intuitions. To make sure that the world as we see it is in fact the world as it is. Absent that reassurance, we wander in clouds of questions and tentative assumptions.

And if we know that words are that powerful, why not use them instead of violence, when a misunderstanding arises? Why not talk to someone at a traffic stop, and not shoot them dead, just in case? We have evolved to use complex language, a gift rare in the natural world. If we are to be worthy heirs of so many years of evolutionary development, we should use that gift to make our world a better place.

Words matter. And so do lives.

Words Matter

by Matthew Broyles

I used to pick on language pedants. Certainly, I'm a stickler for grammar and spelling, but my militancy on that front has tended to be self-focused. Hijacking an interesting discussion about a larger topic by nitpicking the vagaries of someone's language use always struck me as petty and stupid.

That said, there is power in language. When we use 'illegal' as a noun to describe a person, for instance. I noted yesterday the feeling I got when someone described another person as "a black." Not "he's black," but "he's a black." That little article between two perfectly ordinary words opens a huge window into who it is that I'm talking to, their history and presumptions.

The same is true with 'terrorist,' or 'patriot.' Each of these words come fully loaded with assumptions of meaning that are very specific to the segment of our society with which we self-identify.

Some terms have had their meanings change over time by way of cultural combat. I proudly call myself a 'nerd' now, but 30 years ago, that same word had no other meaning but as a pejorative. Likewise with friends who refer to themselves as 'queer,' a term with nothing but negative connotations in times past. The use of certain words best left unspoken by cracker-asses continues to be a hot potato as tonedeaf white people attempt to prove their post-racialism by using it as if its already been disarmed by hip-hop and made passe.

We fight over words all the time, insisting that something does not mean what someone else thinks it means. It's the "no true Scotsman" fallacy, illustrated here:

Person A: "No Scotsman puts sugar on his porridge."

Person B: "But my uncle Angus likes sugar with his porridge."

Person A: "Ah yes, but no TRUE Scotsman puts sugar on his porridge."

Our country just finished an election that focused very much on the definition of who the TRUE Americans were. For every issue espoused by one side as an American value, the other came right back saying that no TRUE American really wanted that. Thus the very word 'American,' originally just a designation of nationality, is transformed into an entire set of beliefs and principles that just happens to fit whatever our own personal beliefs and principles are. Anyone else cannot use that word to describe themselves, because they are not TRUE Americans.

I remember when I first heard the title Homeland Security, back in the early W years after 9/11. The word 'Homeland' came packed to the gills with cultural connotations that made me squirm, reeking of nativism and exclusion. This from a nation of immigrants, excepting of course my two Cherokee great-grandmothers, pauperized in their own homeland by newcomers until they married into the dominant, invasive society we now call native to this place. 'Homeland' is a verbal threat to today's newcomers, letting them know that they are not TRUE Americans.

Words circumscribe everything. I ordered a pair of sunglasses online that I thought looked really good. Upon receiving them in the mail, I noticed on the invoice that it said "women's sunglasses." Involuntarily, my guts seized up. Would everyone but me know that I was walking around wearing women's shades? They just looked like sunglasses to me, but that one little word put the nagging doubt into my head. I'm not one to put much stock into traditional notions of masculinity, but the truth is, I still haven't decided whether I'm sending them back. Because of that one word.

Someone told me the other day that they believed in 'traditional values.' The conversation was not political, and it was a sort of side comment, but it was everything I could do not to violate my rule against hijacking discussions with language clarifications.

What the hell are 'traditional values?' Whose tradition? I once worked with Hasidim who thought nothing of arranging marriages for their young teenage kids. I know multi-generational Santeria adherents, and people who won't let their children watch television because demons hide in the airwaves. When I hear 'tradition,' it's in the voice of Tevye, insisting that his daughter will be dead to him if she marries outside the faith.

And yet, I know exactly what was being expressed in that conversation. When a middle-aged white man in Texas says 'traditional values,' he means conservative Protestant Christianity, augmented by gun-lust and Fountainhead-humping economics. I really didn't need the clarification. But I object to him usurping the words 'traditional values' to only mean those things that they mean in this region, to his ethno-religious demographic. The debate required to set all this straight, however, would have taken hours, so I ditched it, as most of us do when it comes to language in daily interpersonal interaction.

And of course that's how they get you. The less you question a word being co-opted by one agenda or another, the more it becomes the standard meaning, and bam, before you know it, any conversations using that word are automatically loaded.

So maybe I've been wrong on this. Perhaps the only way to keep language from being hijacked is to have those nitpicky conversations. To be that guy. Although do it enough, and people will probably go out of their way not to have conversations with you. Somehow we have to make sure that everyone knows how much words matter.

Until we all switch to communicating by emoji, anyway.

Words Matter

by MC Dalet

Words matter.

Words explain things.

Try to explain things well.

Words help us to understand.

Try to make an art of understanding.

Words create reality.

What reality do you want to live?

Words can wound --

a curse or a condemnation.

Words have started many wars...

Of many kinds...

The shots and bombshell and planes

are always secondary.

Words can bridge worlds

Above and Below --

A prayer or a plea.

The answer is always the effect of the causal

request.

Words fail to describe

the horrors of human history.

Nor can they capture, as a photo cannot,

the beauty I've seen.

But they get us closer.

Always closer,

If we craft them with consciousness.

They can bring US closer.

They are doing it now.

From my Awareness to yours.

We transmit meaning through

an arrangement of symbols --

Symbols of consequence...

and creation.

Words matter.

So I leave you with these:

I love you.

Words Matter

by Paul Williams

Kellyanne Conway is a spokesperson for the current (45th) president of the United States, Donald Trump. She is a vile creature, a lying witch, completely devoid of integrity, honor, of honesty, just a gruesome wound of a human being. Today she commented on a recent tweet by our supreme leader saying that he was being "ironic." What he said in his tweet was that he was being "investigated for firing the FBI Director by the person who told him to fire the FBI Director."

Donald Trump's tweet is not a case of being "ironic." He made a statement describing a situation that could plausibly, under normal circumstances, be seen as being ironic. But HE was not being ironic. The situation is not "ironic" for a number of reasons. First of all, he is not being investigated for firing the FBI Director. The president has the right to fire the FBI investigator at his own pleasure. He is being investigated for MANY things, among them: 1) Collusion with a foreign (and by the way, adversarial) Government to interfere with the 2016 United States presidential election; 2) For financial improprieties, including possible money laundering; and 3) for Obstruction of Justice by trying to sabotage an FBI investigation (this is the only issue being investigated that has anything to do with the firing of the FBI Director, though it is NOT the same thing). These are the ones we know of…. Back to the pathetic explanation by the vile witch Kellyanne Conway - Trump's tweet claiming that he was following the suggestion of someone else in firing the FBI Director is ludicrous! The man HIMSELF, on a National televised interview SAID, that he was firing the FBI Director because of the "Russia thing," and that it was his decision, totally independent of any suggestions he was given by the Deputy FBI Director. I believe his exact words were "I was gonna fire Comey."

I must offer my sincere apologies to the words "irony" and "ironic," two of the most wonderful and important words in the English language, for the assault committed against them.

This same grotesque version of a human form, Kellyanne Conway, had set at one point that one of the other White House stooge crew had simply given "alternative facts" when giving the media a clearly bullshit explanation for some damn thing, I forget now what that was… "Alternative Facts!" That is not a thing that exists!

When the topic "Words matter" was offered for this week's Essay Club, I kind of assumed it was the chosen topic because of this breathtakingly dishonest and corrupt administration. It is certainly a timely, fitting, and important concept to consider, as the dark forces rising against human decency and dignity embrace, in very obvious ways, the concept that Words DONT Matter, and then proceed to vomit all over us with example after example, proving their evil nature…confirming their evil intentions. It would be enough to make a cat laugh if it weren't so insidious…AND, if it weren't so goddamn sad how stupid and wretched about 40% of the population is.

If I were to try and begin a list of horrible deceits, lies, errors, ignorant and bigoted statements, treasonous utterances, etc, puked up by this insane posse of clowns, I would be writing until the 4th of July. A couple that come to mind, just for the sake of example, are "2nd amendment remedies," "Health care will be better, cheaper, and it will be easy," "Mexico will pay for the wall," "Russia, please, leak her emails." Oh God help me, impeach this fraudulent traitorous fuck for God's sake… Anyway…

When I think about the idea of "Words Matter," whether it's with regard to this current clusterfuck of a president, or another application, I feel the need to push the concept deeper. What really matters is truth. TRUTH matters. Words can be misconstrued, or misunderstood at times, and done so when the intent was innocent, and not devious. What is the real truth behind the words? Did i misunderstand your intent? Ok then, we can clear that up and no harm no foul, we all hope. Truth matters! We are watching minute by minute, day by day, the devaluation of Truth! This compulsive liar Donald Trump has spent his entire adult professional life slaughtering the truth (not to mention dignity, honor…oh fuck me, I can't stop). A simple cursory examination of his career and statements reveal the most blatant and compulsive liar we've ever seen. It's as clear as a punch to the nose. And it stings just as bad.

You know, in a certain kind of way I was wrong. I guess words DO matter to these people; the words that poison, that deceive, that line their pockets, that hide and distract… These words are the ones they use. These words matter to them very much. These words are chosen very carefully, chosen SO painstakingly…after hours of discussion and consideration. The truth? Not so much…

○

A Fate Worse Than Death

○

A Fate Worse Than Death

by Anna Bardin

Fates worse than death, ranked in no particular order:

Flesh-eating bacteria.

Fighting a war I don't believe in.

Mandatory church attendance.

A child I don't want.

A permanent Republican majority.

Vogon overlords. (possibly the same as the four items just above, but with bad poetry added in)

A spouse I can't stand.

A lifetime of bad sex.

Rap-country all day long.

A job I hate, and that I can't leave.

Flesh-eating bacteria. (seriously, I can't)

Getting only five of the six lotto numbers. Twice.

The Handmaid's Tale.

Immortality for all. I mean ALL.

Telepathy.

Lack of air conditioning.

Astrology is real.

That bug tunnel in *Temple of Doom*.

Men get to choose all of my wardrobe.

Other women get to choose all of my wardrobe.

Radiation sickness.

Cats can tell us what they think of us.

I have a long-lost twin sister, and she's a Trump voter.

Someone goes back in time and kills baby David Bowie.

Daytime television.

Did I mention the flesh-eating bacteria? Jesus.

No doesn't mean no.

National anthem changed to that Lee Greenwood song. Or *We Built This City*.

Prohibition II.

It puts the lotion on its skin or it gets the hose again.

Interior nose pimples.

Arranged marriage.

The return of the scorpion bomb.

My body is not my own to do with as I see fit.

A white Christian nation.

Karaoke at the airport bar.

Being Melania Trump.

Did you know there's a type of bacteria that eats your flesh? Damn.

A Fate Worse Than Death

by Ashley Van Arsdel

Is death so bad when you're living a life that is slow and painful? When everything is painted a flat shade of grey? When you don't even realize how dead you actually are, until someone taps you on the shoulder and says, "Hey!" waking you from your walking coma?

The living coma is, without a doubt, much worse than non-existence. Trudging through life, carrying out the motions like you are fully present, when deep inside you wish you were miles away. Maybe on a beach, maybe at a zoo, maybe in front of a Baldwin grand with no one around and the candles lit.

I have done this, more than I'd like to admit. Waking, "living", sleepwalking through my life – unable to appreciate the small joys that would astound anyone really seeing them.

I killed two ants today, and I guarantee they were more alive than I have been on my worst days. Though it could be said those ants were simply going through the motions, doing what they had to do, to them that fate was more important than death. I hated killing them, but I did not want to be overcome by them – an infestation of these small guys getting into all the sugar and flour and carpet. Crawling on me, stinging me, biting me, all without doubt of what the future holds or if their day would improve somehow.

Wouldn't it be nice to be an ant for a day? To understand how they think and what they see? To learn what is important to them, the lowly insect?

Sometimes, I envy the ant, even in its death. They have presumably no cognizance, other than basic survival instincts. Only carrying out simple duties to their master, the Queen, and carrying out the survival of their mound. Returning food to her on their tiny backs, without ever worrying if they will be crushed. Then, when the crushing happens, they simply die. No wonder of what will happen to their lifeless little ant bodies when they are gone.

I do stick my head out of the fog sometimes and shout, to see if there will be an answer. I like it when a friend or a loved one shouts back, to remind me I am not alone. The fog does lighten here and there, and there are days where the mundane seems oddly fulfilling. Another ant comes along to help me carry the crumb, before I see the mighty hand of fate, coming down quickly to crush us both.

A Fate Worse Than Death

by James Michael Taylor

All fates are worse than death because no fate is without suffering and there is no suffering in death.

A Fate Worse Than Death

by Matthew Broyles

Over the past few years, I have bumped up against a pillar of our culture that is so deeply ingrained that most of us don't even think about its existence. That is, until we run afoul of it.

The pillar I speak of is the idea that wanting not to be alive is insane.

There are evolutionary arguments to be made for this. DNA's primary purpose is continuity and self-replication, and as products of this material, it should stand to reason that survival would be paramount in our psychological makeup. And for most of us, it is.

Yet as our brains have developed over millennia, we have taken ourselves into philosophical territory that occasionally conflicts with our physical programming. How many of us want something that we know isn't physically possible? I would say that is a feeling the majority of us have experienced, although my sample set is likely biased by a preponderance of artists and intellectuals in my social circle. Still, wishing for the impossible is not a concept foreign to a large number of people in our society.

So what happens when the desire for something is strong enough that the denial of it becomes painful? I know lots of folks whose dreams have been dashed on the rocks, and have grudgingly resigned themselves to a mundane existence. At some point, the ensuing depression might escalate to a level where continuing to live in a way they do not want might be so unpleasant that life itself is no longer enjoyable. Should we, as thinking adults, be able to make the choice to unexist rather than continue in a life we do not want?

This is putting aside entirely the number of people affected by severe mental or physical illness, for whom daily existence can be tantamount to torture. Yet even these people are expected to want to live, despite the clear evidence that doing so means prolonging their suffering.

We cannot bring ourselves to say that in some cases, perhaps more than we'd like, death is preferable to life.

Often this viewpoint is bolstered by the concept of hope, which in the end, is an article of faith. That hope always exists is not a provable contention. Yes, the future is unknowable, and in that uncertainty might lie the potential for improvement of one's circumstances. But equally, things could get worse. Or more likely, stay the same. The insistence upon placing more emphasis on a positive outcome rather than a negative one is not a stance that can be defended with logic. It is faith, based primarily on a sense of universal justice. Which is more or less religion. Which, for my money, is often based on a fear of death.

Why do we fear death? It is the same sort of unknown murk that the future holds. We don't know how it will feel, or if we will feel anything. Again, DNA's imperative for survival and replication could argue for a resistance to non-existence. But when an organism does not possess this reluctance to deactivate, is it in fact a critical fault? If so, it wouldn't be the only inconsistency in our behavior. Most organisms don't shit their nests, but we have a nasty habit of doing that as well. The next century or so might show us how very bad we are at survival, with all of our instincts seeming to drive us to destroy the very habitat upon which our existence depends.

Perhaps self-destruction is actually baked in.

To be clear, I would much rather that this were not the case. Life offers many pleasures to be enjoyed, and I'm in no hurry to stop enjoying them. But that can change. Has changed for people I know, who decided that on their own P&L analysis, there was much more loss than profit. It could be that depression and other mental ailments blurred their thinking about this, and that they are not seeing the picture clearly. But it could be that they are right. And if so, would it not be reasonable to allow them a full range of options to remedy that situation?

We do not allow for this possibility in our culture, except in cases of terminal illness. Life is seen as the most precious of all gifts, a phrase which reveals its provenance from the realm of the mystical. The fact that we regard it as something that some higher intelligence has bestowed upon us circumscribes our thinking on its value.

For much of human history, life has been extremely cheap. Peasants relegated to little more than livestock, soldiers sent to die for the whims of their masters. That this has changed somewhat is an unmitigated good. The concept of equality, enshrined in the foundation of democracy, allows us to place unprecedented value on each individual's existence. Facilitating life, liberty, and the pursuit of happiness for all should be our primary goal. This despite the fact that in practice, we often fall back on our belief that some lives matter more than others.

In the best light, though, the desire to prevent people from committing suicide speaks to our better natures. It shows that we care, and that is beautiful.

But if we truly care about the happiness of others, we must be prepared to believe them when they say that enough is enough. We must be willing to accept the possibility that a feeling we do not share is nonetheless real to those who are feeling it. We must be able to let go of our fear of death, and refrain from imposing it on others.

Maybe this belief makes me a bad person. I rather think that it is the most realistic outlook, and that we owe each other that level of honesty.

I want you all to stick around. But I'll understand if you can't.

A Fate Worse Than Death

by MC Dalet

This prompt left me at a loss. There are the trite fates worse than death, like a life without love, self-examination. . .a life not truly lived, and so on; but I am fulfilled in all of those ways. I can't connect with those ideas because I can't relate to them. There is one thing, though, and it may seem kind of strange, but when I think of *a fate worse than death*, my irrational fear comes to the surface: the fear of being wrongfully imprisoned.

Trust me, the fear is irrational based on my current life experience. When I look back on my 20s, I often remark that I should be dead or in jail. I did nothing that would have kept me imprisoned for long, but I carried illegal substances. I ingested them and went into public, sometimes in dangerous public places. The fact that I was not jailed or gravely injured during the follies of my youth serve in some way to prove to me that I actually need not fear lockup. If it didn't happen then, what could possibly happen now that my law-abiding days are upon me? Add to this the fact that I am white. Let's please not pretend that doesn't work in my favor.

Still, the fear persists. Maybe documentaries like *Making a Murderer* and all of the true crime programs my wife loves – the ones where they have the wrong guy, and years later reopen the case – have somehow planted themselves deep inside my monkey-mind. Maybe it's a past life experience haunting me from deep within my soul memory. Maybe it is simply that I am, generally speaking, a fearful person, if I'm being honest. Afraid to make a mistake. Afraid to be misunderstood. Afraid to be misrepresented. Afraid of being in the wrong place at the wrong time, looking a little too much like a suspect, and separated from my freedom and everything and everyone I love. . .for something I didn't do. That would be a fate worse than death. The prospect of being alive but unable to enjoy life, my family, my wife and children, my band(s), road trips, a cold beer on a warm evening; it would be too much, I think.

I wouldn't do well on the inside. I'm neither crazy nor tough enough to get a bluff in. And I have the world's worst poker face. Maybe that's the real fear: the fear of being in a position that I've convinced myself I can't handle. . .like climbing out of debt, or reaching my true potential. Perhaps this apparent fear, like most fears, masks something more deeply seeded and ultimately more insidious. A lack of self-confidence. Of courage.

In truth, it's layered: there is a very real threat of wrongful imprisonment. NBC News reported that 149 wrongfully convicted inmates were exonerated in 2015 alone. The Innocence Project has orchestrated 350 exonerations. The average time spent in prison, according to both sources, is 15 years. A staggering number of wrongly convicted individuals are African American or Latinx. This is where one might say that it is an irrational fear for a White American male to have. And one would be right. Of the factors that would contribute to my wrongful imprisonment, race would not be among them. But ideology might.

Ideologically, our right to think – and speak – as we choose, as we feel, is protected not just by *a* constitutional amendment, but by the *First Amendment*. It is literally the first right to be included in a list of those liberties the American framers chose to explicitly set to record. Yet, as we have learned by simply observing the world, all rights are negotiable. . .and conditional. It would not take much to tip the balance. If ever a theocracy takes the reigns, I'm toast. Perhaps I have a fear of where my beloved country may be headed. This is a fear of the external given a specific face: speak the wrong words. . .have the wrong idea. . .lose it all. This threat has always been in my consciousness. The fact is even when I was in my careless phase, it was my fear of consequences that eventually changed my behaviors, rather than some sort of moral turnabout. Now I simply have too much to lose. Yes, my consciousness has changed, but fear is still ever-present.

Then there's the internal core: fear of being misunderstood. For individuals exonerated by the Innocence Project, the leading cause of wrongful conviction was misidentification, which contributed (sometimes in conjunction with other factors) for a staggering 71% of wrongful convictions. Nothing hurts me more, I'd say, than being misunderstood, especially when it comes to my intentions. When I am accused of exhibiting a negative quality that I did not intent to display, it is crippling. I withdraw. I sulk. I anger. I *fear* it, as I fear, irrationally, my imprisonment.

But that is the prison, isn't it? The fear. When I let it have the wheel, I *do* miss out on enjoying life, my family, my wife and children, my band(s), road trips, a cold beer on a warm evening. Perhaps my fear stems from my knowledge that I am already in prison and the fact that I know that I must face the discomfort of finding the self-confidence, the courage to exonerate myself.

o

The Pale Blue Dot

o

The Pale Blue Dot

by Anna Bardin

"They're beautiful, aren't they? The stars. I never really look at them anymore, but they actually are quite…beautiful." – Agent K, *Men In Black*

The other day, I'd had enough of screens, drywall, and sunlight filtered through melted sand, so I decided to go for a walk by the lake. Out among the trees and birds, it took a full hour for me to shake off the nagging babble of normal life and actually notice what was around me. When I did, I began to feel that familiar knot between my shoulders loosen a bit, and realized how very tense I probably am during a standard day. I let the scents and sounds of nature fill my senses…

…and then stepped on the sharp edge of a beer can, poking through the sides of my sandals and causing me to curse out loud, alarming the squirrels, who rushed to escape the crazy human lady in their midst.

It can be difficult to think of our world as beautiful. Though many of us create astounding works of art, architecture, and sound, our chief occupation seems to be erecting bland, functional forms, ringed by vast expanses of featureless concrete, with the background noise of combustion and tire rumble as an omnipresent soundtrack. We do not consult nature in these plans, imposing our wills as if we owned the place. Which, in the absence of verbal opposition from our nonhuman neighbors, we've decided we do.

To find a place relatively unmolested by human hand requires driving—DRIVING, on artificial roads—far outside where most of the population can reasonably exist in an industrialized society. That we have had to establish gates to protect our pristine places is an indication of how rapacious we are. Yet even in state and national parks, human detritus can be found snagged in bushes, creeks, and under picnic tables.

There is no planet B, and as such, there is also no trashcan B. We shit where we eat, because the cost of propelling the shit up via rocket into the sun is prohibitive ($10,000 per pound, if Neil DeGrasse Tyson's figures are correct). We are resistant to creating less waste, so we simply come up with creative ways to either re-use our leavings or bury them as best we can.

Of course it's not sustainable. Not with 7 billion of us. I've done my bit by not reproducing, but statistically, I still have a good three to four decades' worth of offal to contribute to the pile before I'm done.

How much longer can we say that our planet is beautiful? Parts of it are, certainly.

Usually the parts we haven't gotten around to despoiling, either due to inaccessibility or unprofitability. When I watch documentaries featuring breathtaking locales full of color and teeming with wildlife, it seems beamed in from some other planet than the one I inhabit.

Right now I'm looking out my apartment window at a green sward of trees and grass. Pleasant enough on this side of the building, since I can't see the parking lot on the other end. Yet even here, I spot a candy wrapper tumbling out from one of my downstairs neighbors' patios. Soon it will lodge in the fence, and I'll either get irritated enough to go retrieve it myself or hope the maintenance guys will take care of it during one of their leaf-blowing excursions, a cacophonous ritual that always gets me shaking my head. I would much rather see nature's leafy debris on the ground than inhale more oil-flavored carbon dioxide, thank you very much.

I wonder how long it will be before our pale blue dot is more of a sepia splotch. I do what I can to minimize my impact, to give my niece and nephew some remote chance of having a pretty place to live when I'm gone. But it never seems like enough, and I feel silly sometimes collecting all the empty soda cans from the office trash, cursing my lazy co-workers for not taking the few seconds required to drop them in the recycling bin down the hall. Am I making any difference at all?

Back at the lake, it doesn't feel like it. I squint a bit to blur out the manmade parts of the view, to imagine that I'm really in nature. Not that I would survive long in the true wild anyway. Which, of course, is why we are in this pickle at all. We have optimized the planet for our convenience, and I'm as guilty as anyone of wanting it my way.

The cost doesn't become apparent until the moment I feel the artificial environment closing in around me, and some extant piece of primal DNA begins to panic, seeking greenery and birdsong. A walk at the park will quiet that voice for now, if I tune out my bleeding foot and the distant thump of bass somewhere on the outskirts.

As someone dead once said, in the end, the love you take is equal to the love you make. I encourage all of us to love our pale blue dot a bit more in the years to come. Asteroids and supervolcanoes can do the destroying for us, but until then, let's try to pick up after ourselves, K?

The Pale Blue Dot

by Matthew Broyles

It seems like every few weeks, there's an announcement heralding the discovery of a new potentially Earth-like planet somewhere off in the cosmic distance. Human ears perk up at the possibility of colonizing a completely new land, one whose ground hasn't been spoken for a thousand times over by the marching feet of history. I used to react similarly, my head full of Star Trek visions and clean-slate dreams.

But now…

Do you know someone who comes up with a new scheme every so often? One that will fail miserably like all the other ones they've tried in the past? Because although the idea is new, the person pursuing it possesses the same critical flaws that sank the previous ventures?

This is increasingly how I view humanity.

I would really rather not be like this. The cynical life chose me, not the other way around. By nature, I am an idealist of the Henson school, *Rainbow Connection* and the whole nine. Those are the instincts which scream in protest every time I pronounce negative judgment on the human capacity for positive change.

But look at the facts. As a species, our record on prudent resource management is plainly abysmal, as is our scorecard when it comes to environmental sustainability. Certainly there exist exceptions among us, people who pour all their creativity and knowhow into designing and implementing brilliant systems that allow us to harmoniously coexist with our world.

Yet most of those innovations do not make their way into mainstream culture. When a choice is presented to the average citizen, familiarity wins more often than not. Especially when those with entrenched profit interests in old methodologies employ elaborate public relations campaigns and lobbying dollars to keep us dependent upon the products and services they provide.

We are easily led, and that more than anything else has darkened my optimism on our prospects. We believe what we are told to believe, to a degree obvious to anyone who's read about Stanley Milgram, the Third Reich, or pretty much any epoch since the codification of propaganda by Edward Bernays a hundred years ago. Not that we were all that individualistic before that, but the modern science of opinion-making frankly makes controlling human beings so easy that the temptation is irresistible to anyone with a few million to blow on it.

They don't even lie about it half the time. Elon Musk says he wants to leave Earth before it becomes unlivable. Other billionaires spend heaping great wodges building their opulent bunkers for when the shit finally goes down. The concurrent plundering of national treasuries by the banksters and corporate scumlords should surprise no one. They know we're fooked, too.

Yet these methods of avoiding catastrophe are pitifully inadequate to escape true global disintegration. Sure, go to Mars. Then guess what? When something goes wrong, you're even more screwed than you were before, having only barely wrangled a hostile alien environment into something approaching a home.

Has no one read *War of the Worlds*? Can you imagine the sorts of microorganisms that might exist on one of these Earth-like planets? Our bodies freak out at exposure to unfamiliar chemicals and microbes all the time. We are only recently learning how dependent we are on the right mix of bacteria in our guts for our health and well-being. Now let's plop ourselves down in an environment with which our immune systems have ZERO experience. Like Wells' Martians, we may drop dead within days, if not upon the instant.

Our dreams of colonizing new worlds come from science fiction, but so do the cautionary tales. A truly Earth-like planet will have developed at least some form of life, evolved optimally to survive in that environment. Do we want to meet the apex predator of Trappist 1-D? And if we do, can we claim the right to decimate it, as we have with other threats to our own existence here on Earth? You can bet we will.

The truth is that I don't trust us. While humanity possesses a wealth of beauty and compassion, we are also rife with avarice and selfishness. Our pendulum between the two swings constantly, both within each individual and in the society as a whole. Where there is a fresh opportunity for personal gain, the worst elements among us rise to the fore, the bleeding hearts and the artists lagging behind. It is not that we will not make something good and precious in our new worlds. I don't doubt that we will. The part that scares me is the price that the planet and the pawns will pay en route to that shining city.

I really hate to be a party pooper. But I tend to think *Star Wars* had it closer to the mark than Roddenberry. Corruption, evil, economic caste systems, all of this will follow wherever we go. It's baked in.

That said, I don't really have much say in the matter. If we can, we will go to the stars. That is certain. Good will fight evil, those in the gray areas between will struggle to determine which is which, and people will do what they must to survive, for themselves and their progeny. We are creatures of DNA, whose goal is propagation at all costs. If our efforts fail, our line on the evolutionary tree comes to an end, leaving room for others.

For the moment, I will enjoy my time on this pale blue dot, the one whose contributions to our existence we take for granted as we look for newer and shinier. It is our mother, and mothers never get the credit they're due. I for one will appreciate it, and continue to insist that we treat it with the respect it deserves. For in reality, it may be the only home we'll ever have.

The Pale Blue Dot

by Paul Williams

Pops sat on the little balcony of his 5th floor apartment downtown one night looking at the mysterious windows in the brick building across the street. Mysterious not in the usual sense of intrigue or chilling suspense, only in that Pops had no fucking clue what went on in that building. Not that he was overly curious. He just wondered…and occasionally dreamed up a story about what could be going on there. He spent a lot of nights like this, on the little balcony looking across the street.

This night, in one of the windows in the old brick building across the street, he saw a pale blue dot. Very pale, slightly jittery, a glow about it. A light maybe. He searched his memory for other recollections of seeing the pale blue dot, but couldn't find one. No big deal…he enjoyed staring at the dot. He liked the way it made him feel. It was definitely a light of some kind.

Computers give off what is best described as a "BLUE" light. This type of blue light causes the brain much activity, and anxiety. Staring at the computer before bedtime is not such a hot idea, follow me? Pops had learned this from his beloved wife. She had learned that "RED" light before bedtime was the ticket. Calming. Relaxing. And all because of some deep shit physics fact about the frequency spectrum, how our eyes interact with it, blah blah… anyway, Pops had stopped geeking out on his laptop before bedtime a few months ago, per the wife, and, well…he was more relaxed at bed time, without a doubt. But he quite enjoyed seeing that pale blue dot across the street from his little balcony in the window of the old brick building.

Fairly often, Pops liked to go across the street to have lunch at Carmine's, a pizza joint and bar on the bottom floor of the old brick building across the street. He knew and quite liked most of the people who worked there, although he could only recall a few of their names. Pops sucked with names…always had. He knew Josh the bartender for sure. Josh was a great bartender. He would talk bands with Pops, and would sometimes pour them both a shot of Jameson. Pops always assumed that Josh was buying (he didn't ask for any damn shot of Jameson), but sure as shit, when he got the check, Pops was paying. Like I said, Josh was a good bartender. There was the cashier and general gadfly Doris, who had four kids, yet still seemed genuinely happy despite it. Lots of good people. But Damien was the name belonging to the only Carmine's employee that Pops really loved.

Pops didn't actually know Damien all that well. Their conversations were mostly the shallow, on the surface small talk types. But they had a connection, and Pops just thought Damien was the best, mainly because Damien would often say "Pops, you're the best!" Verbatim. Pops had done a few favors for Damien. Helped him out of a couple jams, ya know? And Damien was grateful as hell.

One night when Pops was sitting out there watching the blue light, he thought about how he wanted to be an astronaut as a child. A "real" astronaut had once described the earth as a "Pale Blue Dot," upon seeing it from outer space. What a thing to be an Astronaut! Pops never became an astronaut, but he was extremely lucky and extremely successful. Extremely successful in that he made millions in business and was able now to give back as well as live a comfortable life. Lucky, in that many times along the way, someone was there to help Pops out, to pay for his education, to make sure he had everything he needed to compete in life. Sometimes his parents, sometimes the government, sometimes a family friend, sometimes a coach or teacher. Always a benefactor. Pops was well aware of his good fortune. He was no fool.

About 2 years later, on an otherwise uneventful afternoon while having a beer at Carmine's, Pops asked Josh how Damien was doing.

"I don't see him too much these days", Pops said.

Josh said there was good news and bad news: Damien had been accepted into college, but he didn't know how he was gonna pay for it. Pops knew how.

He told Josh "Tell Damien he has had a stroke of good luck! It will all be taken care of. Don't tell him how, just tell him not to worry about a thing. And don't mention my name, got it?" Josh nodded.

College? Pops was stunned... Damien didn't know how to read English worth a damn...at least that what he remembered. How the Hell did he get into College?

"Josh", asked Pops, "How the hell did Damien get into college? I thought he could barely read English!"

"He taught himself, Pops. He's a hard working kid. You know that." Josh said.

Pops made arrangements, anonymously, to pay for Damien's college tuition. A going away party was help in the middle of the summer.

One night a few weeks later, a week or so before Labor Day, the dot didn't appear. It wasn't there the next night, or the next night either. It never returned.

o

Carpe Diem

o

Carpe Diem

by Anna Bardin

1989 was a fairly good year. For a lot of reasons…sophomore in high school, *Full Moon Fever* by Tom Petty, first year of *The Simpsons* and *Seinfeld*, driver's ed, somehow not noticing Taylor Swift's birth…but one thing I remember very well was going to the movies with my dad.

Dad never decided what we were going to watch until we got to the theater. That still blows my mind. I don't leave my apartment without a very good reason, and I certainly won't bump elbows with strangers in a dark room unless it's for something I really, really want to see. To just wander into a theater and make a 2-hour commitment based on a poster is insane, and dumfounded me even then.

But that was how he rolled, and so when one night he rubbed his chin and pointed to a placard that said *Dead Poets Society*, it didn't really faze me. We got our popcorn and settled back to see what this particular toss of the bones had gotten us.

About midway through, I began to notice that my father was paying an unusual amount of attention to this film. A story about New England prep schooler problems seemed an odd fit for the sensibilities of a man raised in rural Arkansas, but something about the vibe seemed to grab him. That made me pay closer attention, too, to try and see what it was that had gotten into that often unreadable head of his. We both cried when Red Forman made Puck kill himself, and I even patted Dad's shoulder, a rare opportunity for me to comfort him instead of the other way around. It was all rather beautiful, and most importantly, I didn't tell Mom. This was our thing, just us.

For the next couple of weeks, anytime Dad would leave the house in the morning to go to work, he'd come up behind me and surreptitiously whisper, "Carpe diem." I would smile at our secret reference, one which seemed to double for him as parenting advice. A concept he'd tried to verbalize so many times, without much success. But here was a vivid illustration, although in hindsight, using words which ultimately drove a movie teenager to commit suicide might be seen as a bit sketchy. Still, I knew what he meant.

Or I thought I did. A few weekends on, I was sitting in my room, reading. Throughout my childhood, and continuing unabated in my teens, saying that I was in my room reading was the same thing as saying I was respirating and had a pulse. If you wanted to find me, behind a book was the surest place. I never got much flak for it, since my mom was so happy I wasn't out tearing up the neighborhood or the house like my brothers. Let the girl read, my mother's indifference said. We won't have to bail her out of the clink for that.

Yet on this particular day, my literary revels were broken by the sound of an authoritative rap on the door, one I immediately recognized as my father's. I glanced up instinctively, wondering what chore I had forgotten to do.

"Carpe diem," he said, raising an eyebrow and jerking his head towards the general direction of the front door.

It perplexed me, but I smiled gamely, thinking that was the cosign. But still he lingered, with an expectant look that I recognized from his previous efforts to impart fatherly advice that wasn't penetrating my bespectacled little head.

"Okay," I offered, lamely, nodding as if I'd gotten it. I hadn't.

"You know," Dad said, reaching down deep for some hidden font of patriarchal wisdom he never seemed able to fully access. "You won't be fifteen forever."

Lost. I was totally, completely lost. My frown must have shown it.

"There's a day out there," he said, inclining his head at my open window. "Wouldn't be a bad idea to seize it."

It hit me all at once, like a knife in the chest. Oh, my god. My dad thinks I'm wasting my life by reading all day.

I was hurt, deeply. To me, reading was the greatest possible use of my time. What did he want me to do? Go out and terrorize the town like my brothers? Get knocked up like my classmates? What activity could possibly be more rewarding on a Saturday afternoon than curling up with a book? I literally could not think of a single thing I could be doing that was better than what I was already doing. I WAS seizing the goddamn day.

But there in the glare of my father's gaze, none of these thoughts would force themselves up into my throat to be spoken. Instead, I swallowed them, until they lodged in my heart. Slowly, deliberately, I closed my book and nodded.

He smiled. The bastard smiled when I stopped reading. What the hell? And just like that, he was gone, trundling off down the hall. I waited in my room for a minute, and sure enough, I heard the Oldsmobile crank up outside. Dad was off to seize a two-hour trip to the auto parts store, to have an afternoon's peace while my mother dealt with the kids, one of whom was apparently far too quiet enjoying her book all by herself. Failing, somehow, to seize the day.

I can't watch *Dead Poets Society* anymore. Haven't been able to since Dad died. Somewhere in there is an ideal that in some way unbeknownst to me, I failed to live up to. As, I suspect, my father did, too, and tried to tell me, in that singularly ineffective way of his. I'll never know what it was, and it's entirely possible he didn't, either. But then I pick up a book, find a comfy spot in my air conditioned apartment, and for me, the day is seized.

Carpe Diem

by Matthew Broyles

"The day is short, the task is great, and I am idle…" – Toad the Wet Sprocket, *Enough*

I've seized a lot of days in my time. Yesterday I was looking through a bunch of old photos documenting days seized in the past. Stages stormed, pens put to paper, flesh pressed, keys clicked in fervent hyperproductivity. It all looks like a lot of work. And it was.

It's curious, then, that these days I often find motivation lacking. Because for all of that seizing, at 43 I still reach the end of the week holding my wallet tightly, hoping nothing unexpected appears to blow out the meager remainder of my budget. While profit has not been the primary motive for my creative endeavors, it cannot help but be an integral piece, so long as there is rent to pay. And when it doesn't pay sufficiently to survive, I find myself back in the cubicle, the one place where activity equals a living wage.

#FirstWorldProblems, yes. But as a person who is geared to value creativity above practicality, it is nonetheless depressing. I am ill fit to function optimally in this environment, and always will be. Every minute spent hacking away at the inbox is a minute where I can't create anything that I perceive as having value.

So when some free time does come my way, one might think I would jump on it. But there is a reservoir of bitterness that builds throughout the mundane hours spent in the cube mines, and sometimes it takes a while to drain before the clean spring of creativity can flow. Sometimes it takes all day, and then the time is gone, never to return.

It wasn't always like this. There was a time when the struggles of dayjoberry felt like they were part of a larger plan, to pay my way into the ranks of the professional creative class. Alas, I find that the missing ingredient now is hope. Math was always my weakest subject, but over the years, the power of statistics has become clear to me. And the odds do not favor hope.

In 2012, I attended the Folk Alliance festival in Memphis. An entire hotel teeming with wannabe full-time musicians. It was an absolute meat market, the halls cramped with guitar-wielding younglings, fresh-faced and brimming with potential. I was 38 at the time, and as I gazed upon the overwhelming crush of youthful hope all around me, the only thing I could think was: Most of these people aren't gonna make it. And if these sparkly pretty things can't break through, what chance do I have?

Do it for its own sake, I know. And I do. For if I don't have writing or music to lean on, then all that's left is the humdrum of daily life, which on its own is no life at all, in my estimation. But it can't help but hurt one's pride when a day's worth of key-punching brings more financial reward than a year's worth of painstakingly baring the deepest secrets of one's heart. The world shrugs, and I head back to the cube.

This is not the sort of thing an artist is supposed to say out loud. It's terrible marketing, the poor pitiful me bit, and I react badly to it myself when I see people post this stuff on the Facespace. But I think it's important for someone to say it, on the off chance that another sad bastard reading this also feels the same way, and thinks that they are horrible and freakish. Maybe you are. But you're hardly alone.

One thing I've learned about the universe: It's not personal. Running afoul of the odds is as ordinary as a sandwich for lunch. You have not been singled out for existential torture. You share it with all the misfit souls howling away in their garrets, sorting inventory asset numbers for some suit or another and trying to care, because the moment you can't get up the gumption to click the little buttons and earn your rations, you're out on the street. Satan does not laugh at your pain. If he existed, he certainly couldn't be bothered with something so unimportant. I increasingly feel like a Lovecraft protagonist, shocked and horrified at how very tiny and inconsequential a human life truly is.

Why did I ever believe otherwise? Hope, of course. That desperate clinging to the ass end of the odds, pleading with fate to be granted entrance into the kingdom of the exceptional. It makes no sense. But in this system, art never does.

"Each one's waiting on the chance

To be lifted off the ground, but then

To discover that we'll all be dust again…"

-Jukebox the Ghost, *Adulthood*

Siddhartha knew all of this ages ago, of course. The secret to happiness is low expectations. I understand why people lash out at celebrities who proffer bon mots on the good life. Dammit, can't you see we're all slogging through the grind down here? Don't remind me that there are those who beat the odds, it just makes things harder for the rest of us. Crabs in a bucket, yes, but what asshole put the bucket there in the first place?

It can be tempting to just shut off the world of successful creative types altogether. It opens the scab, reminds me of the summit unclimbed. Far better to watch videos on cooking, home repair, and any number of things I can actually succeed at. Combing through those old photos is worse, a hoard of participation trophies worth precisely bupkis.

Seize the day, by all means. But not all days are created equal. Each of us gets a different one, and some are a bit more sickly than others. Most are ordinary, though. And when I look at a picture of an orphaned Syrian refugee child, perhaps even I can learn gratitude for that ordinary day.

○

Happily Ever After

○

Happily Ever After

by Anna Bardin

I'm not sure I ever believed in happily ever after. Not entirely.

Maybe because of the *Sound of Music*. It was one of the Betamax tapes my mom would put on regularly, and I always wondered what happened to the von Trapps once they fled over the Alps. Ostensibly, they lived happily ever after, but it's not explicitly stated. Maybe they got snatched en route by a patrol and went to Bergen-Belsen.

Or perhaps it was the failed marriages of so many friends over the course of my childhood. Meeting someone whose original parents were still together in the 1980s was unsettlingly rare. It made my parents' union seem oddly fragile, like it could break at any time after one of their simmering tiffs. Had my dad lived a bit longer, they might well have split. Or not, it's impossible to know. But believing the fairy tale was just too painful, lest the hammer shock come one day. I buffered my heart, to keep it from breaking.

Maybe I still do. It could be that fear of believing in happily ever after is what keeps me from fully committing to a long-term relationship. I don't like to think so. I prefer my usual explanation, that love is too big to restrict to one person. I do believe that, truly and sincerely, and am an ardent proponent of polyamory. But I also know that somewhere in the clockwork depths of my soul, there's a tiny regulator that goes off when someone gets too close. The force field goes up, and the potential disappointment of a broken happily ever after is banished again.

I know people who do believe in it, though, and appear to have lived it. Not perfect lives, certainly, but deep commitments to loved ones and lifestyles that are heartbreakingly beautiful to witness. People who have truly found someone who completes them, and to whom they pledge their all. I can't say that I'm not envious. For all my solitary ways, there are moments when I would like to have someone to lean on.

My love life is haphazard, my traveling bf the closest thing to an anchor that I have. But we mesh because neither of us expects the other to be all we need. I take comfort in strangers, as does he, and when we do meet at the other end of our explorations, we bring all the passion we've collected along the way. It is exhilarating, and I can't imagine living without that fresh injection of outside adventure.

But clearly I'm an outlier in that. Why, though? Because I'm weird, or because most people accept the conditioning they're given, that happily ever after exists out there somewhere, if you listen to your heart and believe? Do I refuse to buy that line because I'm emotionally damaged, or because I see through it?

To a degree, we create our own reality. If we believe happily ever after exists, we filter everything through that lens, confirming our bias. If we believe otherwise, we do the same. Perhaps it's not a question of whether happily ever after empirically exists, but whether we want it to.

Happily Ever After

by Chris Dashiell

The Hollywood ending is only a beginning. And if you knew how much wisdom depends on grievous mistakes, you might prefer to stay a fool.

When I decided to be married, I thought I would be great at it. True, no one had taught me how to do it, or even dropped the slightest of hints about what it involves, but no matter, I thought. My innate wisdom and sincerity, not to mention the power of love, would guide me right.

But by some mysterious process, everything seemed to change once we put our signatures on a license, and indulged in that absurd ceremony where family and friends are invited to witness a show of false hope. Now there were expectations, powerful and unnamed. Somehow I was now in charge of the happiness of another human being—I who couldn't guarantee my own. And I must confess that I assumed she was in charge of mine as well. It was an impossible task. Whenever we were disappointed, we fought, and not the kind of fights you quickly get over. These involved long fruitless attempts to explain and prove ourselves right, ending in bitter tears.

We thought this was a phase, a necessary stage of growth. We thought it would lead to something greater. We were unable to account for the strength and endurance of our grief. What did we grieve? The loss of the original romance, the passion, the limerence. When we were fascinated by everything about one another. When sexual attraction was the constant background to anything else we might do, not as a goal but an unfailing present enjoyment. That was gone, but oh not forgotten. It was longed for. How to return to Eden? What new behavior must we learn in order to recapture the brilliant time of "in love"? New beliefs, new thoughts? Might a good therapist solve the problem?

We were enlightened, forward-looking people, but in the blind center of our hearts we believed all the rubbish we had picked up from movies. Actually it's more than just Hollywood. It's a constructed world of belief about "love," centuries in the making, which shrouds us all in sweetness. It says that to love is to be united, for the two to become one, and thereby to heal the wounds of separateness. It is a beautiful wish, and it is false. How cruel it is that we labor under this false belief, sometimes never awakening from it. I will spoil the suspense and tell you right now that only when you recognize that this belief is false will you begin to know how to love.

In the meantime: an endless series of fights, punctuated by making up and going along as if all were well, until of course the next fight. Most terrible are the words said during the fights, words that can never be unsaid. The resulting guilt, the "marriage shame" someone called it, is crushing. Guilt at having violated the sacredness of our feelings because—because what? I can't even remember sometimes. Because of pride and anger and the fear of being humiliated. Whatever we said and did reminded us of what we didn't want anymore, and of pains endured before we met, which our love was supposed to have healed but only re-wounded. A lot of what initially attracted us to one another became precisely what annoyed us the most. Also, a great deal of it was justified. Oh yes, there is behavior which you just can't live with anymore if you've been together long enough. There's no question some things must change.

There were declarations of hatred, slamming doors, separations, even suicide attempts. We are more passionate and stubborn than most, I think. But the same reality is true for other couples, with differences in degree. I know this to be a fact. Well, I tell myself that at least there was never any hitting, any physical violence. "At least" is the right term, because that really is the least one can expect, don't you think?

We haven't left. What a strange thing that is! Our friends say that's a kind of success. How ridiculous. But I won't deny that love exists with us. The important thing is that "love" isn't anything like what we thought. It's not getting our shitty needs met, I can tell you that. No melding of the hearts, thank you. What I know is the complete difference between one soul and another. Being brave enough to recognize and accept that another person is utterly not me. So that the honor and respect and kindness, and oh hell I guess the love we feel is founded on separation. A seeming distance that hints at more than anything a poor sucker could wish.

Happily Ever After

by Matthew Broyles

We all love a happy ending. It is, of course, one of the reasons why movies are so popular. A satisfying conclusion, a definitive cut-off point at which we can say, "there, that's sorted."

I was thinking of this while watching *The Force Awakens*. A benefit of the *Star Wars* franchise extending beyond the sixth film is that we get to peek beyond the happily ever after. Of course killing the Emperor and getting Han & Leia together wasn't going to fix everything. Roll forward a few years, and things have gone to shit again.

Entropy comes up a lot when we discuss the future. The intrinsic path of all things towards eventual unraveling, documented in science to a fairly convincing degree. However, before things fall apart, they must come together. The chaos of the universe's beginning gave rise to the organization of stars, planets, life, ecosystems. One cannot have destruction without creation, else there is nothing to destroy.

Humans exist in such small pockets of space and time that it always strikes me a bit odd when someone throws up their hands and says, "yeah, but entropy." Okay, sure, over millions of years, yes. But within a human lifetime, hardly.

Except, of course, for the destruction we bring about ourselves. Humanity has a penchant for self-fulfilling prophecies. World War I happened because an awful lot of people wanted it to, from leaders to artists to restless youth, as expertly dissected in Modris Eksteins' *Rites of Spring* and elsewhere.

I'm not sure why I felt such a pull to study WWI back in the aughts and early teens of this century, but I'm not alone in feeling that a similar flash point has been barreling towards ignition for the past few years. It's one of the only things Steve Bannon and I have in common, except that he would like to rush the process, whereas I would very much like to hold it back. Perhaps Howe and Strauss are right about the Fourth Turning, and there is nothing anyone can do to stop the inexorable cycle of conflict and reconstruction, fall and rise.

But it's a bit like telling yourself not to think of pink elephants. If you have it in your head that the whole thing is going to implode anyway, you behave differently than if you actually think something better is possible. I've seen that on a personal scale, hope giving way to resignation, and I think it is inarguable that this has been happening on a national and global level as well.

Witness the gleaming vistas of the early atomic age. Dreams of bright futures, comfort, convenience, and plenty. Even then, of course, there were dissenters. Orwell, Huxley, Bradbury, reminding us that human behaviors had not changed much along with the technology. Shakespearean tragedies still ring true today because people are still people, and we make very much the same mistakes centuries later, cautionary tales or no.

We will never live happily ever after. And yet we want to. If only we do this, this, and the other, then everything will be set up, and we can coast through the rest of our lives. I thought the same thing in my twenties. Establish the right starting conditions, and the rest should take care of itself, so I won't be fighting the same battles at 43 as at 23.

Welp. Guess not.

Cat posters and helpful coffee mugs remind us all the time that happiness is a journey, not a destination. But being constantly in motion is exhausting, especially when even the smallest errors in judgment carry far-reaching consequences for those with few means to recover from them. Have one too many beverages on a single night, risk a DWI charge that upends your entire life. Fumble too clumsily with an attractive stranger, subtract 18 years of freedom. Spend one day uninsured, and one big hospital trip might leave you in the red for the rest of your life. Seize the day, but not too hard, or it'll slice your palm and you'll bleed out.

I remember the days of D.A.R.E. back in school. Pledges by teens eager to please, swearing they'd never touch an illegal drug. I lasted longer than most of them, waiting till my late thirties to inhale any greenery, but that was due to job-related screenings, not promises to counselors. It's easy to make a promise when you don't know the future. Much harder to know whether that promise is worth making.

People and circumstances change. Are any of us who we said we would be? Some, perhaps. For the remainder, do we reassess and reconfigure our lives, or is that an abandonment of principle?

Now expand that thought outward. We know what America has been. What we dreamed of becoming, flush with resources and surrounded by decimated competitors after the second World War. After the fall of the U.S.S.R., after the killing of bin Laden, after the democratization of Iraq. The happily ever after never happened. Because it never will.

With that in mind, are we brave enough to step back and decide that the thing we want to be, the uncontested world champs, is not the best thing for us to be? Can we get enough distance from that fairy tale future to see ourselves as true partners in the global community, as invested in the success of the other inhabitants of our fragile planet as in our own?

Ironically, if there's any chance of us living happily ever after, that would be it.

○

The First Time

○

The First Time

by Anna Bardin

Okay, so...erotica writer, essay titled *The First Time*...my, the way that this could go...

In pondering how not to turn Essay Club totally blue in one 900-word swoop, I made a list of all the various first times from which I might pluck a suitable story. There are plenty of perfectly G-rated ones, but I sort of feel like I'd be disappointing readers a bit with a complete dodge. As the resident sex writer, I feel a compulsion to provide at least a little spice.

Virginity is a shifty target. Determining at what point it has officially been banished can be tricky, especially in Middle America, where church-addled youth devise ever more convoluted loopholes to get their rocks off while still technically remaining pure. (Garfunkel and Oates have an excellent song on that topic, which you should google forthwith)

As puberty gave way to full-blown adolescence, I was hardly immune to the temptations of the flesh. Though shy and bookish, my blossoming chest and hips did not escape the notice of boys, most of whose attempts to gain access would have been laughable if not for the weight of social consequences around every inquiry and refusal. Part of me lived in fear of my body. It seemed to call out to the lads without my bidding, inviting commentary and false friendships, causing me no end of trouble. I envied the plain, flat girls, able to pass a mob of dudes without generating a spray of pheromones.

I got so good at ignoring guys that I did not have any boyfriends all throughout junior high and the first few years of high school. Having instinctively waved off any hints of interest, I kept myself in a protective bubble, hiding out in the library with my books, the only friends I could trust.

The flaw in this plan we will name Kevin, for the purposes of this essay. For as much as I told myself I didn't want boys, the fact was that I REALLY wanted some of them. And Kevin more than most. Like me, he was quiet, and kept to himself. Nerdy, but cute, behind the tattered glasses and unkempt hair. We'd never said a word to each other in Algebra class, but he was a lot of the reason why I wasn't paying attention to the teacher. Already prone to daydreaming, under Kevin's influence my brain spent hours spinning tales of romantic rapture, warm kisses, heartfelt words, and...other things.

What did I know about those other things? Probably more than I should have. I had older brothers, mouthy ones who liked to brag to their friends about the magazines they kept hidden in their rooms. Their troublemaking ways kept them out of the house a lot, so when I was home alone, I'd sneak into their room and see what was what.

I didn't think much of the pictorials, lurid and clinical as they were. But I was utterly riveted by *Letters to Penthouse*. The scenes my mind created around this new, suggestive vocabulary elicited physical sensations that took me aback, sending me running for a blanket to cover myself up as I read, hiding my furtive hands as they struggled to release the excitement in whatever clumsy way they knew how.

The power of my compulsion shocked me. Though a silent skeptic, I was nonetheless still full of apprehension about purity and what God—should he exist—might think of my prurience. But watching Kevin's big hands fiddle with his pencil in class, I could not keep from imagining them doing other things. Things that maybe wouldn't count as sex.

In an unusual display of bravery, I cornered him at lunch one day, and asked him out. It was the most terrifying conversation of my life up to that point, but thankfully he accepted, himself rather shocked at my forwardness. Although I wanted the romance and all the other, I confess that the agendas of my illicit reading—and increasingly, writing—were paramount in my mind when I met him at the movie theater for our first date. There in the dark, I thrilled to feel his hand in mine, and shuddered inside at our first kiss, sloppy as it was. That was enough to keep me interested for a few weeks. But I knew what I wanted. What I really wanted.

Stoked by some nameless fear that my opportunities were slipping away, one night I inveigled Kevin into the back row of the theater. Ignoring the movie entirely, I swallowed hard as I insinuated his hand between my legs. In my mind, this wasn't losing my virginity. It was a pressure release, so that I wouldn't feel the need to. Little did I know. Nonetheless, fueled more by my desire than by any particular skill on his part, it worked, and I got my first jollies delivered by someone other than myself. I returned the favor, the all-important clothing barrier somehow insulating us from God's judgment, and thankfully he had on dark enough pants that no one appeared to notice as we left the theater that anything untoward had transpired.

Although back then, I did not classify this as the first time, really it was. The 'official' first time would not occur until college, but by then I'd been flying under the radar fairly extensively, learning how to get what I wanted with as little breach of decorum as possible. Many more first times would follow, on more incremental scales, but in hindsight, I proudly award Kevin the prize for first contact.

That said, I don't think there is only one first time. It can take years to truly reach what you seek, and when it happens, it can make the technical First Time seem like nothing.

In the end, the journey's the thing, the destination ever-changing. And thank goodness for that.

The First Time

by Matthew Broyles

I used to say 'never' a lot.

Never do drugs, never get drunk, never give up on a dream, never never never… absolutism is easy when you've only been alive a couple of decades, and been a bit sheltered to boot.

So there have been lots of first times. I remember going to my first after-work happy hour, at the tender age of 25, trying a couple of wines, and being shocked when my legs wobbled as I got off the stool to attempt to drive home. Being walked through my first proper pot hit at age 39, and noticing how easily smoke went down my throat after two decades of playing nicotine-encrusted clubs.

Breaking nevers voluntarily is one thing. Simply deciding that the never was a bit silly, and clearing it off the table, can be very liberating. Less pleasant is breaking the never that you don't want to break.

For the first few years of my son's life, a fair number of my nevers were challenged. Biology was a lot of it, as long-neglected health issues finally reached levels critical enough to require surgery and re-behaving. This, coupled with a sleepless child whose erratic schedule kept me at an average of 4-6 hours sleep per night, sent me into an emotional tailspin that I probably still haven't quite recovered from.

In 2007, I learned that my thyroid had been slacking off for quite a while, and upon starting Armour supplements, I regained a certain amount of strength I'd been lacking. But the doctor who'd put me on it left his practice, so I went to another one, who sent me to an endocrinologist.

If you wonder why I don't trust corporate healthcare, the following events may explain my apprehension. For it turns out that Synthroid, a manufacturer of synthetic thyroid supplements, has over the past couple decades completely out-marketed Armour, which derives its supplements from pigs. You'll see this when you go to any endocrinologist's office and notice the Synthroid logos on every available surface. So when the doctor prescribed me Synthroid instead of Armour, I figured he knew what he was doing.

Over the next few weeks, I began to feel really bad. I pinned it on lack of sleep and the array of turbulent forces on all sides, of which there was no shortage. Poverty, marital strife, imposter syndrome as I flailed at fatherhood, plus my ongoing sinus issues, the extent of which I would not be aware till the following year. The truth was, there was really very little reason for me to feel good. At least that's how I saw it, and as the weeks dragged by, I found one of my nevers hanging on by its fingertips.

For the first time in my life, I felt like I wanted to die.

It's difficult to convey what a shock this was. Up to that point, even in the throes of penniless musicianry, I had never once felt even the merest pinprick of the desire to end my existence. My songs, my writing, the world of ideas there was out there to explore, all of these kept me rapt in hunger and fascination. But steadily, that interest in life began to disappear, and the horror I felt at not being able to recapture it kept me up nights, even after the kid finally knocked off.

Where had I gone? This person I was becoming, so tired and defeated, this was not me. I hated him, and I wanted to get rid of his miserable ass by whatever means necessary. Such was my hatred of this man that it blinded me to the possibility that a medical issue might be to blame.

On a trip to Possum Kingdom with my parents and son, my self-loathing was palpable enough that my father asked me about it; an unusual occurrence, to be sure. I knew then that it couldn't last much longer. Soon I would be so miserable that I wouldn't be able to carry on the daily tasks of fatherhood. My son would lose his dad, yet another never I feared to break. Fitfully, I retraced my steps. What had changed since the last time I felt like I didn't want to die?

For all the hell the internet has brought us, its existence was key to me uncovering the underlying source of my discontent. Some people's bodies react badly to synthetic thyroid, it turns out. Not that Big Pharma is concerned about outliers. But it could be that I was one, and so I hunted down a doctor who would put me back on Armour. Within a couple of weeks, the desire to die dimmed. It was as if I'd been pressed into a shrinking box all that time, and suddenly the walls were retreating, allowing me to breathe. To live. To want to live.

There have been many more first times since then. Some monumental, others less so. But I was changed by that first experience of suicidal thought, perhaps the scariest never I've ever faced down. Having thought it once, the inkling still peers out from the shadows when times get hard. 'I'm still here,' it seems to be saying. Sometimes knowing it's really in there is good, and helps me focus on living, keeping it at bay. Other times, it whispers into the howling winds, a perpetual backup plan that I swore I would never entertain.

We say there's a first time for everything. Personally, I rather hope not.

○

No Remedy

○

No Remedy

by Anna Bardin

When I was a kid, we lived in Kansas City for a year. And every time I was in the car when we drove past a certain dilapidated old farmhouse on the outskirts of town, my father would grimace as he saw the rusty metal shell quietly disintegrating in the weeds.

"That's just a shame," he would say, before launching into a list of seemingly simple things that could be done to rehabilitate the 1966 Oldsmobile Toronado that lay wasting away in this lonely field, forsaken and alone.

These remedies weren't things that my dad could actually do, of course. He'd seen them done by friends of his, and particularly by his brother, a master mechanic in St. Louis. I'd heard my mother's little "hmpf" on the occasions when she was present for these drive-by oglings, so I knew he'd been disabused of any aspirations towards buying it. Still, it called to him like a siren at sea. You could save me, it sang. I know you could…

I've had that feeling about a lot of things myself. Kids in bad situations who need a sane adult. Young artists dealing with the gap between their dreams and their wallets. Kickass boots just a little past their prime, that could be re-tooled if I knew anything whatsoever about leatherworking.

To know that something could be fixed, but not by you, is disconcerting. It makes decay seem like waste. If only I were handy, that house wouldn't have to rot. If only I had money, that theater group wouldn't have to shutter its doors. All the if-onlys pile up, and a feeling of helplessness takes hold.

The inevitability of decline would seem to be something humans could accept, given the abundance of evidence. Things get old and fall out of use all the time. What screws that perception up are the stories of reclamation. The old art deco theater that escaped the wrecking ball to become a community center. That 1947 Hudson that passed on the boulevard the other day, still ticking. Exceptions baffle our senses, and we think, why couldn't I do that?

It's not as if we need to. New housing is ridiculously abundant, as are vehicles with capabilities far in excess of the old ones, and with nowhere near the amount of maintenance. And hell, shopping for new kickass boots online is one of my favorite pastimes. Why would I want to go fix up some old crap when I can get new things so easily?

Perhaps it's a sense of our own mortality. Like our belongings, we age out of our prime, too. The day will come when I cannot climb the stairs to my apartment. Younger men won't give me the surreptitious once-over at the coffee shop. I will have developed wisdom, yes, and will probably be a better writer, but a lot of my original capacities will be diminished. Maybe I identify a little too closely with timeworn objects, feeling some of my own expiration dates bearing down as I adjust my bifocals, the latest reminder of impending dotage.

With that in mind, I understand my dad a little better. He was my age when that Oldsmobile caught his eye. How much of himself did he see in that car, slowly being eaten away by time and the elements, consigned to obsolescence on the windswept Middle American prairie? If he could fix it, then maybe he himself was not doomed. Of course he didn't know that he only had another decade on the planet. Even typing that, my stomach seizes up. I am my father's daughter. It's possible I might not live long enough for the long decline. Maybe it would be better that way.

Or maybe, as the script-fonted posters say, age is a state of mind. It could be that my best years lie ahead, suffused with creativity, love, and friendships yet to be made. Maybe there is a remedy for decrepitude, and it lies in reinvention, adaptation, loosening the shackles of previous expectations to become something new rather than a faded version of a past self.

There is no remedy for getting older. But if we can see ourselves less as a car that needs fixing and more as a caterpillar that is slowly turning to a butterfly, then maybe we can move past longings for repair and towards aspirations of metamorphosis.

Easier said than done, of course. But what isn't?

No Remedy

by Chris Dashiell

In my thirty-three years of professional experience working with business leaders, professionals of all kinds, married couples, children, professors, radio hosts, and other white people, I have noticed one problem they all share: the fact that they have a problem. One young woman, whom I will call Arlene (her name is Heather), summed it up perfectly: "No matter how much I achieve, I'm never satisfied. I feel an emptiness inside that can't be filled." Others complain of dissatisfaction with relationships, inability to get ahead in their careers, hidden resentments towards friends and family, boredom, ennui, enervation, and repetition compulsion.

Working with all these people who are unhappy with their lives, there's one thing of which I'm certain: I know more than they do. Clearly they would not be seeking my advice if I were just as much in the dark as they are. The solutions that you will discover in the pages of this book are the results of a synergistic process developed within my multivalent experience, and with the help of leading experts in the human potential field. I believe I've discovered the key to solving the problems of unhappiness and dissatisfaction. And how did I, a man wearing a Givenchy suit and a bright red tie, attain where philosophers and religious leaders down through the ages have failed? Because I learned to *manifest* the truth instead of just talking about it.

The secret of human life is that we create our problems by believing that we have problems. Then we waste precious time struggling to find solutions to each problem. However, each solution creates new problems, plunging us into an endless cycle of anxious striving. But once we have pinpointed the real source of the problem—*the belief that we have a problem*—our task has become radically simple. We must eliminate this destructive belief that we have a problem. At all costs!

This is only the introduction to my book, so I can't outline all the techniques that I've developed to eliminate the "problem belief." If I did, you might just scan these few pages while browsing in the book store, put the book back, and never buy it. The truth is, you will need lengthy explanatory chapters explaining all the implications of your problem, interesting graphs and charts, many stories of completely ordinary people like yourself whose experiences will illuminate the text with concrete examples, and more *bold italicized phrases* for emphasis, before you will be entirely ready to incorporate my solutions into your life.

I'm reminded of some of the mythic insights from *Star Wars*. (Joseph Campbell affirmed the wisdom of these movies when he moved in with George Lucas on a ranch before he died. Campbell was an important thinker who was on TV.) The Jedi knight did not have to believe in "the Force." He just used it without bothering to explain what it was. Darth Vader seemed like the enemy, but it turned out that he was Luke's father. In the same way, our problems become opportunities when we stop believing in them as problems. I hope this pop culture reference helps you to understand the paradoxical truth I am choosing to manifest.

Each chapter in the book you are about to read presents a new technique for "disappearing" your beliefs. As the illusion of belief fades away like smoke or some other metaphor, your original problem-free essence will become more and more in focus. You will say and do whatever you want without fear. Others will instinctively accept your decisions and actions, because your lack of limiting beliefs produces self-assurance, and this in turn inspires confidence. You will discover that new cars, houses, speed boats, and great sex constitute your true heritage. More importantly, your spirituality will blossom, creating a soft gentle pulsating sense of inner well-being that will radiate calmness and peace while attracting the most beautiful and exciting people into your aura.

I can see you shaking your head. "That can't be true for me," you're thinking. "A life like that is only won by driven, hard-working people. I don't deserve it." But the wonderful thing is: *you don't have to work hard.* Just learn and implement a few simple techniques, and I guarantee you will go with the flow.

After reading this book, you may be interested in attending one of my world-famous seminars. They cost just $699 for two days. This means that only those who are already making good money will be able to attend—but those are precisely the people who can most effectively spread this message through the power of their networking. But never fear. You can always *manifest the money* through the power of no belief!

I may never meet you in person, but know that I deeply love you. Namaste.

No Remedy

by Matthew Broyles

So how does all of this play out?

In the Constitution of the United States, checks and balances are set in place to make sure that no one branch of the government can act unilaterally. This works so long as all branches are not under the thumb of the others.

When both the Congress and a majority of the Judicial branch are in thrall to the Executive, this creates a Constitutional crisis. That many of us do not recognize it as such is of course by design. Waiting rooms pipe in Fox News, AM radio blares brownshirt apologetics and redirection towards minorities, and the opposition party is in complete disarray, unable to call a spade a spade without being perceived as the hysterical zealots they've been stereotyped as for the past several decades.

Where does this take us?

The obvious destination is dictatorship. Not official, like third-world countries, but de facto, like Russia. Elections take place, but with gerrymandered districts and hacked equipment, the outcome is controllable. It could be that 2012 was the last free and fair election in our history, and even then, who knows if test runs of manipulation on local and congressional races were being carried out at that time.

Alongside dictatorship comes oligarchy, a situation we already find ourselves in. Laws are written to benefit the top tier, and protests from the plebes echo uselessly off the walls of the tall glass towers, who spoon out ever more immersive opiates to distract and entertain while the bedrock beneath our feet is mined away.

At some level, we know all of this, but feel helpless to combat it. We march, we call our congresscritters, we encourage our like-minded friends to vote, and we end up in the same hole regardless. Is there more we could do? Probably. But it would require abandoning normalcy almost entirely, committing ourselves to politics the same way we commit to, say, the new *Game of Thrones* season, or our kids' extracurricular activities. It has to be a lifestyle shift, and at least so far, we have shown reluctance to place that need over other perceived needs that, in hindsight, we might consider wants.

I struggle with this myself. Knocking on doors of known like-minded voters and encouraging them both to vote and volunteer, making them believe that it matters…it would be easier if I believed it myself. But with every revelation of election fraud and electronic meddling that comes out, my hope sinks. Can we fix it? I don't honestly know.

It's at this point that Pascal's wager should take hold. Sure, you don't know if it helps, but on the chance that it does, wouldn't it be better to try? That makes total sense. Certainly more sense than heaving a sigh and settling into another video game or *Mr. Robot* rerun. Yet that lack of belief nags at the back of my head, and I hesitate too long, until the moment is gone, and inertia takes hold.

Shame me if you want. Maybe that would help. Engaging in behaviors I criticize others for is shameful. Nothing ventured, nothing gained, it's true. But of course venturing does not mean gain. On the contrary, often it ends in disappointment. The odds whisper their dirge-like melodies, and effort seems to be a mug's game. Carpe diem, have fun while you can, before the whole thing burns down, which it will do whether you fight it or not.

But then I get mad, because I realize that this is exactly what I'm being conditioned to feel. Helplessness is part of the cultural message, has been since marketers seized upon the GenX proclivity towards nihilism. Not caring makes you cool and worldly-wise, enlightened to the futility of it all. Resisting that siren call was part of what separated me from my peers in youth. Falling victim to it in middle age is frustrating, and difficult to fight as so many pre-existing responsibilities jostle for time and attention. It shouldn't be this easy to give up. Not with so much at stake.

So the dark tower rises behind the gates of Mordor, the eye's gaze penetrating farther into our lives by the day, the bulwarks of its traditional foes failing…where are the tiny heroes to beat the odds and banish the shadow back into the mists?

Obviously that job falls to us. And because this isn't a movie, we don't know if we will succeed. But it is increasingly clear that we are the only remedy that exists anymore. We cannot rely on the push and pull of legacy politics. The old ways are gone, replaced by wholesale plunder of the 99% by those who so many of us aspire to be, and who we defend while they pick our pockets and consign our sick loved ones to death.

We will be told that there is no remedy. That entropy will have its day, and the best we can do is ride out the Ameripocalypse as drunk and well-entertained as possible. How much of that is a self-fulfilling prophecy will be left for historians to sort out.

The American empire is falling, that much is unstoppable. But the rate and severity of its collapse is something we may still have power to control. If we care.

No Remedy

by MC Dalet

If I was titling this essay myself, I'd call it "Mid-age Wasteland." Whether the youthful rock 'n' roller that resides in my aging flesh suit wants to admit it or not, this is my demographic, middle-age white male. According to my research and life experience, it is also the demographic at greatest risk for suicide. Though suicide rates for American Indians and Alaskan Natives tops Caucasian rates by a narrow margin overall, the rates peak during adolescence and young adulthood for this group. Rates for those identifying as African American and Latinx scrape the bottom of vertical charts, present, but barely registering. Social justice scholars weigh in here, suggesting that there are too many external threats to these lives. The object is to survive a socially skewed game, not to throw the thing yourself. But for middle-aged white people. . .it's the Killing Fields, and the mines are our minds, the hand on the trigger our own. We are trying to survive our forties. . .and our fifties, and the enemy is within.

That enemy is stealthy in its approach, deafeningly loud when it reveals itself. It is a master of infiltration, creeping into the subconscious, waiting to surface, often in the guise of virtuous pursuits. I WANT TO REACH MY POTENTIAL AS A CREATIVE ARTIST. I HAVEN'T. I MESSED IT UP. And the conscious, logical mind recalls all the ways in which I have. I WANT TO BE A GREAT FATHER BUT I'VE FAILED AT X, Y, AND Z. And the conscious, logical mind, having defined the perfect father through an amalgamation of film's best dads, Hallmark sentiments, and your social media feed, conclusively decides that because you hurt your child's feelings in a human moment of frustration, you are a deadbeat dad the likes of Homes Simpson – but much worse, because you are not part of an animated satire. THIS IS REAL LIFE, BUDDY, AND YOU SUCK AT IT! If you're still in the game to find solutions, here comes IF ONLY I COULD…BUT I HAVEN'T YET. And when you hit middle age, the clock is ticking.

I've mentioned demographics not because I want to racialize the conversation, but to establish a bit of ethos. I speak from the position from which it is most likely to "end it." I think I know how this works. Here's how it looks from the mid-forties, in my experience: we are in the "No Remedy Zone." If we're going to lean on statistics, I've passed the halfway point of my life. FUCK, I'M TOO OLD NOW TO BE A PROFESSIONAL FOOTBALL PLAYER. Okay, not that that was ever a goal of mine. But I like football...and futbol. I admire the players. And then I realize how young they are. My sports heroes were once much older than I, and seemed to be still when we were contemporaries. Somehow this meant that I could still achieve their skill. They were someplace I could go. I am at retirement age for a professional athlete. I will never be that. It's one possibility collapsed. It doesn't matter that it was never a viable possibility for me. Then the dominos start to fall.

Awareness is tricky. It is one's ultimate ally if and only if one gets to the second level of awareness, the one where you are meta-cognitively aware that you are making something out of nothing...or that you are letting that nothing lead you, in a dangerous way, to something. The trick is getting past the first level of awareness where you think you realize all of the things you'll never do and all of the ways you've contributed to your failure to do so. Ironically, if you were really on the lookout for self-sabotage, it's right in front of you, but you're thinking about all of your mistakes and missteps as proof positive that you always self-sabotage and that it's all for naught. Concisely: when the enemy surfaces, my forty-three-year-old mind is a landscape composed of two basic thought-groups – 1.) all the ways I'm not meeting/cannot reach my potential, and 2.) ALL of the ways I planted the seeds of my discontentment in a past now unalterable. Remember, the clock is ticking. Pressure. Fight, flight, freeze. Suicide combines all three.

I'M FROZEN HERE. NO WAY OUT. NO REMEDY.

NOTHING TO DO BUT CHECK OUT.

It is possible, even probable, that you fight yourself with more ferocity than all the enemies that could ever crash your gate.

I write this following the suicides of two famous middle-aged musicians, both iconic in their respective milieus, and the death of a childhood friend at his own hands. It is a concentrated dose of heavy. I respected both artists. And, remember the pro footballer analogy? Rock star is something that is actually in my possibility sphere. I'm not saying I have the goods for stardom, but I do play and sing in bands. HOW MANY ROCKERS BREAK INTO THE BIG SHOW AT 43? CAN'T NAME ONE, CAN YOU? But my enemy digresses. The point is – two middle-aged white men. Actually doing my dream job. Both with families (a blessing which is most important to me). With money (a source of stress for me, and an omnipresent object of my enemy's sentence, IF I ONLY HAD...). And it wasn't enough to stem the self-slaughter. My friend is not as well documented, but externally, he had the markings of someone who had the checklist covered: family, friends, a good job. None of it is enough to quite the enemy within. Not for the men who irreversibly finalize their battle.

Why do we do it?

Perhaps when there is no enemy without, the enemy within, this Satan who wants to knock us out of the game, has no competition and grows powerful and emboldened.

I'll close by responding to a particularly distasteful post that crossed my social media feed the day that Chester Bennington of Linkin Park took his life. The post read, "Breaking: man who sings about suicide for 18 years commits suicide." It may "just" be dark humor, but its sentiment is misguided. As an artist, I think it is often the art that drains the enemy. If I can externalize the enemy, identify and separate it from my Self, I can face it down. When Bennington sang "Crawling in my skin/these wounds they will not heal" some 17 years ago, he took what was inside and cast it out. But he was twenty-something then, as was Chris Cornell when "things [weren't] looking so good." The forties (and fifties, evidently) are a different game.

My conscious, logical mind once thought suicide the selfish act of a coward. After all, I battled through the angst of late adolescence and the clinical depression of my twenties and early thirties having never truly entertained the option. Here in the forties, I find myself in the Valley of Death itself, the No Remedy Zone, and there is a unique and dangerous presence here. We must be constantly vigilant against it. What is more, it is imperative for you to know, so that when you address us, and observe us, you know that, no matter how grateful we are for what we have, this is the age when we are tested against our enemy, and we need your assistance. We want to defeat it. We can. As long as we are alive, we can do anything.

○

Nemesis

○

Nemesis

by Anna Bardin

Growing up, I had brothers. When people ask me how many brothers I had, I usually say, "All of them." All through my young life, it seemed as if there were no end to the great herds of sweaty, rambunctious, hurr-hurring males tromping all over the house and yard, some of them related to me, some not, but every one of the confounded creatures were in my damned way all the damned time.

Siblings closest in age are often at greater odds, and this was certainly true of my brother Tommy, only a year my senior. He was everywhere I was. On the bus, at school, at birthday parties for friends…the bastard was in my face all the time, and I resented every second of it. He bothered me about reading too much. Invented boy crushes to tease me about, usually for dudes I had zero interest in. Stole and hid my toys, to which I retaliated, spurring hostage negotiations for G.I. Joes and Rainbow Brites that resembled Israeli-PLO summits.

For years, Tommy was my nemesis. There was no parade he would not rain on, no silence he would not break, no secret that was safe. Except one.

When we moved to Des Moines, one of the many mid-sized cities we inhabited in my gypsy childhood, for once we were close enough to the school that we could walk instead of taking the bus. This was a huge relief to me, as someone with personal space issues and all the brothers in the world constantly running afoul of them.

The first day of school, I made a point to get up early, and leave before my brothers. I didn't want them tailing me all the way, else the whole no-bus thing would be for naught. I also didn't want them catching up to me, so I took a route that was not terribly direct, skirting a large, overgrown field that appeared uninhabited. Looking back now, walking alone in a little-traveled area was probably not the safest plan for a 10-year-old girl. But my drive for solitude overpowered any fear I might have had, and so, with time to kill, I took a detour through the lot to root around in the tall grass.

Lo and behold, I found an abandoned shed, quietly moldering in the weeds, forgotten and alone. Just exactly like I wanted to be. Over the next few weeks, I commandeered this hideout, decorating it with little totems and shoring up the sagging walls, lest it collapse on me in the middle of *Watership Down*. I couldn't believe it. I had finally found a place free of boys. Drunk on power, I brought a marker one day and scrawled ANNA'S HOUSE on the doorframe. There could be no mistake. This was MY sanctuary.

So imagine my shock and horror when, barely a few days after officially claiming the shed, I arrived to find my name scratched out. STEPHANIE'S HOUSE, read the legend now, and my blood boiled. Stephanie WHO? That fucking bitch! I didn't know any Stephanies at school, but I was new in town and hadn't met all the girls. I didn't even know what grade she was in. This hussy might be a pipsqueak third grader, or a haughty teen. What I did know was that this was war.

I stole a can of white paint from the garage that Saturday, and spent all day brushing over those words. Then, with infinite care, I artistically drew ANNA'S HOUSE on the longest wall. I don't know why I thought this would solve the dispute. Surely the attention to detail would shut the interloper down. But of course by Monday afternoon, the little shack was covered in STEPHANIE STEPHANIE STEPHANIE, over and over again, covering the frame in bossy black marker. Something about how complete her rejection of my sovereignty had been sent me into tears, and I rushed home, slamming the door to my room, sobbing and cursing the evil Stephanie, a nemesis I'd never laid eyes on, but whom I hated with a fire easily triple the one that scorched when Tommy's face hove into view.

I didn't go by the shack the next morning, nor that afternoon. I couldn't have anything that was my own. If it wasn't brothers, it was evil faceless bitches with markers. People ruined everything.

I'm not really sure what made me go back the next Saturday. Just to make sure, I guess. To verify that I was beaten. But my face fell slack when I spotted the shed there in the waving grass. It had been painted solid black, neither my writing nor Stephanie's visible on any part of it. I approached with caution, suspecting a trap. And nearly burst a blood vessel when my brother Tommy's head poked out of the door. I lost it.

"This is MY house, Tommy!" I fumed, balling up my fists, ready to clock him.

His smile, though, was not the usual self-satisfied grin I knew so well.

"It is now," he said, cryptically.

I frowned, confused.

"I met Stephanie," he said, twisting the corner of his mouth. "She won't be bothering you anymore."

The bottom dropped out of my world. All sense of order had vanished. My brother knew about my house, and hadn't trashed it? Indeed, had run off the only rival who dared challenge my claim? I stared, gobsmacked.

Tommy just shrugged and beat a hasty retreat through the weeds towards some unknown boy destination, leaving me to enjoy my castle in peace. On one level, it rankled me to owe him anything. But on another, I felt a gratitude so profound that it changed our relationship thereafter. Sure, we fought, but beneath it all there was an undercurrent of mutual understanding that hadn't been there before.

It seemed that the only thing Tommy couldn't abide was me having another nemesis.

Nemesis

by Cristee Cook

The first week that I was an Uber driver, I learned that my problems are small.

And being an Uber driver is a nightly adventure in surprising ways. For example, you could potentially get your first ride of the night while sitting in your driveway. An hour later, you could be on the complete opposite end of the metroplex in a neighborhood you didn't know existed. Each customer is a dice roll, people and groups, and the places we go, an endless variety. I am a happy Uber driver overall. I enjoy the people.

The first week I was an Uber driver, probably my first Saturday night shift, I found myself in North Frisco in a neighborhood I didn't know existed. It was getting later, close to midnight, and I was annoyed when I pulled into the apartment complex to pick up my rider. There was no apartment number. There was a gate code and no one answered the phone on the account who had hailed my car. After a few minutes, a man pulled up in a car and told me he was my rider. I was nervous and visibly agitated because the name on the account was a woman's name. Also, he had driven up in a car. He explained that it was his wife's account. That he had to leave the car here for someone to pick up. I called the account holder again from the Uber app, and she answered, and confirmed everything he had said. He was getting on my nerves, but my gut told me he was harmless, so we got our trip started.

He knew I was annoyed. He was apologetic. He wanted me to trust him. He began explaining that he didn't have a phone that could carry a lot of apps, so they had to use his wife's phone for Uber. He didn't need to use Uber a lot, so they didn't think it was a big deal. He was switching cars with so-and-so, over at so-and-so's place, which is where we were going, and his complicated explanation forced me to reconsider my initial judgment that he was a nuisance, or worse, dishonest.

"Where are you from?" I asked. He had a heavy Spanish accent. He spoke in broken English. A sign of bravery.

"Venezuela." He answered. "We have been here for almost a year. We had to leave our country because there was no food."

He continued. His wife and children, and his parents fled Venezuela and came to a Dallas suburb to live with a distant cousin. In Venezuela, he was an Engineer. Here in Frisco, he is a cook at a mom-and-pop hamburger shop. His wife is cleaning houses.

He carried with him a substantial load of groceries and based on the aroma, hamburger and fries for everyone he was going home to. He talked about his hopes and dreams, not his problems, and he had a determination I seem to have lost.

When I dropped him off, three family members came outside to help him unload his items. They said nothing, just nodded and took a portion of the bags dutifully. He wanted me to know his story. That he was no lazy mooch. That they had no choice but to start over.

I felt admiration for him. I felt humbled by our conversation. I didn't realize it at the time, but the experience planted a seed in my thoughts. I watched him go back into their home, and I thought about my attitude an hour earlier: annoyed, inconvenienced, and a little judge-y. I knew, in that moment, that I have it so much easier. I am privileged. I know that by societal standards, I'm not The Other.

In the United States of America, to be an Immigrant is to be seen as a Nemesis. A large portion of our native population believes that hardworking people who want the best life possible will somehow be the downfall of our country. That they are an external threat for which we must keep vigilance. That they will take something from us, and we will be less because of it. When focused on a collective of disenfranchised, the arguments against Immigration are generally based on the fear of loss.

I don't receive that kind of judgment just for existing. I grew up in the suburbs of 5 states in America. My existence here is forged and expected. My Nemesis isn't an outside force. It's the part(s) of me that still fall to the limited perspective, the "mine!" mentality and the separation. Even if it's over something as small as an Uber ride.

Nemesis

by Matthew Broyles

I've always heard that if you're not making enemies, you're not living right. It's the sort of thing that a certain type of person might say, one who is confrontational in nature, and goes around seeking conflict in order to right wrongs. I am not that person, and consequently, I can't say that I have a large list of enemies.

At least, not people who know they are my enemies. Someone like the Tangerine In Chief has a lot of enemies, and can't be bothered to pay attention to little old me in amongst all the other detractors. That's a general enemy, though. The personal sort, where gimlet eyes are exchanged, seems mostly a waste of time to me, so I haven't bothered.

That said, maybe I should. I've been known to let injustice slide on occasion, with an eye towards the bigger goal of harmony. That mostly works, but in the process, little bits of bad behavior are allowed to go unquestioned, and sometimes fester until inevitably, they must be dealt with by the sort of conflict I was trying to avoid.

I mean well, I really do. But I've also been disabused of my hippie notions over the years, and will not keep a straight face for the people who tell me that all we need is love and understanding. That does work a lot of the time, but anyone with the barest modicum of historical perspective has to know that there are times when fighting is required. Ugly fighting, not chanting and waving placards. Like, fist-to-jaw fighting, the kind with blood. Not my forte, but certainly not out of the question where the well-being of my loved ones is involved.

I'm reminded of this every time I see men like Richard Spencer or Alex Jones. Demagogues who think nothing of whipping up hateful emotions in the hearts of their followers, exhorting them to violence against those they perceive as weak. People like me. I remember years ago someone telling me that only dykes and beta males go to Tori Amos shows. I'm not sure why it continually surprises me when I'm confronted with that sort of blunt tribalism. I never seem to be ready for the argument when it pops up in casual conversation. One minute you're two reasonable people, and the next, one of you is a caricature.

Stereotypes exist for a reason, of course. Mostly because we like categorization. And more than anything, most of us want to be clearly catalogued for easy identification. Goth girl. Craft beer dude. Soccer mom. Metalhead. We go out of our way to festoon ourselves with the trappings of our chosen identities, and blink in confusion when someone is not clearly labeled.

Back in the aughts, I had a furious argument with a now-prominent blogger about poses and music fandom. Her contention was that it wasn't possible not to have a pose. You like this thing because that's part of the pose you throw. To the point that if you say you don't have a pose, but you just like something because you like it, then that itself must be a pose. I may still have the scorch marks from the steam that shot out of my ears.

Funny, I've seen arguments like that create nemeses, leading to a flurry of blocking and social media trash-talk. I'll tell you, it takes a whole lot more than an ideological disagreement to make me block a person. It can happen, but you gotta work pretty hard, and get really personal. Yet I know people who hit the block button at the first sign of opposition to whatever opinion they're posting on the goddamn world wide interweb. On the one hand, as a conflict-avoider, I understand it, but on the other, as long as someone's not actually spouting ad hominem hate speech or threatening you, isn't debate part of why the internet is there? I mean, apart from the cat pictures.

Or rather, do we see the intertubes as an opportunity merely to amplify our own worldview? Recent events would suggest so. Thus, the blocking is seen more as pruning, cultivating a garden of unanimity in which our self-assurance can bloom unchecked.

But if we so casually remove oppositional viewpoints from our private worlds, are we slowly creating a mountain of nemeses? An entire cohort of people we cannot begin to communicate with, for fear that they may contaminate our rightness by their mere presence? By putting off the conflict today, are we stoking a future showdown between utter strangers who see the other as aliens, unfit for coexistence?

It seems a foregone conclusion at this point. We fight via the ballot box and pocketbook, but do not see each other directly, except in passing. I do it myself. Do I ask the guy with the stars & bars on his truck why he believes black people should be property, as the bearers of that battle flag did? Take one guess.

So perhaps I have more nemeses than I think. Maybe the polite avoidance of unpleasant confrontation is in fact feeding a much larger conflict to come. One in which people will kill and die. Maybe I should go out and make enemies now rather than wait until critical mass overtakes us all.

Maybe my nemesis is America.

Nemesis

by MC Dalet

There is no Nemesis.

There is only choice.

My enemy is my teacher.

Will I pass the test?

Push me to oblivion,

I fade,

fall,

or rise.

The hero has no home outside the quest,

the defender no cause without calamity.

To be the best in a field of one does not

　　make one a legend.

It makes one lonely.

And trivial.

Push me so I fly.

Shove me so I feel.

Try to take me down so I learn to stand.

I can't stand you, but I need you.

Without you there is no me.

Light shines brightest in the heart of darkness.

Joy ascends to divinity when it is challenged most.

Mashiach is born from the broken shards of the decimated Temple.

A path to the stars born from The Bomb.

So crush my body; it will only unleash my soul.

Dash my dreams so that I may find new ones -- clearer, cleaner, grander that all that came before.

You are my enemy, and I love you.

Because I choose to.

I choose to rise.

I choose to fight.

I choose to fly.

I choose to feel.

I choose to stand.

I choose to shine brighter in the face of darkness, to laugh with joy at the brink of defeat, to bring Mashiach, and to find a path to the stars.

I choose to unleash my soul without losing my body, and to let go the dream if in dreaming I forget to live.

I choose to live.

You cannot stop me.

I know you must try. If you did not, how could I appreciate every breath that brings me closer to the hero within? I could not. So I thank you.

Enemy mine, I see you now. Though you are inescapable, you are not omnipotent. No longer invisible, I meet your gaze across the field of battle. And we smile, knowing.

You are a part of me. But you are not my Nemesis.

There is no Nemesis.

There is only choice.

○

Without Whom

○

Without Whom

by Anna Bardin

The transition from high school to college can be trying for anyone. But I don't think I'm out of line by saying that I had a worse time of it than most. Bad times come and go, but spring and summer 1992 were without question the worst months of my life.

I still get angry at my father for being one of those men who never went to the doctor. If he had gotten his regular checkups, maybe his cancer would have been detected, and I wouldn't have had to spend the last days of my high school career in absolute emotional ruin, watching him die, powerless to do anything but cry, cry, and hate the world.

It's a testament to the sympathies of my principal that I was given accommodation to take my finals late and graduate on time. Still, I really don't know how I did it, given the perpetual state of turmoil in my head and heart. I remember sitting next to my psychologically deteriorating mother at the funeral and thinking, 'I have to get away from here.' Maybe that makes me a bad person. But that determination propelled me headlong into college.

Standing there in a brand new place, in my brand new adulthood, in a brand new world in which I was half-orphaned, my compass spun like a top. What was I for? This life, this person? My career goals had been murky enough before the tragedy, but now I couldn't see past anything but the Liberal Arts degree plan, some vague notion of escaping a fry cook job, a future that didn't involve living in a trailer.

Unmoored from parental expectations as my mother descended into hyper-religious madness, there was one node of my brain that began insinuating itself very strongly in that place. I was surrounded by men, many of them attractive. Having spent the past few months feeling utterly horrible, I desperately wanted to feel good. And I had very intense and creative ideas on how to achieve that.

It is not entirely accurate to say that I spent my college years throwing myself at men. 'Hurling' is a better term. 'Launching,' even. Uninterested in ambiguity, I let the lads who caught my fancy know in no uncertain terms what benefits they would enjoy, and more often than not, they accepted the invitation. I did not have many female friends during this time, because I had boinked a lot of their boyfriends before they got the chance. What the hell did I care? I had to have the rush of carnal fulfillment, NEEDED it to stay afloat, to keep sadness at bay.

Word got around, and I started getting invited to more parties, for predictable reasons.

Being That Girl made me feel dangerous and powerful, any niggling sense of shame drowned out by the desire to be wanted, no matter how briefly. This power subsumed my introversion in amorous settings, both alarming and exciting me at what it might mean.

It was at a one of these parties that I met a man we will call Troy. Tall and tanned, with devastating brown eyes, I could not help but follow his body language as he motioned us out to the tree-covered patio for what I expected would be something quick and dirty in the shadows. I was more than ready.

"I liked your poem," he said, pulling the rug out from under my brain, keeping his hands to himself as he leaned on a railing.

Poem? What poem? I struggled to access the parts of my mind I'd stowed for the evening, irrelevant as they were.

"Oh," I replied, remembering my little submission to the campus quarterly. I honestly had no idea anyone had read it. I leaned in closer, stroking his big hand. "You don't have to say that."

He gave me an amused smile and laced his fingers with mine. Okay, I thought. Pleasantries done.

"Would you read some of mine?" he asked, sheepishly.

I eyed him. Surely he knew he didn't have to come up with a pretense. I was already on board. But I played along.

"Sure," I said, with a knowing grin.

Lo and behold, when we got to his place, he actually showed me his poems. They were…problematic, but earnest. I gave him honest feedback, which he took in thoughtfully before finally kissing me with breathtaking tenderness. When we did get down to business, he spent as much time on me as I did on him, a first in my experience. It was damned good, the best I'd ever had at that point. As I basked in the afterglow, I started thinking that maybe I'd been selling myself short. Choosing quantity over quality. It woke me up from the haze of the chase and made me ask some serious questions about what it was I truly needed.

Alas, such considerations also sent me into a panic about Troy. He called the next day, and it was clear he was after something serious. As much as he'd thrilled me, I was in no state to seek attachment to anyone that might stand a chance of breaking my fragile, wounded heart.

I let a beautiful man go that day, but he gave me a gift I still treasure. A sense of worth. Of being someone you might have to work to win. I don't know how I would've turned out without Troy, but I'm glad he cared enough to see me as a person and not a toy.

In the words of Billy Gibbons, you didn't have to love me like you did, but you did. And I thank you.

Without Whom

by Matthew Broyles

A lot of things happened in 1987. *The Joshua Tree* was released, as were *Raising Arizona* and the *Max Headroom* series. Weird Al did not put out an album that year, noteworthy for me, nerdboy that I was in the small-town wilds of Weatherford, Texas.

Nerdery was not celebrated then to the degree it is now. I lived in a jock and roper town, where status was determined by thickness of neck and tightness of Wrangler. An eighth grader in '87, social prospects for skinny bookish types were largely nonexistent.

Which was why getting James Hamilton as my American History teacher that year was a big deal. Bespectacled, learned, and totally uninterested in the social standing of anyone in his class, he loomed large in my daily routine. I had not been an avid student of anything officially sanctioned by public school, but in Mr. Hamilton's class, I paid attention.

I still hear people tell me they don't care much about history, and I'm always gobsmacked by that. But then I remember that prior to 1987, I didn't really care much about it either. Hell, the prior year, I'd had two whole semesters of Texas History, most of which drifted right past me like a musty odor, registering somewhat, but more as something to be endured than to be engaged with.

Not so the lessons of Mr. Hamilton, who, yes, was related to Alexander, long before there were any smash Broadway musicals on the topic. We learned about Alex & Aaron, the clashes between Founding Fathers, all the ugly details that often get glossed over in our national zeal to portray ourselves as the perfect specimen of democracy. But great storytelling contains a lot of conflict, and my teacher knew that, focusing as much on the troubled times as on the victories.

So when, upon learning that Mr. Hamilton was taking a group of students to Washington, DC over the Christmas break, I completely lost my mind. It was $500, a not-insubstantial sum for a one-income family with three kids, but clearly my parents saw my excitement over the prospect and somehow made it work.

The trip was my second time out of state (Oklahoma does count, barely), but my first on an airplane, and certainly the first without my parents. Our group numbered about 20, and was made up largely of high academic achievers, which I was not. I was there for the history, and to hang out with my favorite teacher of all time.

At the Capitol in DC, we met Charles Stenholm, then the congressman for our district, and Mr. Hamilton's future employer after he left teaching to work in politics. In '87, the Speaker of the House was Jim Wright, who had once been the mayor of Weatherford. I knew next to nothing about current political affairs, something that I would remedy in the years to come, but I did know who the president was. While walking along the Mall one night, the big black motorcade drove by. We were told that the hand waving to us from the limo belonged to Ronnie himself, and it could have. The extent of Reagan's dementia wasn't officially known at that time, and it's interesting to remember the fleeting encounter in that light. Who knows what he thought was going on just then.

We saw as much as we could in our brief visit. The Lincoln & Jefferson memorials, the National Archives, the Smithsonian Air & Space Museum, Colonial Williamsburg, Mount Vernon, and the Vietnam Memorial, among others. The significance of the latter was lost on me, as it was a war seldom elucidated upon by the adults I knew. Nobody liked to talk about it, and with the benefit of hindsight, I can see why.

Mr. Hamilton had plenty of details to give us all along the way. In the impressive environs of the capitol city, history seemed vast and full of hidden mysteries, especially when told by our enthusiastic guide. That week, I felt the hook sink into my brain, where it has lodged ever since.

It's possible I would have developed an interest in history some other way, but I doubt it would have been quite so intense. Upon returning to Texas, I took up reading historical markers in our town, and paying closer attention to TV documentaries and the news. '88 was an election year, and even while I didn't understand a lot of the issues very deeply, I did follow the campaigns as best I could. It would be four more years until I could weigh in officially with my ballot, and I like to think I was more informed than the average 18-year-old in 1992, due to the influence of my former teacher.

The only problem with having a great teacher in junior high is that you have four more years of relative mediocrity to slog through. I got a disinterested coach for history in 9th grade, a bit of a let down from the Hamilton heights. But as is my autodidactic wont, my studies continued separately from official sanction, as they do to this day.

For all the mixed blessings of social media, I will say that I'm glad it has enabled me to reconnect with James Hamilton, and even get him to write an essay for this page once. He is a man without whom I would not be who I am, and for that I am grateful.

Without Whom

by Paul Williams

My mother, Paula Jo Williams (maiden name Foutz) passed away around midnight last night. Mom, without whom I clearly wouldn't be sitting here writing this, had been quite ill for a number of years with various maladies and discomforts. She contracted Hepatitis and liver disease a few decades ago from a blood transfusion. This was back when they didn't properly test blood donations to the extent they do now, and this particular tainted donation had somehow slipped through the cracks. Dumb luck... It took approximately thirty years of incubating and damage-doing before any of the symptoms revealed themselves, at which point her life turned into a constant battle with the disease and all of its unfriendly side effects. She also had a hereditary degenerative eye condition, which resulted in severely reduced eyesight and then virtual blindness for the last few years. These last few years were low-lighted by many trips to the hospital, many surgeries, constant discomfort and frustration, and very often, agonizing pain, not to mention disorientation, and of course the treacherous and constant swim through the criminal dark lord that is the United States of America Health Care system.

Paula was an incredibly kind woman, and without an enemy. She was well loved by all she encountered, by her four children, and especially by her beloved husband, my father Ralph Dean Williams, who is currently sleeping on a couch a few feet away from me. He is suffering from late stage Alzheimer's disease, and the death of his wife of more than sixty years is barely registering with him. I feel that maybe this fact is a merciful blessing, in the same way that I feel my mother's passing is mostly merciful relief for her.

This is sounding something like a eulogy, and I guess so be it... But I'll shift gears here to offer a few words of criticism for my now late mother, and those like her. My parents were extremely religious people, a full bloom of fundamentalism, judgement, intolerance, and fear. God bless us everyone... My father was a fire and brimstone pulpit preacher for more than fifty years!

When I began to question my religious upbringing, and the "sacred" nature of the Bible, my parents and I travelled a path leading to great separation, to great loss. They were horrified by my passive departure from the church, and by that I mean specifically the "Church of Christ." At one point (a few years after my older brother had died), my parents excommunicated from me, refusing to even eat meals with their only son. They never refused to talk with me or refuse my coming to visit them. But generally these visits were brief and always ended with a perfunctory admonition to change my ways or risk eternal damnation by Hell Fire.

I was never an atheist. I still don't consider myself that...more of a searching agnostic, but open to inspiration, to truth, to justice, whenever these things show themselves. In other words, I consider myself free, free from the chains of dogmatic thought and free from the insanity of defending to the death nonsensical points of view or claims. I've seen so many families, not just mine, ruined by dogma, by the refusal to allow the light of logic into the room.

As my parents' health declined and they needed enormous aid, even in performing basic functions of existence such as eating or showering, our religious chasm gradually lost its importance. My father's dementia has resulted in him not even mentioning religion to me at all in the last couple years. Before he laid down to sleep a few minutes ago, I told him that Mom had gone to be with the Lord, that her suffering was over, that she was in a better place. These thoughts connected with him, and he voiced his appreciation for them.

I certainly don't know if there is a heaven. I'm pretty sure if there is, then my late Mother is there. If she couldn't get in, no one else has a chance. But I'll be Damned if I will spend one second of my time driving wedges between myself and anyone else because I think I know what is gonna happen to them after they die. It's a pathetic and sad kind of damage we do to each other.

And I can't help thinking, as I watch this country teetering on the edge of so much chaos and violence, fueled by hate and greed...that so many people are like my parents, and these voters, without whom Donald Trump would never have been elected president, continue to find new ways to inflict pain on themselves, their neighbors, their families, our nation, and our planet.

RIP Paula Jo Williams (1934 - 2017)

RIP Heather Heyer (1985 - 2017)

○

Ouch, Right in the Heritage

○

Ouch, Right in the Heritage

by Anna Bardin

It's funny when you go back and study important moments in your life, tracing all the threads that led to them, seeing how they put in motion the now-inevitable conclusion. Thus it is that to tell one tale, I need to tell another first.

In my 11th grade year, we lived in Wichita, Kansas, one of the many largely interchangeable Midwestern cities my family occupied for no more than a couple semesters at a time. However, one thing did differentiate this minor cosmotropolis from the one that preceded it: Our local library had a very nice genealogy section.

Digging up ancestry at the merest dawn of the Information Superhighway was no mean task. No websites to click around on, and no email for most people, including myself. No ma'am, what we had was microfiche, and a lot of it. And that's if you were lucky. Some records hadn't been fiched, and still lay dusty and obscure in county courthouse basements.

At Christmas in Arkansas the previous year, my Aunt Diane had brought us all spiral-bound copies of the genealogical research she had painstakingly carried out over several years of visiting physical archives and shuffling through fiche. My dad didn't appear to care much about his sister's pursuit of our origins, but I found the document mesmerizing.

Aunt Diane was pleased about this, because there was a branch of our family that she hadn't fully mapped out, and it so happened that they had resided in Wichita back when it was barely even a town during the 1870s. It was a rather important piece of the family tree, because that was when my great-great-grandmother had birthed her four children and promptly died of pneumonia shortly after the fourth one's arrival. Her husband remarried, but did not have any kids from this new wife, based on the chronology laid out in the document.

So the hell of it was, nobody knew who the biological mother of my great-grandfather had been. This, Diane and I decided, was a mission for a bookish teenager, one I took very seriously.

After a fruitless fiche-fest, I ended up having to go to the courthouse to peruse legal and tax records. Lo and behold, there I found an entry listing a marriage performed in 1872 between my great-great-grandfather and a Helen Zuckerman.

I blinked. I was no linguist, but Zuckerman sounded pretty Jewish to me. Another search found the tax records of her father, an Abraham Zuckerman. Nothing was cut and dried, but a variety of scattered info led me to believe that yes, I most likely had a Jewish great-great-grandmother.

This might not sound all that interesting to a lot of people, but for a misfit teen in the terminally Protestant Midwest, the prospect of Jewish ancestry was incredibly exotic. Unbidden, my brain formulated wild tales of Helen's life, a Jewess out on the Kansas prairie, doing her best to assimilate until ill health took her before age 30. Never one to resist a good story, I took my slightly embellished version of the narrative to Christmas the following year, along with copies of the records.

To my dismay, this exciting new development in our family history did not thrill anyone, least of all Diane, who was a good churchgoing woman in Little Rock. With a bit of a haughty sniff, Diane at last concluded that of course Helen would have come to accept Jesus before she married her husband, who we know raised their children in the Christian faith after her death.

I supposed this was probably true, but it saddened me. I wanted Helen the Super-Jew Frontierwoman to be part of my family. A sparkly sequin in the otherwise monotonous parade of stern-browed Calvinists that made up our lineage. Super-Jew Helen became the private occupation of idle moments, a way to tell myself I was part of a secret line of American history. Despite knowing that by now, the bloodline was well diluted, I decided that I was part Jewish.

Fast forward a few years. First job out of college, a forgettable little accounting firm in Dallas, now long absorbed into some corporate megamass. There were less than twenty employees, but to my secret delight, over half of them were Jewish.

It sounds silly now, but some part of me had allowed itself to feel so Jewish, regardless of my hyper-crackerized Christian upbringing, that actually being in a rare cluster of fellow tribe members felt like an opportunity to finally come out of the shafe. That's "closet" in Yiddish. I think.

In a blurted confession, ON MY FIRST DAY, I regaled my co-workers with the tale of discovering my Hebrew ancestry, and how special it made me feel to be part of such a distinctive tradition.

To my astonishment, their reaction was not altogether different than that of my aunt. Surely, they ventured, she and her children had converted. And as there were no female children from that brood, the line was broken, insofar as the Judaica was concerned. These people seemed rather irritated at me, and I couldn't tell why.

In hindsight, I feel like I understand. Just as a child of mixed race with white skin does not have the same experience as one with black skin, neither does someone with distant

Jewish ancestry experience the trials of being a minority population in this Christophilic culture. By appealing to what I saw as our shared heritage, I had used the wrong entry point to try and be their friend. Had I simply been myself, a product of this continent's dominant society, which was of course who they saw before them, there would have been no impasse. But by presenting my barely legible carbon-copied bona fides as a point of commonality, I merely showed how very little I understood about either my culture or theirs.

Silly as it is, I still think of myself as part Jewish. Amid the current xenophobic roil of our nation, Helen's contributions to my DNA ground me. A reminder that American stories are not as homogenous as we often think. Part of me will always be Other, and if that helps me be more compassionate to actual minorities as the great orange parade float bounces through America's cities, knocking out windows hither and thither, then I'd like to think Helen would be proud.

Ouch, Right in the Heritage

by Matthew Broyles

Let's do a bit of a thought experiment.

Suppose that one day you find out that your grandfather, whom you love, has been convicted of human trafficking. He is unrepentant, even proud of what he's put his captives through, everything from kidnapping, rape, beatings, not to mention the enslavement itself.

Now, you are related by blood to this person. He is part of your heritage. Do you celebrate him? Do you keep his picture on your wall, and go out of your way to mention him to your friends when you talk about where you came from?

Many people in Germany and other war-torn countries face this conundrum. People who they know personally, and have good memories of, nonetheless guilty of monstrous crimes. It is something these children and grandchildren have to reckon with, to fit into their picture of who they are, who they aspire to become.

A lot of us have this experience on a smaller scale. Uncle Frank, the wife-beating drunk. Cousin Jimmy, locked up for sexual assault. People we wouldn't mention our relation to unless pressed. Certainly not people we'd like to spend any time glorifying.

Clever reader, you've no doubt deduced where I'm going with this. For those of us with long roots in the American South, it is difficult to avoid a connection to an ancestor who was not involved at some level in the slave trade, arguably one of the largest mass murder/rape/abuse institutions in human history.

For many of us, it is an inconvenient truth. We know it happened, we regret it, and we strive to be better than those whose genes flow in our veins.

And then there's the rest of us.

It often starts with the line, "I'm not racist, but…" and predictably deteriorates from there. Born and raised in Texas, I've heard it too many times to even begin to count. In most places, it doesn't even need to be said. Drive past Jefferson Davis Park, or Confederate Parkway, or any of the myriad memorials to our ignominious forebears, and the voices of the past whisper insistently in your ear: 'This happened, and we should have won.'

The next bit is always that the Civil War was not about slavery, but state's rights. That's a pretty little dodge, of the same ilk as "I'm not racist, but…" and of course it is just as irrelevant. It doesn't actually matter whether you say you are racist or not. Any child can tell you that it doesn't matter what someone says. It matters what they do.

If you believe that the Confederacy should have won, then you believe that my African-American friends should still be in chains. You really believe that. Because there was no Emancipation Proclamation in the South, and thus, with a CSA victory, all of those people would still be slaves. There is absolutely no getting around that conclusion, try though you might.

You truly believe that one group of human beings should legally own another. And you're proud of it. So much so that you protest when reminders of that preference are torn down, requiring you to actually speak your monstrous evil aloud rather than let the statuary speak for you.

I hear "But it's history!" That's right. It's over. The outcome of the Civil War was decided over 150 years ago. And you disagree with it. Which incontrovertibly means that you continue to support the moral reasoning behind slavery. Which means you're an asshole.

I don't care how nice you are to your kids. I don't care how polite you are to the black lady at the grocery store. If you celebrate the parts of your heritage—and mine—that contributed to the kidnapping, torture, rape, and murder of millions, then you are not only an asshole, you are a racist, and un-American.

If we're talking history, the record shows clearly that the United States of America, a slave-free nation as of 1863, defeated and annexed the Confederate States of America over a century and a half ago. Any desire to rewrite those events to favor the South is a de facto admission that you do not wish to be a citizen of the USA.

Especially if you're one of the Texas secessionists I run into all the time, whose threats of withdrawal from the union are as feeble as they are toothless. Take the vote today, and see how many of this state's citizens wish to leave the protective embrace of the world's largest economy. Who's the minority now?

But I digress…

I keep being told I'm a sore loser. That's pretty rich coming from people mourning a loss incurred before the invention of toilet paper.

Let's be clear, though, about what you lost. About the fact that not being able to own other people is such a burdensome state of affairs that veins pop out of your head when symbols of that failed human trafficking operation are consigned to the dustbin of history, along with swastikas and hammer-and-sickle. Slavery was always a terrible idea. And your insistence that its proponents were great people only serves to render my estimation of your judgment rather low.

"But my heritage!"

It's my heritage, too. And I am rightly ashamed of it. My relatives who fought in the Civil War were wrong, and those who died deserved to. If they hadn't, the African-Americans I call friends today would still be property. That is not a legacy I want to be part of. And if you do, then we have nothing more to discuss.

Ouch, Right in the Heritage

by MC Dalet

Look up "heritage" in the dictionary, and the first definition you get is, in paraphrase, something that is legally inherited, passed down. Subsequent entries address more abstract forms of inheritance, such as behavior, attitudes, and traditions. As an academic and a student of a specific spiritual wisdom, part of my heritage makeup is that of a student in a lineage of teachers. In my academic life, I am a performance scholar, which means that I view pretty much all human activity as some kind of performance. It also means that I am versed in the LANGUAGE of different performative modes, and one of the most powerful modes we employ is comedy. Like all language, performative languages evolve. But they change slowly, in large part due to the fact that all performers also have a lineage of teachers. This is especially true of comedians, perhaps more so than any other brand of contemporary performers, aside from tap dancers. Additionally, all performance modes have conventions, overt and subtle, that audiences know how to "read." This is also especially true of comedy...until now.

Something has shifted, and the conventions of comedy, particularly that delivered by white performers, have not shifted in kind. How do I know this? "Sheet-caking."

Look, as a performer, I know you can't please all the people all the time, but I am confounded by the kerfuffle surrounding Tina Fey's now (in)famous sketch on *Saturday Night Live*. So I have to put on my scholar hat to make inquiry on the matter. My academic heritage begs me to view the conventions, content, and context of Fey's performance to try and come to an understanding of its divisive reception.

Conventionally, the "Sheet-caking" sketch is textbook satire. Actually, it's not just textbook, it's exemplary. Fey delivers a layered satire, sending up stereotypes about women (white women in particular), race relations, and socio-political apathy, all while tapping into a historical arc reaching as far back as the American and French Revolutions. The performer employs a subversion of the phrase "let them eat cake," uttered by an elitist member of the ruling class, claiming the phrase for the "plebeians" who feel helpless to affect change, giving the phrase an implied twist -- let US eat cake. This use of subversion and juxtaposition are long-honored tools of the comedian, and should be read as such.

It should be obvious that "Sheet-caking" is satire. 1.) Satire is a common convention for *SNL* sketches. 2.) Satire is a common COMEDIC convention. It doesn't always endear you to audiences. As an example, George Carlin pissed a whole lot of people off, but his comedy was not often misread as straightforward sentiment. One of my quandaries, then, is wondering why so many people, people literate in the language of Satire in general and *SNL* in particular misread Fey's sketch as advocacy for complacency.

Putting these detractors aside, we move on to the argument that the text of the sketch is white privilege in action, or to use a direct quote, "the epitome of white privilege." Yes. Yes, it is. From a social justice point of view, the text of Fey's guest appearance is paternalistic, patronizing, and privileged. It is also purposeful. When examining content in context, one contextual element that MUST be accounted for is the performer herself. Fey is a master of her craft, a craft she has honed for decades. She is intentional with her language and her delivery. To dismiss the efficacy of the performer is to miss the communication.

I make this point with students when we watch Jimi Hendrix's Woodstock performance of the *Star-Spangled Banner*. I once had a classically trained musician in class on Jimi day. I think I actually saw her face melt. "He's switching keys! He's shifting tempo. He's throwing in screeches and pieces of other songs. It's not even music!" she said. But she didn't know who Hendrix was or what he did to advance the rock genre. Understanding this didn't make her like the performance, but it sure as hell changed her READING of it. Regarding his "violations" of musical convention (here analogous to Fey's "violations" of PC convention) as intentional and calculated allowed her to read a rich narrative into the musical text. We owe comics the same type of reading.

And usually, we give it to them. Not everyone, of course, but certainly many of the folks I've seen lambasting the sheet cake sketch. So what changed? Where's the block? Have the conventions of comedy changed?

No. But the social context in which comedy is delivered has. In a profound way. Satire depends upon using the absurd and hyperbole to make a point. This technique is nearly impossible to employ when the behavior of the commander in chief is absurd and the actual news seems both hyperbolic and absurd. More than once over the past six months, I have assumed headlines shared in my social media feed to be *Onion* headlines, only to scroll down and see CNN, *The New York Times*, and *News and Guts* as the authoring entities. When factual reports seem satirical, a new convention arises in the reception of communication. Let's call it audience confusion. Or fact/satire conflation. Or just plain ol' end times shit.

Aesthetic performance (film, plays, comedy) and social drama (real-world events) have always reinforced one another in an infinite feedback loop. The War on Terror and the rise of reality TV create a response in the form of Suzanne Collins' *Hunger Games* trilogy, which in turn becomes a reference point for contemporary revolutions; Henrik Ibsen's *A Doll's House* incites riots and advances the conversation that becomes feminism; Jimi Hendrix's rendition of *The Star-Spangled Banner* grows out of the counter-cultural hippie movement but reinforces the philosophy that one can be in dissent and patriotic in the same breath.

But what happens when the feedback loop collapses -- when an absurd candidate plays the presidential election like a reality show...and wins? When Godwin's Law, a rule of engagement crafted to prevent hyperbole in online conversation, must ostensibly be abandoned because one can legitimately call someone a Nazi or compare public figures and their strategies to Hitler and his strategies? When aesthetic and social drama become one and the same, that context affects the convention of satire, calling into question content that would, even a year or two ago, be read with the critical distance that comedy generally affords.

Ouch! There goes the lineage of comedy scholarship and a nice little chunk of literary analysis. Since aesthetic and social drama are now collapsed into a performative singularity, so too go the conventions of comedy itself. And the discussion of social access and privilege have now become the discussion of who can and cannot write and deliver comedy. I'm white, so, in my liberal circles, I'm not even supposed to weigh in on the discussion. I will keep it academic.

It leaves me with some questions, though, and fascinating ones. DO our performative paradigms -- social and aesthetic -- have to change drastically or risk not being heard at all, much less heard properly? If so, how do we quantum leap conventions that usually take centuries to evolve? What does post-Trump comedy look like? If we are now in the age of proprietary commentary, who decides what group gets to tackle which issues? And of course: what kind of icing should I cover my sheet cake with -- cream cheese or butter cream?

o

The Road

o

The Road

by Anna Bardin

We seek destinations, despite the fact that we never quite leave the road on which we're traveling to them. Aphorisms tell us that there is no arrival, only the journey, and that makes sense. But still, I can't help feeling like there's a location I keep trying to reach, just over the next horizon.

I don't know what I would do if I found it. Relax, look at the scenery, enjoy the feeling of accomplishment? It wouldn't be long before I got restless and set off in search of another destination.

Not everyone is like me. Friends and family lock down the lives they want and keep them pinned, fretting when they start to shift. To a degree, I'm not altogether dissimilar. A romantic nomad, I get nervous when things aren't changing. Perhaps the road is my destination, like those country songs. An odd hankering for a woman who's lived in the same apartment for over a decade.

Adventure is in the eye of the beholder. To some, it's extensive travel. Others crave thrills like skydiving or rock climbing. For me, the prospect of a new lover is utterly intoxicating. There doesn't have to be anything wrong with the previous one, but at some point I want a strange body to explore, new and delightful responses to discover, an unfamiliar voice whispering in my ear.

I know this about myself, but I also have a faint mirage that floats into the back of my head sometimes. An arrival, a denouement. The One.

Truthfully, I don't believe in The One. It's a remnant of fairy tales and movie tropes. My behavior refutes the premise that all women want the forever prince. I do want the prince, but eventually I want him to go home so I can find a new one.

I concede that it is probably different for others. Many women and men cling to their partners with a grip that would send me running away. Who seek to be needed, not just wanted. That need makes me suspicious. It speaks of gaps in the self that need strengthening, or at least patching. Judging people for this is nonsensical, though. I've used love as plaster for my insecurities my entire adult life. I use it to feel good, to banish the destructive demons in my head, and to give some of the more salacious ones an outlet. Clearly I need it.

Maybe it's when the need stays fixed on one person that I get jumpy. Or worse, when that need is focused on me. The bf wants me, to be sure, but he doesn't need me. Some nights, he wants someone else, as I do. Still, it is nice to know that he's there. Maybe it's more of a need than I'll admit. Someone I trust to reliably push my buttons, so every encounter doesn't require a fresh hunt for a talented partner. That's worth a lot. But if I thought I needed it, I'd probably start feeling like one of those crazy girls.

Perhaps I am one. I just have better camouflage. I don't frantically text, but I do pine. When the bf is out of town, and no stopgap has been secured, I ache a bit more than I let on. Sometimes that drives me to take the chances, surprise someone who didn't know I was scoping them. Someone I might not have scoped if I had other options. But once awakened, new love fills my bloodstream with endorphins and adrenaline, and I ride the high as long as it can last.

It does raise a few questions about maturity. I know this chase will get harder the older I get. Infirmity and gravity will exert their influence, and not all who catch my eye will be interested. I will have to find another road on which to find adventure.

Or maybe that's when a destination will become clear. A home, with someone who has also aged out of the game. Someone who knows me, and accepts my physical flaws as I accept theirs, the inevitable march of time, no one's fault. But from here, that feels like settling. What to do when the new shiny flashes into view? Maybe it becomes easier when the shiny passes you over. Or maybe you just feel like an old hag.

Maiden, mother, crone…the cycle of womanhood. I've skipped the middle stage, so it shouldn't surprise me when the third one hits. Part of me feels like I'd make a pretty good crone. The wise woman, whose counsel is sought by the young. She who knows the secrets of life. To a degree, I fill that role for my niece and nephew already, helping them navigate the often confusing world around them.

Still, though, doesn't the crone get pent up? Who gets the crone's rocks off? Does she find a man-crone for that?

Perhaps that consideration subconsciously drives my thoughts towards a destination, knowing that the road will not always provide as it has so far. Maybe there does have to be a goal. Or maybe I'll just load up my wagon and keep croning on down the road like Baba Yaga, frightening the villagers and confusing the horses.

"If my life is for rent, and I don't learn to buy

Then I deserve nothing more than I get

'Cause nothing I have is truly mine…"

– Dido, *Life For Rent*

The Road

by Matthew Broyles

When calamity strikes, it can be easy to focus attention on the nearest scapegoat. Who made this happen? That guy, get him!

Such has been my attitude towards our current president, I confess. The Angry Creamsicle is such a ready target, a perfect mishmash of everything I hate about our society. But when you boil it all down, Tangerine Hitler is not actually the problem.

For the Stay-Puft Cheeto Man is merely the inevitable destination of a road we have been on in this country for many decades now. Possibly centuries. It almost doesn't matter that Adolf Twitler is the man in the Oval Office. At some point, we would have gotten someone else equally as incompetent and hateful.

We know what happens when you build a house on sand. The foundations for the United States of America were laid thus, a lot of pretty words about freedom laid over the festering sore of a slave economy. Little wonder it burst open inside of a century, flooding the basement and ruining the floorboards.

That's history, though, over and done with, right? Apparently not.

Reconstruction didn't solve the problem of our parallel societies. White people never got over the belief that we needed to exist on a higher social plane than our darker neighbors. I was about to say "especially in the south," but the record shows that racism is as rampant in Union states as it is here, evidenced in part by the number of Confederate monuments in states which were not even part of the CSA.

We like to tell a national story that separates us from other corners of the globe, whose ancient rivalries go back generations. Serbia, still angry about Ottoman annexation in 1459. Sunni and Shia, still arguing over which of Mohammed's heirs are the most worthy. But we will not release the death grip on our own history any more willingly than other nations. Implicit in #MAGA is the Again, a reference to the way things were at some unspecified time in the past, back before the underclass got uppity.

Here again, The Fanta Fascist is no self-made man. Certainly he possesses the demagogue's gift of reading a mob and giving them what they want. But the mob pre-dates Hair Fuhrer, and has been steadily building up steam for a long time. The road to November 2016 stretches back quite a ways, winding through Roger Ailes, the Moral Majority, the Southern Strategy, John Birch, George Wallace, Jim Crow, and right back up to the doorstep of our eternal patriarch, Manifest Destiny.

The European settlers of this stolen land decided long ago that there could be only one kind of rightful owner here, favored by divine will. That hasn't changed, no matter the massive demographic shifts of the past few decades.

And this, when we get down to it, is the reason why the Real Americans are so angry. In the years when white dominance was demonstrably secure, the pitch of the resentment towards the dark armies was kept at a murmur.

The sheer terror that has been unleashed in the ranks of white America could only reach such frothy heights by their worst nightmare: A black man in charge.

I hear you warming up your keyboards, ready to give me the what-for. While you're at it, include an apology. From everyone whose guns were not confiscated by Obama. From everyone who was not rounded up and put into martial law FEMA camps by Obama. From everyone who does not currently live under the sovereign control of the United Nations. From all you armchair eschatologists who predicted the collapse of civilization under the reign of a black, somehow Nazi president.

Repeat after me: "I was wrong."

Because it is your desire for righting the racial ship of state that has brought us ACTUAL Nazis waving swastikas in the streets. YOU did that.

But I can't even blame you. Because you, like all of us, are caught up in the gears of a machine built upon the whip-worn backs of slaves. It is so baked in that we don't blink when it gets outsourced. We are not offended by our smartphones being built by children paid a pittance to work 12-hour days in dangerous Asian factories. We are only incensed when we find our own lily-white selves unable to procure a job because they've all been moved overseas.

We're used to shunting all the shit work off onto the swarthy folk. What we're not used to is paying a price for it.

The road to King Leer is the same road we've always been on. It is the American story. But our destiny did not manifest as we believed it would, because some of us started questioning its underlying assumption that there is a permanent underclass, and that it is anyone but us.

The Emancipation Proclamation elected Mango Mussolini, as did *Brown vs. Board of Education. Citizens United* sped the process up, but it would have happened eventually anyway. This is our desperate lurch to return to the default settings.

And therein lies the only hope. That the cry of restoration means that it's already too late. That critical mass has been achieved, sufficient to displace this country's original owners. If their reign were not in danger, the spittle would not fly so freely upon their tiki torches.

The trick now is to recognize this, and leverage it. Already municipalities are striking while the iron is hot, removing monuments to our shameful past and stepping up to defy federal inclinations towards insular white nationalism.

We are still on the road. Where it goes from here is less up to Vanilla ISIS than it is the rest of us.

○

Poking the Bear

○

Poking the Bear

by Anna Bardin

My dad and his brother Tim were never close. Or rather, they were a bit too close. Growing up, they shared a tiny room in a tiny house, and according to family legends, were at each other's throats the entire time.

Their manner around each other at holidays certainly backed the stories up. The tension when these two men were in the room together caused the backs of everyone in range to seize up, bracing for some unnamable conflagration which could explode into being at any moment.

This despite the fact that year after year, it never actually did. Credit my grandfather, whose gimlet stare upon any exchange of thinly veiled nastiness cut right through the warring brothers' wills and steered them towards more congenial conversational waters.

Until…

One of the problems with growing up in a small town is that the dating pool is limited. Thus, Dad and Tim dated many of the same girls in high school, which didn't help their already strained relationship. In fact, Tim's wife was originally Dad's girlfriend, something that Tim insisted on bringing up at every inappropriate opportunity, always when the woman in question wasn't in the room.

"You know, Cheryl loves dancing," Tim would say. "Some men don't pay attention to that kind of thing."

To his credit, Dad never took the bait directly. But he couldn't leave it be, either.

"Some men don't pay attention to the temperature gauge on their truck," Dad would throw back, reminding everyone of the time Tim had been late to Thanksgiving due to a dry radiator overheating his Datsun.

Predictably, the exchange would escalate from there, voices kept low to avoid alerting Grandpa, until ultimately one of the wives would return. Tight smiles ensued, and it was back to sports and the weather.

My brothers and I endured these melees in tense silence, fearful of catching any stray shrapnel. But as we got older, Tim seemed to insist upon bringing us into the conversation, mostly to irritate our dad. Successfully.

"Tommy, let me tell you, girls don't like it when you go dutch on a date," Tim would tell my brother. "Ask your dad."

Visibly holding back his first twelve responses, Dad would stare into the middle distance before smiling thinly at nothing in particular.

"They really don't like it when you tell them you're about to go off to Vietnam next week," he would respond. "And then don't."

These exchanges were uncomfortable, but we youngsters, though spoken to, were at least not being spoken *of*. Until Christmas of my freshman year.

Uncharacteristically, I'd worn a nice dress to the gathering. I don't know why, just trying on different ways of presenting myself. Tim noticed, not in a creepy way, just sort of surprised that the girl who usually hid herself behind as many layers of sweaters and coats as possible actually took some care to doll herself up a bit.

"Wow, look at you," Tim said, smiling at my dad, who shrugged his shoulders in false modesty as the contributor of half my genes. For a moment, I thought I might have instigated a détente.

"Makes you glad you didn't marry Sharlene, huh?" he continued, and the air between them snapped taut.

I froze. I didn't know who Sharlene was. But I knew that look on my father's face. I'd seen it only a couple of times before, and I knew what happened after. With effort, I didn't wince.

My dad clenched his jaw and took a deep breath. Turning to look Tim in the eyes, he closed the distance between them to less than a foot.

"Do not…" he said, extending a finger and poking Tim hard in the chest. "…talk about my daughter."

My cheeks flushed red. Horror overtook me. The prospect that I would be the cause of the final showdown filled me with unspeakable dread, but I dared not say anything.

Tim's brow furrowed in confusion, transforming quickly into anger.

"Hey," he said, poking my dad back. "It was a compliment, genius."

Dad's voice went low and vicious, almost too quiet to hear. But I heard him fine.

"You can talk about me all you want," he said, cold as the grave. "But do *not* talk about my daughter again. Ever."

"Robert!" my grandpa's voice snapped from the kitchen doorway. In charge, as if the two men were still just quarreling children. "Go put up the chickens. Tim! Get the firewood."

The heaving of the brothers' chests calmed, their steely gazes splintered as they looked over at the old man. The spell broken, they separated and left.

I stood there, stock-still, afraid to breathe. As my dad and uncle left the room, Grandpa saw my distress, and came over slowly. I leaned into his hug, needing something solid to hang onto.

"It's not your fault," he said, patting my shoulder.

I knew it wasn't, but at the moment, I was glad of the confirmation from an authoritative source. I stared up at Grandpa, seeking some explanation for the maelstrom that had unfolded on my behalf. Grandpa sighed heavily.

"After Tim stole Cheryl from your dad," he said, shaking his head in irritation. "He mocked him for dating Sharlene Carson. She…wasn't known as a looker. But your dad loved her."

I swallowed. An alternate history. My eyes asked the question.

"When she dumped him after they'd been engaged for six months, Tim had a field day," Grandpa groaned. "But when Robert came home with your mother…well, it shut Tim up, I'll tell you."

My brain boggled. I thought of my mom's high school picture on the wall, next to my dad's bowling trophy. How radiant she'd been.

Oh my god, I thought. A trophy.

"Kids…" Grandpa grunted, giving my shoulder a quick squeeze before ambling off to the kitchen, leaving me in the charred ruins of my illusions.

Poking the Bear

by Cristee Cook

"I said that's enough!"

"You're not listening to me!!"

"I told you I needed a minute. You're pushing me!" my husband yelled before he ran up the stairs and slammed the door.

I sat on the bottom step and cried. I looked for a way to escape the profound discomfort I was experiencing, but there was nowhere to run. Leaving in the car would only make the situation worse.

It was the early days of my marriage and I had taken a small disagreement and expanded it to door slamming and tears. Back then, I was exceptionally good at this.

My husband and I have changed a lot since that day. Knock-down-drag-out fights rarely happen now. When they do, we are both embarrassed and after we have calmed down, will sheepishly wonder how we even got to that point. How had the argument even started?

For a long time, I thought that these passionate quarrels were a sign that we had passion between us. That we were fiery soulmates destined for greatness. Now, I see it differently. And because I am a person who wants to keep the peace, to create peace, and who always (at least) tries to see many sides of a situation, my ability to take a volatile event and make it worse has always bothered me. Why can't I just stop? Why must I always poke the bear?

A need to be right.

Fear of abandonment.

Unkempt rage.

A lack of healthy boundaries.

Like I said, we have both changed a lot since those early days. I have learned to let go, to be ok with being wrong, and I have worked hard to transform my rage into allowance and patience with myself. I'm better at not needing "closure." I've learned that I don't need to understand, or even know, every second of my husband's inner life.

We have also changed because we chose to have children, which inherently changes everything. My kids are the two best teachers I've ever had. Children are a wild paradox. They are experts at letting go. They are also experts at poking the bear.

It must, therefore, be a human impulse, illustrated through a common and overused joke: "Don't press that big, red button! Whatever you do, don't press that button!"

So what do we do? We press the button, and act surprised when disaster unfolds.

How and when did we learn to poke the bear? To disregard blatant consequences and give it one final shot, just to "be sure?" I did it as a kid and younger adult, and now I watch my kids do it. Just the other day my daughter spilled some paint during a craft project and I asked her not to touch it for fear that the paint mess would only spread. So what did she do? She ran her fingers through it and got paint all over her new t-shirt, and became so upset about her new t-shirt getting stained that she actually spilled more paint. I didn't say "I told you so." I just cleaned her up and told her we'd get the stain out, and to be more careful next time. And I thought about myself at her age because I see that we are remarkably similar.

The first time I remember hearing the phrase "poking the bear" was when I was about 8 years old. I grew up in the 80s and early 90s – a simpler time when parents left their kids alone in the car while they ran into the dry cleaners. A simpler time when cars had built-in cigarette lighters. I knew those things were hot. I had seen my grandparents fuse countless cigarettes against the gray coils inhaling until the lighter burned hot-orange and tobacco smoke wafted into the air.

This time, at 8-ish years old, I just had to be sure. My mom was inside the dry cleaners and my sister and I were in the back seat. I leaned forward, yanked the lighter out of the dash, and poked the gray coils with my right pointer finger. I burned myself so bad that I screamed, dropped the lighter, and cried. Then my sister started crying because I was crying. And, needless to say, when my mom returned to the car, she was exasperated and worried.

"What happened? Why is everyone crying?!"

I showed her my finger. I didn't have to explain what happened because the built-in car lighter had branded the coil shapes into my finger pad, and in the painful moment of contact I had flung the lighter onto her seat.

"Well, why did you do that??? You know it's a hot lighter!"

"I just wanted to see if it was hot when it was gray," I whimpered.

"Well, it is, Christi! Why do you always have to poke the bear?"

Upon reflection, I giggle at the story. I defend my younger self and push it off to curiosity and the childlike ability to be so in the present moment that consequences are not considered. My mom was right, though. I think about all the times I wasn't, or haven't been willing or able to let go, and find I'm more contemplative.

I think it's something we can all change, but maybe we are addicted to physical confirmation. We don't trust. We have to "be sure." We can't help but poke the damn bear.

Poking the Bear

by Matthew Broyles

Life is a bear. We all know this.

It doesn't really take much to disturb the slumber of the beast that lies at the borders of mortal survival. An unexpected injury, an ailment gone chronic, a natural disaster, loss of insurance, a stock market crash…as a civilization, we have added to the legion of calamities that can bring one closer to waking the great hairy executioner. There are as many ways to die as there are ways to live.

With that understanding, it would seem logical that a careful life is the only reasonable sort of life to live. If he's right outside the gates, snoring away, why the everloving heckfire would you poke the bear?

Yet day after day, year after year, that is precisely what I have always felt driven to do. Save that extra money for retirement, or go somewhere I've never been? Shore up the rainy day fund, or publish another book? Stoke the college kitty, or pay for a unique summer camp experience? By feeding the imp of the present, I poke the bear of the future.

Verse and cat poster alike extol the virtues of seizing days, of not leaving till tomorrow what might be done today. Thus do those of us in the dead poet's society front-load our lives, not trusting that the golden years are assured, fearful of the early deathbed realization that that was it, no do-overs. There is wisdom in this, but foolishness as well.

Art in general tends towards bear-poking. Something about the sleepwalk of prescribed paths chafes at a certain sort of person. The sort of person I never have quite been able not to be. The unpoked bear lying in the corner, a temptation rather than a warning.

We big-shirted folk refer to the group of chimps in a cage, sprayed with cold water when they reach for the banana atop the ladder. Cycle the chimps out over time, and each carryover warns the new ones of the danger, long after anyone has actually seen the sprayer in action. Things are feared because they have always been feared, dread passed down the generations for perfectly understandable survival reasons.

Yet some of us are seduced by the idea that maybe something fundamental has changed since last someone climbed that ladder and got a face full of aguamenti. Maybe this time it'll work.

But it's too easy to blame the bleeding hearts. In the business world, too, blinkered optimism reaps the grizzly. Highly valued securities composed of thin air, real estate hiked up to the limits of credulity, the inverse relationship between profit and environmental sustainability patched over until nature breaks its bounds, raining devastation on rich and poor, summoning the bear. Play by the rules or not, our ursine companion remains on guard, ever vigilant.

It might be said that living itself pokes the bear. The universe does not require life. Stars and planets wheel through the void with no need of sentience, no thirst for self-awareness. The chance arrangement of atoms into formations capable of making their own decisions needn't trouble the vast cosmos, which takes little notice of their deliberations as it plows on mindlessly, the chain unbroken, the billiard balls set in motion eons ago, falling into their pockets, creating new reactions that will play out indifferently to our fretful cogitations.

Our very existence pokes the bear. Given to us by happenstance, we do our best to figure out what the hell to do with it in the time allotted. Seek the secrets of the universe? Bask in the pleasures of the flesh? Help others less fortunate endure the ordeal of living with as little suffering as possible? We make our choices, tiptoeing past the furry guardian, ascribing potency to our actions, telling others how we have survived, guiding them to do likewise.

Certainly there are courses of action which hasten the creature's appearance. Drug abuse, wanton violence, failure in the arcane arts of pattern recognition. Unexamined behaviors, under-examined motivations. Yet even if we do correctly divine our true selves, what to do when what we find that poking the bear is the very basis of our being?

What to do when we realize that the bear is us?

Poking the Bear

by MC Dalet

Some figurative phrases just capture the actions we humans take perfectly. My current favorite is "poking the bear." I find I've used that one a lot lately, both to describe the self-perpetuating state of global strife and to point out the folly of some within my personal sphere. "Poking the bear" takes "borrowing trouble" and levels it up. Humanity is notorious for doing both. Borrowing trouble begins at an intrapersonal level. We are – or have become – quite a pessimistic species. Without ever knowing the whole story, we jump to conclusions and assume the worst. We take a personal bias or challenge, read our world through that lens, and let the accusations (sometimes against ourselves) fly. This is bad enough; it brings undue anxiety and chaos. Even if a true external problem exists, by internalizing it and focusing on what's wrong, we've borrowed on the original trouble and begin accruing interest at an unfathomable rate. When that angst becomes too much to carry in our account, we go interpersonal, lash out, and start poking the bear.

It seems ridiculous when viewed from the outside. Why on Earth would one, metaphorically speaking, agitate a creature capable of ripping us limb from limb, or at least causing us a great deal of pain? What's really in it for us except the backdoor validation of our "rightness"? "See, the bear IS bad!" It's not even sound logic. YOU did the poking. I'd take a paw after you too if provoked with such focused intent. But bear poking seems to be an instinct that is hard-wired. But unlike most outmoded primordial programming, like profiling, that may once have served the survival instinct in ancient tribal societies, the bear-poking instinct reads as faulty programming, for it is counter-intuitive to survival and to long-term survival's spiritual foundation, unity.

I can painfully admit to poking many a bear in my time – loud, aggressive rebellion in the name of principles I couldn't even clearly define; mouthing off to really REALLY big dudes. I am especially guilty of poking bears that live in my own personal den.

I recently warned my five-year-old daughter that she was "poking the bear" during one of our little child/parent skirmishes. She was. And she knows it. She knows just where to verbally and behaviorally jab me to elicit a swift, reactive response. I can't just write it off as a kid being a kid, though. She only needs a keen power of observation (which she has) to hone her poking proficiency. As I feel the proverbial stick press against my bear hide, the old anti-drug commercial from the 1980s plays in my head: "From you okay! I learned it by watching you!" It's true. Yeah, it really hurt to admit, but sometimes SHE'S the bear, and I keep a sharp stick. No question of genetic continuity here. Fighting with her is like fighting with myself. It's infuriating. And it's illuminating how quickly I'm able to descend to her level and poke away. I fight. . .no, I behave like a child. I'm embarrassed by it, but I do not at all believe I am alone in the adult world. It seems to me our basic behavioral patterns change very little as we mature. We learn methods of controlling those impulses at best, of masking them at least; but we never abandon the feisty child within, and when the situation presents itself, we indulge it. Some more quickly than others.

This is not a political commentary, so I won't go on a tear about the president's very dangerous bear poking. . .you know, the kind that happens on a nuclear level. The truth of the matter is that the Internet and social media merely allow for the amplification of an impulse that is not just figurative, but literal.

I was surprised to learn about the Elizabethan entertainment known as "bear baiting" while taking my college History of Theatre course. This practice, popular in England, and really across Europe, from the sixteenth through the nineteenth century involved a captive bear aggravated by a man a group of men, dogs. . .you get the picture. It was a blood sport that involved literally poking the bear. Entertainment ensues. And there it is. In addition to baiting the aggravated party into lashing out, thus proving that we, the agitator, are "right" and the object of aggravation "wrong," it comes down to the fascinating anthropological truth that we are entertained by it. It's why internet trolls exist. It's why POTUS hurls incendiary Tweets at people and institutions with far more power than he actually possesses. I've long said that Trump won the election because he played it like a reality show. His business is really as a reality entertainer, and that's the game he continues to play. Why? It's a proven formula. Dangerous when you're the commander in chief, but still. From gladiatorial combat to UFC to The Real Housewives of Wherever, we are actually entertained by physical and verbal violence.

I cannot stand in judgment. It simply "bears" examination. We are childish. Just yesterday, while standing in line for a waterslide, I heard a boy of about nine, a cast around his arm, discussing with his friend that "it is fun to get hurt." His friend replied that it was even more fun to WATCH someone get hurt. You can say "oh, boys will be boys," but until you and I disengage from the self-same actions of putting ourselves in harm's way in the name of being right or watching with simultaneous outrage and blood-thirsty lust as others fail, fall and even die, let (s)he who is without childish impulse throw the first stone. Just don't throw it at the bear.

○

I'm Sorry

○

I'm Sorry

by Anna Bardin

It was easier.

That's not a good justification. I knew it even then. But it was the truth.

Peter arrived in my life at a time of great uncertainty and upheaval. Fresh out of college, struggling with a job that I simply could not bend my mind around, and reeling from years of sorrow after my dad's death, I met this sweet, loving man, and fell into his safe, comforting embrace.

That we were not altogether compatible was something I unconsciously decided to gloss over. He wanted kids, I didn't. He was religious, I wasn't. Little niggling irritations were swept under the rug as I allowed him to hold me, to protect me as he so clearly wanted to do. True to his faith, Peter saved people, and at that moment, I needed saving.

Months went by, and the sticking points became harder to ignore. Asking me to go to church, making asides about names for babies. Yet still I clung to him, because I could not endure the trauma that I knew would ensue if I broke us up. I was not yet healed, and I feared ripping the wound open again, sending me back into despair and hopelessness.

The sweetest man, he brought me flowers. He made candlelit dinners. Every page in the book of woo was exhausted upon me, and I basked in his intoxicating, overwhelming devotion. All the while cringing inside because I knew I would never feel the way about him that he clearly did about me.

I loved Peter. I did. But I could not love him the way he wanted. Giving him his heart's desires: a stable, churchgoing family, the Norman Rockwell painting he tried so desperately to plaster over our unbalanced codependence.

I tried so hard not to lie, ignoring his prodding about faith and domestic bliss rather than challenging it. Asserting myself would mean the end, and I wasn't ready for that yet, though I saw it clearly on the horizon. So I lied by omission, because it was easier.

Or so I thought.

Relationships are an investment. The more you put into them, the greater the sense of loss when they tank, and when at last I felt the strength to tell Peter that I did not want children, ever, I knew I was tearing an intrinsic thread that held his fancy to me. He battled bravely to assert his point of view, to bring me around, but I would not move. The look in his eyes as he realized his dream was falling apart sent my stomach plunging.

Watching his world disintegrate, I felt guilt of a sort I have seldom experienced. I had done this, willfully. Had held off bursting his bubble, because it was easier. Because I needed and used him in my time of suffering, and was not willing to reciprocate, not to the extent he wanted. I burned with shame, loathing myself for what I'd done to him, accepting his rejection of me as the ignominy I deserved. I let him dump me, giving him that point of pride, a poor recompense for his frittered investment.

I could not face myself in the week that followed, and drank heavily, trying to drown my remorse, to no avail. Advances by men sensing my vulnerability were rejected, the spectre of ruining their lives as I had done with Peter's too much to bear. I was a pariah, a selfish bitch undeserving of love.

Two weeks out from the breakup, I heard through a friend that Peter was seeing someone else. The feeling of relief that flooded my heart was strong and soothing. Perhaps I hadn't destroyed the life of someone I loved. And I did love him. But sometimes that's not enough.

I'm still sorry. But not for breaking us up. I'm sorry for taking so long to be truthful about our future, one we could not possibly share. I owed Peter better than that, and I will never be able to justify my actions to my satisfaction. He has told me several times that he forgives me, and honestly sometimes that makes it worse. Remembering that time, I'm not sure I deserve forgiveness.

People are not merely tools to be used by others for their own satisfaction. I have been used like that myself, and ached at the betrayal, which is why I won't entirely let young Anna off the hook.

I'm sorry, Peter. But I'm glad that you are happy now. The pictures of your daughters are the only things that make me feel like I did you a favor all those years ago. You got what you wanted, what I couldn't give you. That this is important to me means I do care about you, and always will.

"There's a danger in loving somebody too much

And it's sad when you know it's your heart you can't trust

There's a reason why people don't stay where they are

Baby, sometimes love just ain't enough…"

-Patty Smythe and Don Henley

I'm Sorry

by Matthew Broyles

2007.

A one-bedroom apartment under the DFW airport flight path. Diaper packages and baby toys litter the floor. The child and his mother are asleep, and a man curls up on the couch in the dark, weeping.

Two years prior, he had held the infant in his arms in a dimly-lit hallway while they stitched his wife up from a traumatic delivery that would haunt them both for years to come. Alone in that silent hall, the newborn stared up at him, utterly helpless, searching for some form of reassurance in the strange new world into which he had just emerged.

Holding this vulnerable, frightened child, the man spoke fervent promises. *Don't worry*, he said. *I will take care of you. I will be there for you no matter what. I will give you what you need. Never doubt that. I'm the reason you're here, and I take that responsibility seriously.*

Yet as the next weeks and months unfolded, those promises were sorely tested. Ripped from the only life he had known, the man plunged headlong into a never-ending tunnel of infant need. His wife traumatized by her birth experience, and weighed down by the necessity of providing a steady income, the task of caring for the baby fell mostly on him.

Day after day, he told himself he could do it. Had to do it. No one else could or would. His friends saw him on that lonely island, but were childless and had no help to offer, no parental instincts or resources to draw upon. As relations with his wife strained, he felt increasingly alone, and the baby pulled nearer, needing more, a troubled sleeper with a worried temperament. The man drowned in the child's need, scarcely able to breathe, but fearful of surfacing, lest he abdicate his responsibility, his half of the bargain.

Driven onto the therapist's couch by compulsive guilt, he was guided to the realization that he could not shoulder this burden. That if he continued to go it largely alone, every day, he would break down, and fail the child utterly. Coupled with the fact that his wife's income was insufficient to truly sustain the family, he had to make a choice.

He knew people put kids into daycare all the time. But he had promised this child that he himself would be there, had acclimated the baby to his daily presence, the anchor, the constant. No longer a baby now, nearly two years old, the boy still could not comprehend the explanations of what was about to happen. That he would be going to a fun place with other kids, and that Daddy would be working somewhere else, would see him at the end of the day. But he didn't want Daddy to be anywhere else, and cried, telling him no, stay with me.

Bent into a fetal position on the couch that night, the man broke down, the echoes of the child's tears streaming down his face. He'd broken his promise, the most important promise he'd ever made, because he was weak. Because he couldn't handle the responsibility he'd committed to.

I'm sorry, he cried to the universe, desperate for it to understand that he hadn't meant to do this. That he had erred by believing he could raise a child. But of course it was too late. The child was here, and his needs would not change anytime soon.

The next day, he left the shrieking, horrified boy in the restraining arms of a daycare worker. The man fought not to collapse on the floor himself and scream his shame to the world. He left his child in the care of others, people who knew how to take care of children, and who would not suffer a mental breakdown during the task. At the temp job he'd secured, he sat at his desk, typing numbers into a computer, figures he cared nothing for, obsessing over his failure, over the child's confusion and sense of betrayal by the one who had always been there, but now was not.

Slowly, with painful languor, a new norm was established. But the time in the evenings after work was not enough, and the boy cried often when playtime had to stop, clinging to his father, the person he wanted more than anyone else, and who was now more distant, troubled by his flagging marriage and resentful of his meaningless employment.

I'm sorry, the man said to the child, who did not understand what he was saying, not fully. *I'm doing my best*, he said, and though it was true, it was not enough.

Years passed, and with the start of Kindergarten, time was secured in the afternoons for more play. It was still difficult for the man to slow his mind down to five-year-old speed, but he tried, and at good times it seemed that the child at least appreciated his presence, if not his full attention. The boy's anxiety level dropped precipitously, and the man knew with aching certainty that his absence had been the cause of the tension.

He resolved not to fail the child again, setting up a schedule that would allow for time together, even if he could not entirely commit his mind to the repetitive, simple play that the boy craved. Nonetheless, he tried.

The child is now older, and more self-sufficient. But his childhood is not over, and in weeks when his father is not as available, he still becomes anxious, though he tries manfully to mask it.

I'm sorry, the man still pleads to the darkness. *For all my weakness, for all my unintentional selfishness. For the mountains of mental debris that have consistently come between me and my child. The one to whom I made the most solemn promise of my entire life.*

I'm sorry, I say, hoping that one day he will understand what I mean.

"I know a father who had a son

He longed to tell him all the reasons for the things he'd done

He came a long way just to explain

He kissed his boy as he lay sleeping

Then he turned around and headed home again…"

  -Paul Simon, *Slip Sliding Away*

I'm Sorry

by MC Dalet

"You're so much like me. I'm sorry."
-- Ben Folds, *Still Fighting It*

One of my favorite musical artists is Ben Folds. His musical ability is divine, and I mean that in every sense possible; but his ability to create character and story within a musical frame is his greatest ability. In his song, *Still Fighting It*, Folds paints a poignant portrait of a father speaking to his young child while ruminating on his own experience of how much "it sucks to grow up." This father, the speaker in the song, knows, as I do, the inevitability of his child facing the same challenges and heartaches he himself confronts. The part of the story that gets me every time is the clear layer of the narrative that reveals the speaker's fear that his son will feel growing pains IN THE SAME WAY, and perhaps with the same intensity, as the father because, as he says, "You're so much like me."

I can say without hyperbole that ever since my daughter reached the age of 3 and her personality began to manifest in earnest, I have yet to make it through the song without a tear. I find myself looking in her direction as the chorus drops as I shakily sing along, my eyes locked on the yet innocent creature: "You're so much like me. I'm sorry."

Of course the last bit, the apology, while it puts a stake right through my heart in the context of Folds' song story, accomplishes nothing of consequence in the real world or, I suspect, the world of the story. First, one cannot apologize for genetics. DNA does what it does, brilliantly combining parental traits into a uniquely beautiful individual, like his or her parents, but distinct. It does this automatically. We have no control, and can offer no apology. Then there's the part a parent can claim, behavioral modeling. Tell the child anything you want. What they absorb, internalize, and replicate are your actions, the overt and, as I have discovered, the subtle. Even the things you thought you were concealing. Model negativity, fear, lack of confidence, and no amount of apology or explanation will deter the child from familial cultural assimilation.

"Everybody knows it hurts to grow up."

When I was a child, I was praised by teachers for my good behavior, even my intelligence. But my lack of confidence was betrayed by my pencil strokes. My whisper soft writing became a recurring topic of parent-teacher conferences. Oh, in music class, I would sing out loud, having yet to be told I wasn't a brilliant singer, but when it came to academics. . .Every time I faced the possibility of getting an answer wrong – which, of course, describes every assignment – fear of rejection, of my potentially wrong answers somehow revealing a wrongness inherent in my being, crept over me. Simple homework took hours as I checked and rechecked my math, my spelling, my reading comprehension. I talked myself out of self-evident correct answers.

I would later come to realize that this was a lack learned from my own parents – from my mother, who learned it from her mother, and even from my father, who concealed his fear of inadequacy through an outward appearance of what we jokingly refer to as "waking up and pissing excellence," which he does. But remember, even the things you think you are concealing, a child receives.

By the third grade, I was cloaking my work. Afraid of being wrong, I wrote so lightly with my pencil, my teachers could hardly make out what I'd written. For verbal interactions, I would raise my hand, eager to please, but speak softly when called upon. If I couldn't be read or heard, technically I couldn't be wrong. This pattern of behavior has followed me into adulthood. Afraid of criticism, I do nothing at crucial junctures. I consistently recheck my "math" until the time for calculation has passed. I whisper discontent under my breath instead of facing life's inevitable conflicts and moving on.

Then came my daughter, the Great Mirror.

"I can tell you about today, and how I picked you up and everything changed."

In pre-K, she came home with songs learned at school and shared them with us, singing loudly, executing the attendant hand motions. She continues to share her school life, and seems happy. She's also a brilliant reader. Sincerely, I am amazed at how well she can read at 5 and a half. But I have noticed a development: "the quiet read." The words she's sure of are vocalized clearly and brightly, but one little question about whether she's got it or not, and the volume drops to a whisper. Sure, a fairly normal child trepidation, but paired with her determination to actively deny that her lower case "d" is actually a "b" and a recent post-fit discussion during which she stated "I'm just mad at myself…"

"So weird to be back here. . .It was pain; sunny days and rain; I knew you'd feel the same
    things."

But no amount of apology works here. The only way to break the cycle, to "stop fighting it," is to change my behavior. . .and my consciousness. It is interesting that I write this in the Hebrew month of Elul (or Virgo), leading up to Rosh Hashanah. It is a time of "teshuvah," or "repentance." In traditional Judaism, this means admitting your wrongdoing before the Creator in an attempt to be written into the heavenly "Book of Life" for the coming year, a cosmic "I'm sorry." Turn to the deeper roots of the practice of teshuvah, those illuminated by study of the Kabbalah, and one finds that true repentance is the admission of negativity, yes, but also an acknowledgement of times we fail to take positive action, or in my case, any action. Furthermore, the purpose is not to say "I'm sorry" and be done. Saying "I'm sorry" does not change the effect of our negative actions. Instead, one must RECOGNIZE one's own negative behaviors and in so doing expose them for removal, like taking the garbage to the curb on trash day. The idea of Rosh Hashanah, the beginning of a new year, in this deeper understanding is to step into a new story, a new movie, by recasting ourselves as NEW CHARACTERS. "I'm sorry," is a beginning, so long as we really mean it. Changing our behavior, at its core; that is, as the maxim goes, the best apology. To get to a point where "I have all the CHANGE"; it's a hard battle.

"The years go by and we're still fighting it."

My Created Life

My Created Life

by Anna Bardin

A problem writers have is separating truth from fiction.

Lord knows it's happened to me enough times. A perfect scene that flows so well in my head somehow clanks around jerkily when I see it in live action. Pairings of lovers that work much better on the page than in their meat suits, bashing each other's neuroses together in vivid technicolor.

Logically, I shouldn't build up expectations. I should let things happen organically and see where they go. But it's so tempting, in idle hours, to paint a pretty picture of people you know, and bask in its sublimity. The trouble arrives when you start mistaking the fantasy for reality.

I set up a couple one time. I'm not in the habit of matchmaking, but Carol and Lee were both single friends of mine from different circles, and for whatever reason, I couldn't stop thinking that they would be adorable together. This was in the days before Facebook, so the date was truly blind. I gave them both the sunniest representation of each other I could come up with…not lies, but omissions were made…and I even made reservations for them at a restaurant I knew they both liked. It was going to be perfect.

Meeting Carol for lunch the next day, I was all bubbly, and totally unprepared for the dubious scowl on her face. I sat down, a chill seizing my heart.

"What the hell, Anna?" she asked, lighting up a cigarette on the patio. I'd never seen her smoke before.

I blinked, dumbfounded.

"Did something happen?" I asked, stupidly.

Carol blew out a disgusted breath and shook her head in annoyance.

"Your friend is a piece of work," she said, rolling her eyes. "I'm not sure I've ever dated anyone more rude."

My brain imploded. Lee had never been anything but sweet to me, and to every woman I'd seen him around. Did she meet the wrong guy?

"This is Lee we're talking about?" I asked, tentatively. "Blue eyes, brown hair?"

"Oh, that's him," Carol scoffed. "He made sure I knew all about him."

That sounded ominous.

"Did he try something?" I asked, horrified.

"Ha!" she barked. "Didn't get a chance. I paid for my meal and got out of there too fast. You need better radar, girl."

Now I was pissed. What the hell had Lee done to put her in this state? After lunch, I called him.

"Oh man, Anna," he said, upon picking up the phone. "I hate to say it, but bad call."

"What the fuck happened?" I growled. "Carol was livid. What did you do?"

"Do?" he snorted. "I didn't have a chance to DO anything! She was so obnoxious, I couldn't get a word in edgewise."

Anger gave way to confusion. These people were not liars, at least not that I knew of. How could their personalities be so incompatible? In my head, they made scintillating conversation, and stared lovingly into each other's eyes, grateful for the chance to meet someone so nice, smart and attractive.

The more I thought about it, though, I started to understand. Both had trust issues from broken homes. Both were bullheaded, which I found cute, but in a date setting, maybe not so much. In my mind, I had edited the rough edges of their personalities for a smoother narrative. Somehow I thought that if they just met each other, they would see what I saw. But how could they? They were in their real lives, not the ones I had created for them.

This is one reason I've always been scared of having children. I can totally see myself inventing versions of these little people in my brain that bear only a passing resemblance to the ones running around at my feet. *This is how it should be*, I would explain to them, right before they promptly ignored me and went back to beating each other with pool noodles.

Oddly, it hasn't seemed to be a problem in my love life, probably owing to the temporary nature of my entanglements. I can make the dreamworld happen for a night, or a few weeks, long enough to fulfill the vision in my head. Once the inconsistencies start piling up, it's time to move on to the next story. Novels or epic trilogies are a bit of a stretch. The shorter the sweeter.

This is the life that I have created, and through experiences like the Carol & Lee Debacle, I have learned not to impose my imagination upon the lives of others unless I can guide the action personally. To show them the story the way I see it. Reality is malleable, in the right hands. It dances if you show it the moves.

So I will continue to create my life to my specifications. And when the facts on the ground don't match up…well, that's what writing's for.

My Created Life

by Cristee Cook

When I began to create my life, when I was younger, I set out into the world with the understanding that there is a "happy life" formula. The rules go something like this: get through school, preferably by making as few waves as possible. Go to more school, especially if you have big dreams. Find your soulmate and marry them. You'll need to have some kids, and buy a house, and have a cute car. For extra credit, love Jesus. I mean really take him into your heart. Your life will be amazing. Cue dreams!

The rules are presented as a successful formula, but the formula is ultimately flawed. They forgot to teach us that we have to learn how to create our little reality in a conscious way. The idea of creation implies, maybe demands, consciousness. I assert that part of the reason we humans experience such profound suffering is because we are largely uneducated about how to actually CREATE. The majority of us follow the norm, unconscious. I will go as far as to argue that our external societal chatter is so strong, it's like the death metal played at unsafe decibels for hours straight to a sleep-deprived, starving, suspected terrorist during an investigation. It will break you. I know I sound harsh here, but I am passionate about the subject.

Creation demands consciousness. You have to pay attention. Constant vigilance. Often we are shaken up from our societal stupors by a life-altering event. Think about it. How many inspirational stories are told about how a divorce, bankruptcy or a medical diagnosis push a person to realize they've been living an unsatisfactory life? Some of us have this realization after smaller events or milestone birthdays, but the effect is the same. The shake-up causes the change. Then, those lucky enough to see that they have another chance, will attempt to create a life that's closer to their personal truth. Consciously. They feel, as the kids say nowadays, "woke." Gone are the days of blind conformity.

So, how do we skip the pain and trauma part and just start creating what we want the first time? Husband and I are on a lengthy process of re-creating our life together. A few years ago we had the stark realization that we had created our life according to the "happy life" formula. We didn't regret everything we had done, but we weren't happy. We felt trapped, wildly unfulfilled, and the pressure of changing our situation was less stressful than staying where we were. So, we are re-creating everything. It's hard. It's no joke. Every choice we are presented with requires that we ask questions. Is this congruent with what we're trying to create? What will it take for _____ to happen? Then, we have to be assassins of our own negative self-talk. Fear is actually not only not an option, but it isn't a luxury we can afford. We can't go back to the way it was before.

To have a different reality you don't burn down or rally against what you've already created. You try to view it objectively, like an uninvolved observer, and see how it can be transformed. You have to create a new way, not choose between either-or. This is the part of the formula they forgot. It's isn't a pass-fail system. There are, in reality, an infinite array of possibilities and you, me, we – can transform anything. I'm not going to present this as though this is easy. It actually really sucks to go against an established paradigm. Uprooting your old beliefs and choosing different things opens you up to judgement, jealousy, and potential isolation. People don't really want to change, and they don't want to be confronted with the need to truly transform. But, there is such incredible power in being able to choose. To choose consciously…I think that's a closer definition of creation. The willingness to bravely acknowledge the lies we tell ourselves, the lies we buy in to, and the lies we perpetuate. And when we recognize something as an illusion, to have the courage to ask: what else is possible?

I challenge you to try it. See where it leads you. I'll be here, waiting to gleefully receive your tales of new adventure.

My Created Life

by Matthew Broyles

"You may ask yourself: Well, how did I get here?" – Talking Heads

We are often given a false set of choices when we consider the phenomenon of life. Either life is something that happens to you, or it's something that you make happen. Which of these is more accurate?

The answer, of course, is both. Obviously life happens to us, in the form of weather, drunk drivers, tax assessment, and all manner of factors beyond our control. But by making choices every day, more than we generally notice, we are also making our life happen, shaping its path, sometimes in dramatic ways, but usually the way a glacier carves mountains, slow and steady.

That so much of the process is gradual is why we tend to miss it, until we look up one day and things appear different than we thought they would. Glancing back over our shoulder, we see the path we laid, and it makes a sort of sense, but in those moments when the remnants of our younger selves wake up in an older person's body, it can be very jarring.

Taking responsibility for the parts of our lives that we are less satisfied with is difficult. It hurts to admit mistakes, especially when they mean a window has passed, and you won't get to make the decision again.

When the weight of all those decisions bears down at 3AM, it can be useful to employ the George Bailey test. Rather than focus on the hypothetical good things that might have happened in an alternate universe, take a look at the existing good things that would not have happened had you not made the choices you made.

Some of these might seem very small, but it doesn't mean they are insignificant. When I retrieve an item from a high shelf for a bent old woman at the grocery store, that might be a mere blip in my day, but I'll wager it means quite a bit to her. Over the years, I've learned that simple emails or bits of information-sharing I did on a whim set in motion a series of important events in someone's life. I know it's true for me that sometimes a random act by someone I barely know has set off a cascade of reactions that alter my trajectory in significant ways, often without their knowledge.

We say we are the creators of our lives, but of course we do not start from scratch. Genetic chance, geographical happenstance, and the good old spacetime continuum set our initial conditions, influencing the paths we pursue. No five-foot-four NBA draftees, nor paraplegic rock climbers. That said, there are deaf musicians, and gymnasts with degenerative muscular diseases. Starting conditions need not always constrain potentialities, but they will make one's journey either easier or harder, and our judgment of success or failure must be adjusted accordingly.

And we cannot forget the years in which our lives are created for us, from conception to adulthood. At that painfully glacial pace, a child is slowly transferred incrementally larger pieces of control over their lives, until at last they are set free to steer their own ship. But we carry our childhoods with us in those early adult years, because they are all we've ever known. We use the lessons learned therein as our guideposts, often discovering to our horror that we possess contradictory programming, and that we must reconcile our view of the world with the world's view of us.

This is a process that can bring us to our knees, and can hit hardest in midlife, when we see the path we've carved, and follow its vector forward, blinking in alarm at where it seems to be pointing. Worse, we can't actually know for sure where it's going, because as we are creating our lives, life is still happening to us from outside, sending waves over seawalls and inflicting tiny cuts in the form of chronic health conditions, socio-economic fluctuation, and the weight of responsibilities taken on bit by bit over many years, heavy enough now to make maneuvering difficult.

Yet even if we find changing course too onerous, staying on the existing path is still an active choice. We cannot stay in one place, because time is passing, and our relationships with loved ones shift and warp as all of us grow and experience the world, which never stands still. It can take as much effort not to change as it might take to change, though we seldom see it that way.

As the original builders of our lives pass on, and we are left increasingly to our own devices, that sense of creating our own lives becomes stronger, and sometimes burdensome. How to know what is right? We know what we know, and it will never be everything we need to know.

In times like this, it can either be comforting or terrifying to realize that no one else has all the information either. All around us, people creating their own lives, in which we play some part, major or minor. And in being a part of others' lives, we find that we are life happening to them, just as they are life happening to us.

If that is so, then perhaps we have more power to create our lives than we believe. To cultivate a garden of lives we affect in positive ways, in hopes that they in turn cultivate us.

○

There Goes My Hero

○

There Goes My Hero

by Anna Bardin

In high school, there is a very definite line between the adults and the students, even though age-wise, they aren't often that far apart.

That got challenged for me my junior year, when I ended up in a desk next to Misty. A pretty girl, thin and smart, she exuded a confidence that I warmed to. Especially when I found out that she was a mother.

Misty was only 18, but had gotten pregnant the year prior, and opted to keep the kid, plus marry the father, another student who dropped out to get a job at a machine shop in town. He was paying their bills while she finished her diploma, something important to her career aspirations.

I knew other girls in similar circumstances, but Misty was the only one who seemed not to be overwhelmed and at least a little ashamed. She talked about her kid with great affection, not the defensive kind I heard from the girls who knew they'd screwed up their lives. Misty seemed to take it all in stride, and although I wanted no part of motherhood, I admired her for it.

Mostly because she was also the only girl in school who talked about sex the way that boys did, unabashedly enthusiastic and saucy. She spoke about carnality the way I wanted to, but I never got up the huevos until years later. Misty could tell that I liked to hear her say those things, though, and would throw me a bone now and then.

"Ooo…" she said one day, sitting down gingerly and winking. "A bit sore from last night…"

It was so hard not to blush at such open admission of sexual activity. Dammit, I wanted to be sore from a drubbing of that kind, though I dared not pursue it at that age. Especially not if it got me pregnant. Middle American teen knowledge of birth control was woefully sparse, so for all I knew, enjoyment itself would get a girl preggers.

I wanted to ask Misty so many questions. Because she knew. She'd been there, and liked it. A lot. Despite myself, I wanted to be like Misty, minus the kid. And the marriage. Mostly I just wanted to be as sexually forthright and fearless as she was. There was never a dark shadow that crossed her eyes when she talked about her husband or her home life. Although she said she hadn't planned the pregnancy, that didn't seem to stop her from making the most of her life as it unfolded.

One of my great regrets is that I didn't keep up with Misty after she graduated. We didn't have the same circle of friends, and in the maelstrom of my dad's death and college, I didn't have any room for tracking down former classmates, especially in the pre-internet age. Sadly, I can't remember her last name, and she never seems to pop up in alumni groups online.

Part of me wants to know what became of her. But another part is a little afraid. What if that confident, vivacious girl got beaten down by the grind after all? What if she married too soon, and left to pursue a different life after a few years? There are so many ways her story could have gone, and I ache a little not knowing how it all turned out. Is she even still alive?

It occurs to me that Misty's daughter would be 26 years old now. Eight years older than Misty was when I saw her as this supremely self-assured young woman. I wonder how her daughter sees her, and if her dauntless nature was passed down. I would very much like to meet her, although then I might learn some of the things I'd rather not.

Sure, it could be that Misty was playing a role. Putting on the wry smile to avoid showing her weakness, to be different from the sad girls fearing the lord's judgment for their sluttery. I don't think so, though. Misty seemed to find the trade-off more than worth it. Makes me want to meet her husband, the more I think of it…

I know, it's weird when your hero is a knocked-up teenage mom. But Misty was never far from my thoughts as I pursued my own sexual adventures in adulthood. Her knowing smile told me that there was something good to find in the tussle of hormones and naked body exploration. She was one of the only voices telling me that back then, and I salute her for it.

I hope it stayed good for her. I would like to think that somewhere in the world today, Misty is sore from the night before. And for the very best of reasons.

There Goes My Hero

by Clark Weddle

Hero. There's a word that gets bandied about real loose these days. Why is a sniper a hero when he's on our side, but when he's a Nazi or Viet Cong he's a coward? Hell, there are some people who'd say I'm a hero. Just because I'm a veteran. I'm here to say it just ain't so. I should know, 'cause I was there, and they weren't. It irks the crap out me when someone feels he has to gush over it. I don't want to hear it, but I'm usually too polite to say so.

When I was fourteen or fifteen, the country was kind of on the down side of the latest of what I later learned was a long line of folk music revivals, the Big Folk Scare as Pete Seeger called it. I wanted to be part of it. I wanted to be a A FOLK SINGER. So I got me a cheap guitar and a book - *The Folk Singer's Guitar Guide*. I still have that book stashed away somewhere. The covers are long gone, and the pages are tattered, but there are still the photographs. Those old black & white photos introduced me to my heroes. I figured if their pictures were in that book, then they were worth searching out and listening to. This was long before YouTube and iTunes. I had to go to real music stores and stand there flipping through the records, after I was done drooling over the Martins and the Gibsons and the BANJOS and kazoos and jaws harps and nose flutes.

God damn what music there was to be discovered. Lightin' Hopkins. Sonny Terry & Brownie McGee. Pete Seeger. Ramblin' Jack Elliot. New Lost City Ramblers. I never knew such stuff existed. But there was one name that stood out from all the rest.

Woody Guthrie. He was my hero. He had a sign on his guitar - 'This Machine Kills Fascists'. How is that not a hero? He taught me that you don't have to be able to sing to sing. It don't matter - just sing. Now that sure don't mean that there's not somebody out there that won't try and make you feel bad about your singing. Don't pay those folks no mind. If you want to sing, then by god, sing. He also showed me that playing the guitar doesn't need to be fast and flash. Learn to strum a guitar, it's fun just to sing and play some songs for your kids or grandkids.

Because of Woody, my very first (and so far last) "public" performance was in eleventh grade English class. I had just recently discovered Woody's song "The Ballad of Tom Joad" in a book titled "Ballads, Songs, and Snatches." Woody wrote it after seeing the movie "The Grapes of Wrath," based on Steinbeck's novel. I was probably awful, but I what I do remember is this - I GOT AN A. The teacher LOVED it.

Now, in Woody's day you didn't necessarily have to sound like all these cookie-cutter pop or so-called country singers on 'American Idol' to get a radio show. And, as I understand it, in spite of his lack of what you might call 'musical sophistication', Woody had some chances to make it big, but another part of his being a hero got in the way.

He was activating for unions, he was activating for the Grand Coulee Dam. He was activating for people in general I think. He was just activating. Couldn't seem to help himself, and all that activating is part of what made him a hero to me. But it also meant that he just couldn't toe the line that program sponsors set for him. All that activating kinda got in the way of things.

All heroes tarnish a bit once you get to know them. Turns out Woody was somewhat of a womanizer, and had a temper. He was irresponsible, or maybe sometimes he just felt a larger responsibility somewhere else. He'd just take off and leave his family, wife and kids, and hop a freight to go somewhere to activate for something. Or maybe to just be somewhere else. Turns out he also inherited Huntington's Corea, a terrible disease of the nervous system. It probably had a lot to do with Woody's nature later in his life.

Still, there were the songs and the music. If you haven't heard "This Land Is My Land," you been living under a rock somewhere. Am I the only one that thinks that should be our national anthem instead of that god-awful "Star Spangled Banner?" Many of his songs were patriotic, but not that "rah rah my country right or wrong love it or leave it" patriotism that leaves me cold. Well, there was "Round and Round Hitler's Grave", but, well, what can I say? That was the "good" war, right? Look up the songs that he was commissioned to write in celebration of the Grand Coulee Dam. Nowadays, some of those songs might not fit in with today's ecological ideas and such, but they were a celebration of the "We can do it!" spirit that made America great at the time - the building, the industry, the "we can do just about anything we put our mind to" attitude. And the songs he wrote for children. Search out "Take Me For A Ride In The Car Car." And there was "Jesus Christ Was A Man," the liberal gospel according to the tune of "Jesse James."

"I hate a song that makes you think that you are not any good. I hate a song that makes you think that you are just born to lose. No good to nobody. No good for nothing. Because you are too old or too young or too fat or too slim too ugly or too this or too that. Songs that run you down or poke fun at you on account of your bad luck or hard traveling. I am out to fight those songs to my very last breath of air and my last drop of blood. I am out to sing songs that will prove to you that this is your world and that if it has hit you pretty hard and knocked you for a dozen loops, no matter what color, what size you are, how you are built, I am out to sing the songs that make you take pride in yourself and in your work. I could hire out to the other side, the big money side, and get several dollars every week just to quit singing my own kind of songs and to sing the kind that knock you down still farther and the ones that poke fun at you even more and the ones that make you think you've not any sense at all. But I decided a long time ago that I'd starve to death before I'd sing any such songs as that. The radio waves and your movies and your jukeboxes and your songbooks are already loaded down and running over with such no good songs as that anyhow."
- Woody Guthrie.

There Goes My Hero

by Matthew Broyles

We first search for heroes as children. Our expanding minds seek aspirational figures, someone to be like when we grow up. In that stage of our lives, we imbue these people with outsized attributes, larger than life, titans who have mastered the art of living.

Al Franken once said that Republicans love America the way a 2-year-old loves their mother. Mom is the best, and anyone who says otherwise is bad. Whereas Democrats love America the way an adult loves their mother. They're aware of the drinking problems, the foibles and failures, and love her for who she is, warts and all.

The example above is a bit simplistic, but it always pops into my head the minute a cultural icon makes a big mistake, and suddenly that person is The Worst Human Ever, no longer deserving of ANY admiration, a worthless piece of trash that we were all fools to love in the first place.

When I see that go down, as it has recently with people like Joss Whedon and Louis CK, it sounds an awful lot like a 2-year-old temper tantrum. Mom was the BEST BEST BEST, and now she's BAD BAD BAD.

Are we not adults? Have we not made mistakes? Do we not realize that other adults do likewise? Should a lifetime of beloved work be tossed unceremoniously into the bin, because its creator made bad choices in their personal lives?

Obviously this is a decision everyone has to make for themselves, but personally, I prefer to celebrate the work regardless of whether the person who made it was an intolerable asshole. Because frankly, if I didn't, I couldn't be a fan of very much at all.

Art only comes into being because of conflict. The friction of life rubbing against the grain of a sensitive soul, the shavings thus created forming a testament to the fundamental struggles we all face. If you think that process happens without collateral psychological damage, you're out of your goddamned mind.

I say this as an artist, but art is not the only realm in which people who perform great acts take a mental toll in the process. They falter, they screw up. Of course they do. So do you, so do I. The difference is that when they bumble, it gets broadcast on every screen in the nation. If that happened to any of us, don't you think the damage from the error would be compounded, leading to further errors? I sure as hell do.

This isn't to say that we shouldn't condemn bad behavior. Even prosecute it criminally, if appropriate. But if a bridge builder goes to jail for embezzlement, do we tear all of their bridges down?

I recently read Phil Collins' autobiography, learning a lot of things I didn't know about the crazy shit that was going on in his life at the time he was making the songs I love so much. Would I have wanted to be his wife or kid? Absolutely not. But that is not my relationship with the man. In fact, I do not have any relationship with him. My relationship is with the music, which, while an integral part of him, need not only be appreciated alongside his personal life.

As someone quipped once, I would have unfollowed Lovecraft on Twitter by now. But will I forsake *At the Mountains of Madness*? Hell no. John Lennon beat his first wife. Will I burn my Beatles records? Absolutely not.

If I demand complete moral purity of all my heroes, then I will have no heroes. With the possible exception of Saint Fred Rogers, everyone who ever made anything worth a damn has demons. Sometimes those are exorcised in beautiful ways, and other times they come out like the creature in *Dreamcatcher*, leaving a bloody fecal mess all over the ground.

Do I judge those people as people? Yes. Do I judge their work through the same lens? No. Phil Spector is a horrible person, but he made wonderful records. So did a lot of really terrible humans.

And you know what? That's part of why the work resonates. Whether we're openly honest with ourselves or not, when we see or hear another person's pain expressed artfully, part of us recognizes it. Knows that these demons live inside us, too, to one degree or another. We all have vanity, selfishness, greed, hatred, envy, and secrets that would destroy us in the eyes of our loved ones if they knew.

So imagine that you take those bad parts and put them out on the table for the whole world to see. That's art at its best, and our society is the better for it. These people are taking one for the team. But don't think for a minute that this act of revelation comes about without consequences. It is a painful process, and painkillers come in all shapes and sizes. There is collateral damage. There is blowback. It is the price of being human.

Thus do I exhort you to love your heroes the way an adult loves their mother, with all the issues and drama and knowledge that this is a human, not a statue on a pedestal. Never blameless, but doing the best they can in shaping your life in ways that no one else could.

Be kind to your heroes, whether they deserve it or not. Truly, they have done the same for you.

○

Bring Me the Head Of…

○

Bring Me the Head Of…

by Anna Bardin

There is a peculiarity in human biology that has always vexed me. It is that one can achieve transcendent physical euphoria with someone who is a horrible match for you otherwise.

The realization of this misalignment can be painful and confusing. It throws your confidence in your own judgment into crisis, and makes you hate your own body for wanting what it wants, even while your brain knows the price is far too high.

Bring me the head of whichever sprig of DNA got morphed years ago to create the conditions for dualism, the split between body and mind.

I know acids don't have heads, but as I don't believe in intelligent designers (much less so when this conundrum is considered), I have to blame what's available.

Our bodies and minds should want the same things. Yet more often than not, they don't. That box of donuts in the break room, for example. My body doesn't want diabetes. It would complain very loudly if I allowed myself to indulge my brain's craving for sweet, fried doughy deliciousness as often as I wished. So I sit at my desk, fighting myself, one set of cells debating with the other instead of focusing on, I don't know, my JOB, which allows both body and mind to survive in relative comfort.

Perhaps it's cultural more so than evolutionary. There are mental practices that bring body and mind into greater alignment, but they often require a degree of separation from the culture at large. This shouldn't bother me, the cloistered writer in her garret, but I suppose my expectations of the world aren't as far from the mainstream as I'd like to think. I want fun stuff, silly fripperies, and on-demand everything.

Or rather, my brain wants that. My body says hey, maybe you should work out more, so we all feel a bit better like you always say we want to. This is the same body, though, which will exhort me to stay up all night with a lover, accepting the next day's baggy-eyed suffering as a reasonable exchange. The same body that resists breaking off the affair because if you can just keep him from talking, he will transport your senses to the ninth circle of OMG WOW.

What to do when neither mind nor body are providing reliable guidance, and giving contradictory advice to boot?

Religion, I suppose. Handing over control to a third party, one that might help you save yourself from yourself, and your other self from whatever other selves are wandering around in there. You really have to believe, though. I've always been extremely glad I'm not an alcoholic, because I wouldn't last long as a twelve-stepper. I know higher powers can be interpreted in unique individual terms, but given that my own religion is basically sex, that doesn't really leave me any better off.

But the third party thing works to some degree. Eventually the lover will piss me off enough to cut bait, and it's on to the next thing. Tempestuousness is a double-sided blade, one I've learned to handle with thick gloves. Distill the essence of the experience, write it down, put it out there, and carry on, ever forward.

Bring me the head of Anna Bardin. That bifurcated, ungovernable hussy. I love her to death, but damn.

Bring Me the Head Of…

by Matthew Broyles

Tracking the breath from a butterfly's wings is a tricky business. History seems obvious and linear when you see it in hindsight most of the time, but here and there one spots tangles, flurries of events that are so tightly knotted that it can be difficult to sort out particular causes and effects.

World War I, for example. I've read numerous books which attempt to nail down the prime suspects, and even allowing for a multiplicity of them—decline of the Ottoman and Austro-Hungarian Empires, the rise of quasi-scientific utopian movements, the depredations of the industrial age, etc.—there is still the sense of something unseen, hiding in the center of the storm, a kink that cannot quite be teased out.

2016 felt similar to me. So many norms broken, for no one reason that anyone could readily identify. The Orange Kaiju was going to happen, no matter the precedents suggesting it was impossible. Countless thinkpieces, both in the run-up and aftermath, attempted to ascribe blame to one thing or another, but as with other great calamities, separating cause from effect has been problematic.

How far back to go? Reagan's union-busting and treasury-looting? Milton Friedman's deconstruction of Keynesian economic theory? Johnson signing the Civil Rights Act? Reconstruction? The Civil War? The three-fifths compromise? Behind each significant development lies its backstory, and behind that, yet another trail of breadcrumbs, stretching off into the misty mountains of history. One might as well blame plate tectonics, separating continents to create the resource and climate disparities that drive the dark engine of colonialism to this day.

With such a wide lens, it can be tempting to go full relativist, letting people off the hook for the historical positions they find themselves in. Thomas Jefferson, freedom fighter or oppressor? Arguably both, but that's not very satisfying to our natural drive for a clean narrative. And if we have to hedge our heroes, surely we must also do so for our villains.

Hitler as victim is a tough picture to paint, yet accounts of daily beatings by his father cannot be read without at least a twinge of sympathy. We like to imagine our monsters are born bad, intrinsically evil creatures, irredeemable. This prevents us from forestalling the creation of new monsters by mitigating childhood abuse and neglect. How many Hitlers have Child Protective Services obviated?

Yet a society free of individual accountability cannot stand. Even if the causes are entirely understood, there are those whose presence in the world is a net negative for the population at large. If provided a bullet and the hypothetical blue police box, whose absence from the historical rolls would benefit the greatest number of people in the present?

Der Fuhrer is an obvious target, but it has been argued fairly successfully that given the state of post-WWI Germany, it was less a question of if than when a demagogue would rise. Eliminate one, another simply steps in to take his place.

Does this change as we go back further? The Atlantic slave trade killed far more people than did the Third Reich, but there we have a confluence of actors rather than a unitary mastermind. Blame the Hebrew scribe who enshrined slavery into the Bible? But of course the practice extended well beyond Christendom, so no go on that front.

In fact, the farther you go into the foundations of our worst behaviors, the more you realize how much of it appears baked in. Greed, oppression, racism...none of these are bounded by time and place. They manifest in cultures around the globe from antiquity to the present.

This points to humanity's intrinsic nature, born either of evolutionary happenstance or infernal supernatural influence, depending on where you fall on the science-religion continuum. On the latter end of that range, the call for the head of the prince of evil makes sense. For those of us lacking that panacea, at whom do we swing our swords?

We live when we live, waking up in a world already in progress, surrounded by others equally hemmed in by their circumstances. We cannot rewrite the events which brought us here, but neither can we throw up our hands when confronted with evil borne of centuries-old animus. Someone's for the chop, but who?

Or rather, what? As the children of empire have rushed towards the top of Maslow's pyramid, have we neglected to maintain its base? What use freedom of expression if the larder lies empty? Like Wile E. Coyote, are we standing in midair, waiting for the drop? Some of us are already falling, and perhaps therein can be found the seed of anxiety that made so many of us clamber onto the gold-plated jet as it blazed through.

Again, too easy. Plenty of well-provisioned Americans pulled the same lever. And so we return to the multiplicity, the reality that no one human's elimination fixes the condition of the rest.

Headhunting for scapegoats will not save us. Honesty about ourselves and our motivations might. But lordy, what a tall order.

"You can see the summit, but you can't reach it

The last piece of the puzzle, but you just can't make it fit

Doctor says you're cured, but you still feel the pain

Aspirations in the clouds, but your hopes go down the drain..."

  * Howard Jones, *No One Is to Blame*

○

Guys (Girls) Like Me

○

Girls Like Me

by Anna Bardin

Two incidents, four years apart...

Junior year of high school. I'm at the hairdresser with my mom, very much against my will, getting dolled up for a wedding. A shotgun wedding, as it happens, arranged hastily by a family friend for her daughter, whose birth control knowledge and/or implementation was found lacking. My coif is done, and I'm sitting on a puffy vinyl chair, nose stuck as far into a terrible magazine as possible, to avoid being drawn into the conversation my mother is having with the stylist, an old harpy with a nose for gossip.

"It's the movies that do it," my mother proclaims haughtily. "These girls today, they see sex on the screen, and they think it's all sweetness and happily ever after. The boys swoop right in to pounce, and the poor things never see it coming."

Like a Martian heat ray, I feel my mother's gaze sweep over to me. I try desperately to disappear into the insipid Cheryl Tiegs interview on the page, but her eyes melt right through the page, and I am forced to look up.

"Not girls like my Anna, of course," Mom says, smiling that smile that is both praise and threat.

I return the gesture, my own smile a blend of fake compliance and back-off coldness. I'm getting good at adding the latter bit in these late teenage years, and the temperature of my grin turns my mother's head away, back to the safe natterings of middle aged matriarchs.

Bitterly, I have to concede that she's right. At this point, I have not had what I would call sex, although I've had boys' hands in places my mom would certainly not approve of. But I'm not one of Those Girls, partially because of the alarming number of my classmates who have suddenly disappeared from school like Central American political dissidents, vanished in the night due to bellies inflated by the wanton injections of the local male populace.

I've been careful to keep the safety on during my handling of any rocketry, and thus 'girls like me' still technically means virgins...by my definition, anyway. And in the back of my head, I secretly despair that it will always remain so.

Cut to junior year of college.

I sit in a deli booth with two girls, one of whom hates my guts. Several months prior, the guy she was dating slipped into a closet with me during a party, and certain things happened which my dear madre would definitely not consider appropriate. The fact that I was not aware of his attachment, or really even his name, did not seem to absolve me of any blame, and my name was spread across campus like a scarlet letter painted by a skywriter. And of course a beacon to the boys, for better and worse.

If I'd known the woman scorn'd would be at this restaurant, I would not have come. But we were both invited by our mutual friend Shelly, who either hadn't gotten the memo about the bad blood or was trying to broker a truce. It never was clear to me, because all I could feel was my enemy's hate radiating across the table like...well, a Martian heat ray.

"Oh my god, I got an invite to Trey's party," Shelly scoffed, rolling her eyes. "What a goddamn jerk convention. No thanks."

I fought a blush. Trey, too, was a notch on my belt, though it hadn't been advertised. Not my favorite guy, but nice enough to me, and talented in important ways. I'm not sure if my nemesis spotted my reaction, or if she already had her bullet loaded in the chamber, but I remember the next words very clearly.

"Oh, I don't know," she said, icily. "Sounds like heaven for a certain kind of girl."

Under the table, my fist balled up. The hypocritical bitch. She'd laid half the campus before sinking her hooks into what's-his-name, angling for her MRS degree once she found out he was loaded. Withering retorts jostled for position in my throat, ready to crack that sneer into little pieces.

But then I paused, and drew a deep breath. I wasn't going to make a new friend here. Nor was I going to say anything that would ever shut her up, ever. A hot spike of pride shot up my spine, and I turned to look at Shelly, raising my eyebrows and setting my mouth in an unbreakable grin.

"I'll be there," I said, though I hadn't even been invited yet. "Carpe diem, motherfucker."

Shelly's eyes popped, at a loss for any response. The scorching beams from the Queen of Cunt Island's eyes burned my cheeks, but I did not deign to dignify her outrage with my attention.

"Gotta go, shit to do," I announced to Shelly, and scooted out of the booth, skipping out of the deli with a jaunty step that made me smile as I thought about what it was doing to the horrid witch's blood pressure.

'Girls like me,' now meaning 'unrepentant whores.' I liked it. Refusing to let someone else's definition of my lifestyle become pejorative would become an important building block in my development into an independent woman. So thanks for that, you horrid, gold-digging heifer.

"I must not fear. Fear is the mind killer. Fear is the little-death that brings total obliteration. I will face my fear. I will permit it to pass over me and through me. And when it has gone past I will turn the inner eye to see its path. Where the fear has gone there will be nothing. Only I will remain." – *Frank Herbert, Dune*

Guys Like Me

by Matthew Broyles

Let's suppose you heard this description of a person:

43-year-old white male, raised in rural Texas, two years of community college (no degree), voted GWB for governor in 1998, father worked at a lumberyard, has one son who's homeschooled, once saw Pirates of the Mississippi at Billy Bob's, sets off fireworks in the country every July 4th.

What's your knee-jerk assessment of this person's socio-political affiliation? I'm betting it's a Baptist Republican, probably blue collar, very possibly a Trumper.

The thing is, that person described above is me. Simply by arranging pertinent facts about my history and omitting certain others, I have managed to present a raving democratic socialist musician and writer as a card-carrying member of Team Camo.

And indeed, as a white southern male, there are enough assumptions made about me when I interact with people that my way is often smoothed. If I don't give anyone reason to assume that the person presented to them isn't on their team, then it's easy enough to just figure I'm in the local majority.

There's a look that people get in their eyes when I finally deem it necessary to break out of the box they've put me in and go full weirdo. The cleverer ones have deduced it already, but more often than not there's a moment of surprise when, lo and behold, before them stands a native Texan with no church membership or red state harrumph anywhere in him. Based on their reactions, it can be quite jarring.

I've been surprised myself when my assumptions about others have been cracked. Seemingly progressive-leaning women suddenly belching forth Fox News wharrgarbl as if it were fact, sensitive musician types whipping out the Leviticus to bash gays, and horribly racist rants worthy of George Wallace from the mouths of LGBTQ community members. You never do know.

I'm often amused by the gentle conversational probing that takes place between two people to figure out just who they're dealing with. Little verbal feelers put out to test for sore spots and potential backlash nodes. The sigh of relief when they realize they've found a like-minded individual, and can dial the cloaking device back a few notches.

Much as it can jack up our public discourse, we do all have a drive to seek out members of our tribe. For a conservative living in a place like Texas, it's fairly easy. Others have to work harder at it, as I have throughout my adult life. In NYC, I was regularly alarmed by just how much racism and basic cultural ignorance exists in a city containing so much diversity. I found I couldn't make the assumptions I thought I could.

Perhaps that's best. If we always get what we expect, we become complacent. The problems arise when we believe our expectations SHOULD always be met. That everyone in our little country town SHOULD go to church and vote red. That people different than us in whatever ways, whether physical or ideological, SHOULD live in separate communities.

This thinking takes the impulse for seeking tribe to a dangerous extreme, putting the focus more on exclusion than inclusion. Get with the program or get out. I see it in the identity throes of the Democratic Party, an organization whose card I do carry, as the various litmus tests for worthiness fly in all directions, branding all factions other than one's own as the enemy, mistaking opposing ideas for malicious sabotage.

We always hear that America has never been more divided. I presume the people saying this have never read anything about the Civil War. Nations of this size will always contain a multiplicity of viewpoints. What makes or breaks a society is its ability to handle such diversity in a functional way. As Aristotle said, to entertain a point of view without necessarily accepting it.

Argument is a central feature of any advanced culture. If we cannot argue productively, then we will continue to divide up the population in terms of Guys Like Me and Guys Who Are Evil And Must Be Destroyed. That way lies barbarism, which looks very much like where we're headed if we can't accept that people who disagree with us are still human, still worthy of understanding, and probably, when you dig deep enough, more like us than we suspect.

Try this: The next time someone blurts out some Bannon fodder, don't fire back. Tell them you haven't heard that perspective before, and ask them about where they came from. What they do for a living. Where their kids go to school, what their parents did. Drill down until you find something you have in common, and build your understanding of the person from that point. That way, at least you're talking.

If we define each other only by the feverish lashings of our anger and frustration with the world, we will see only caricatures. And worse, we will become them.

o

Change Is Hard

o

Change Is Hard

by Anna Bardin

Discovering a gaping hole in one's armor is an alarming sensation. Once detected, the breeze through that weak point becomes distracting in its obviousness, and you know steps must be taken to patch it. This is easier said than done.

Towards the tail end of my college career, the weight of the wreckage strewn out behind my love life began to drag me down. In my zeal to reinvent myself as a fearless woman, I had torn through the castle like Sir Lancelot, maiming suitors and passersby alike, not to mention myself. Four years into the crusade, I began to wonder if such an approach was sustainable, and more so, whether it was desirable.

The alternative, though, or at least the only alternative I saw, frightened me. Settling down, picking a mate and sticking with them…it all sounded frightfully like my mother's path, and I was not in a mental place to put myself anywhere near her shoes.

However, a glaring pattern had slowly insinuated itself into my awareness over the past few years. It had to do with who I chose for my headlong leaps into carnal frivolity. Specifically, the fact that I usually went for the bad boys.

This wasn't all that surprising. If one wants to do bad things, one seeks out those for whom badness comes easily. Half your work is done for you, and you can just surf the wave until it crashes. But the problem with bad boys is that they drag all their bad baggage into the ring with them, and instead of making a clean getaway, I would often end up with emotional scars to show for my efforts, no matter the prior rewards.

There had to be a way to get what I wanted without inviting so much pain into my heart. To find a kinder, gentler class of lover.

However, to do this, I would first have to jettison a lot of instincts, the first of which was fierce attraction to the evil glint in a bad boy's eye. I had conditioned myself to see that spark as desirable, since it got me what I wanted. But now I also saw danger, and my impulses warred with each other when one of these specimens hove into view. In my senior year of college, I made a concerted effort to interpret that glint as a warning rather than an invitation.

With that in mind, I deliberately cast my eye around for softer faces. There were plenty of shy boys about, many of them very attractive, but I found that it was much more work to get them to make any kind of move. I struggled with this, because sure, I was perfectly capable of charging right in and making a date happen, but I also enjoyed being chased, and having to do all the heavy lifting of opening myself up to rejection was burdensome.

I found myself eyeing the bad ones again. Friggin' plug and play, so much easier. At least in the beginning, before the shit started. No, I determined, anything worth having is worth working for.

My prime target was Owen, a bookish guy with beautiful eyes who I'd only heard speak once, in class. I knew he liked me, had seen him looking. I made a point of sitting next to him before class one day, and he got all nervous when I started talking to him.

Yeesh, I thought. Come on, I ain't got all day. Ask me out already, you dithering, gorgeous putz. He didn't, and my fists balled in frustration as I knew I would have to go for it myself.

"Hey," I finally said after class. "You're taking me to dinner tonight, okay?"

It might have come out a little more confrontationally than I'd intended, judging from his wide-eyed stare at my presumption.

"O…okay…" he stammered, and I fought not to shake my head in irritation. Goddammit, grow a pair.

We did go out, and I did score with him, but the fact that I had to drive the bus bothered me, and despite him being a lovely guy, I couldn't muster up enough enthusiasm for a follow-up. He was crushed, of course, and my heart hurt, knowing that even with my reformed ways, I was going to leave a trail of carnage no matter what I did. That's love, no easy outs.

A series of bad boys followed, the last one leaving a fairly significant mark, and I re-upped my commitment to going for the good ones.

Blessedly, I met Charles, who only needed a bit of prodding before he took up the reins and inaugurated a whirlwind romance that swept me off my feet. YES, I exulted, this is what I'm talking about.

Or at least it was, until he started talking about a house and kids. Once again, I had a choice. Change my ways, and become the nice girl he was clearly looking for, or be true to myself as I knew myself, a free romantic spirit who could not be tied down by the world's expectations.

I made the choice, and it broke both our hearts. This, despite the certainty that I was making the correct choice for both of us.

Change is hard, and sometimes wrong.

So here I am, a woman in her mid-forties, unanchored by vows or progeny, and every year it gets trickier to find those men who are similarly situated, and also not evil pricks. Perhaps one day I will have to change. Either that, or I will bask in my memories of the good and the bad, and know that no matter what else happens, there are worse fates than a life of honest solitude.

Change Is Hard

by Grace Joonie Hall

Hard but inevitable. Although some change is easy. Changing my clothes is somewhat easy. Changing my mind does seem to come easier than most people appreciate. And certainly, changing other people's minds is more difficult.

I'm not crazy about this topic. When I first saw it, I thought it would be easy enough. Change is hard. We as humans tend to be creatures of habit. The Devil you know versus the one you don't, so to speak. Is that just laziness? Why are we so content to remain in situations we would be better off changing?

Perhaps it's fear of the unknown. The Devil we know. Or maybe the obstacles to change seem insurmountable. Or we don't know which direction to start. What is the first step? Do I really want to change this? What if.... so many what ifs. I want guarantees that everything is going to turn out "right" and no one gets hurt.

Change is hard. Does that mean hard versus soft? Soft being easy to land on. A nice fluffy pillow landing instead of a hard, concrete, break your back landing.

I suppose this is where I should add a personal anecdote that would tie all of this rambling together and end with some statement. I've never been one to shy away from change as long as it would bring about something new and exciting to my life. For that reason, I've moved around the country a bit; mostly out of boredom. It's been an expensive change but one I've embraced. Relationships are changes I loathe to make. Regardless of who makes them, emotional pain is usually a part of that kind of change. I have many personal stories I could share of when the change has been a blessing and when they extracted just a bit too much from my psychic soul, but I'm not comfortable doing that here on my first foray into this arena. So, suffice it to say, change is hard and good and scary and wonderful and exciting, and and and....

Maybe it's really about how we approach change. The more open we are the more positive it can be? The more fear we bring to it, the greater the negative consequences? I don't think that's true either. I think the closest truth is that it's inevitable. Much like Buddhists say pain and suffering are a part of any life.

Now look what you made me do, as TS would say. I've gone all philosophical and I'm only at 420 words! Damn you, giver of topics!

One thing for sure about change, it is inevitable. Much like the topic for next week will change and I am forever grateful. *smiles* Thanks for reading.

Change Is Hard

by Matthew Broyles

When asked to summarize the plot of his *Sandman* comic series, Neil Gaiman said, "The Lord of Dreams learns that one must change or die, and makes his decision."

Most of us have faced some version of this, from different angles depending on where we're coming from. When the long arc of our lives, shaped by our consistent behaviors, leads us to a bad place, we have to try and fix those behaviors, lest they lead to our doom.

This can be difficult when the behavior in question is considered an inherent personality trait, one that also brings benefits. An impulsive person can take advantage of surprise opportunities more readily than a cautious one, but can also get into trouble easier. Whereas the cautious person, while more stable, can find themselves painted into a corner by their reluctance to take chances.

I myself am a peculiar mix of those things. I have been impulsive and overcautious in varying degrees, and in different arenas. Money, for instance, brings out my freewheeling side, much to the chagrin of my future self who has to pay the bills. Whereas socially I am extremely cautious, forging friendships in stuttering, piecemeal steps, wary of committing to a two-way flow of companionship unless I know more precisely who I'm dealing with.

Career-wise, I have been both, although my ineptitude with money has restricted my ability to take as many chances in that realm as I would like. If the creditors are knocking, taking a year to sleep on couches and live by the seat of my pants carries greater penalties. Maybe I shouldn't be saying all this on the internet, but then, maybe keeping myself too much to myself makes me seem standoffish and inaccessible. Which, in some ways, I am, with corresponding consequences flowing out behind.

One of the greatest change-or-die tests I ever faced was when my son was little. Small children live 100% in the moment, and I didn't really realize how little time I normally spend in the moment until I was forced to reside there day in, day out. Like Luke Skywalker, my mind always drifts ahead to the far horizon, seldom bothering with the mundane details of what is actually going on around me. Bending my brain to exist second by second nearly drove me insane. I did it, but the effort took a toll, one I am still coping with years later.

And as I careen through the rapids of middle age, I find that once again I'm having to change. To think of finances not just in terms of the next few weeks, but the next few years, even decades. Oddly, for someone whose mind spends so much time in the future, incorporating fiduciary realities into that picture is awkward and unwieldy, not to mention depressing.

The deliberation can become more difficult further on down the line, when a number of changes have been made and their results can be analyzed. Maybe one turned out okay, but not as well as you wanted, or maybe it seemed good at the time, but turned out to be a mistake. Or maybe it had to happen regardless, and the consequences of not changing would have been far worse. There can never be a proper A/B comparison once one timeline evaporates and you can only inspect the one you chose.

This can lead to paralysis when dealing with new choices. A recent conversation with my shrink was illuminating:

"So, you're upset because you don't know what will happen in the future?"

"Yes."

shrug "I dunno what to tell you, man."

Exactly.

Change is hard, but deciding whether a particular change is absolutely necessary can be even harder. Especially if you will never conclusively know just how necessary it is/was. Choices which seem powerfully urgent in one moment can look silly and inconsequential in hindsight, and vice versa. How shocking the realization that what you thought was a minor decision turned out to be far more momentous than you could have known.

All of this can create either catatonia or a mad scramble for upsetting every apple cart, sometimes alternating wildly between one and the other. For those of us raised with a notion of universal connectivity, in whatever form that might take, resisting the urge to ascribe deep meaning to any setback or victory can be tricky. Sometimes an oopsie is just an oopsie. But sometimes a mistake does actually tell you something very important about yourself, and the cost of not recognizing it can be catastrophic.

The biggest changes, of course, are the ones you can't undo. The ones that shut off an entire timeline, for better or worse. School friends of mine are in prison for want of a change they could not make. Others are dead by their own hand, presumably hastening the change-or-die conclusion based on their perception of the odds. Again, not knowing the future, and making the best guess available, using the only lens they had.

True change, lasting change, means remaking yourself in a form you will not initially recognize. I have faced a transformed version of myself in the mirror before, and occasionally recoiled at the image. It still happens, and it's hard to morph those feelings of shock into acceptance. Or to know whether the discomfort at the shift should be taken as a warning sign rather than a natural reaction.

Most of us, at some point in our lives, will have to change or die. We can only hope that we recognize the choice for what it is.

o

Except for This One Time...

o

Except for This One Time…

by Anna Bardin

As referenced in this space before, I am wont to sample a wide variety of partners for pleasurable experiences. Some of these are in other relationships, some not. But always, always, ALWAYS, I have an ironclad policy of consent from any other partners with whom this person is involved. If everyone's on board, we're good. If not, the conversation is over.

I've had this policy consistently since college, and it's kept me out of trouble.

…except for this one time.

One day, I met a man named Don. 'Man' is not really an appropriate word to describe him, though. 'Adonis' is more apt. The guy was cut out of a magazine, a perfect sculpture of essential maleness, and I'm sure I wasn't the first woman to be caught staring at him. His knowing smile disarmed me, as did his relaxing voice. I swear he was a hypnotist, because by evening's end, I found myself just nodding along with pretty much everything he said.

It helped that a fair portion of his words were about me. Deftly delivered compliments that made my knees wobble with the increasing likelihood that he was as interested as I wanted him to be.

I say this in the hope that I can be forgiven for sort of deliberately neglecting to ask about his relationship status. So mesmerized was I by this impossibly beautiful face telling me impossibly wonderful things that I decided to trust him. He would tell me, surely, if he had someone already. He certainly wouldn't ask me if I wanted a glass of wine in his hotel room. Right?

Suffice it to say that wine was smoothly transubstantiated into other things, all of which were as astounding as I'd hoped they'd be. Not once did my hormones allow me to question whether any of those activities were violating another's trust in this remarkable man. So thoroughly delighted, I took the note on the bed in the morning as the normal reality of a traveling businessman:

Thank you for a lovely evening. Hope to see you next time I'm in town.

I glowed for about a week after, until a chance series of events unfolded.

Well, sort of chance. I'll admit, I got curious.

The company I worked for had a database of contacts, many of which related to the industry my recent paramour worked in. I might have run his name through the system. And

I might have pulled up his number.

Which might have had the same area code mine did.

Okay, so he wasn't traveling. I ignored the alarm bell that sounded inside my head at that revelation. Maybe this contact info was out of date. Maybe I had a co-worker call him to see. And maybe she got him on the first ring.

Well, shit. Only one lie, though. This was in the days before widespread internet use, so I couldn't Google him. But there was this handy-dandy tool called the phone book. Which had his home number listed.

Bracing myself, I called. And to my horror, a woman answered.

I hung up, and fought a flurry of chills.

No, no, no, I didn't just do that, I told myself. I didn't just sleep with a married man without his wife's consent. I did not.

Maybe it wasn't his wife, I reasoned. He could have a daughter, or live with a sister. My heart was thumping like a hammer in my head, and I had to know just how bad a person I was. Picking up the phone, I dialed again.

"Hello?" the woman's voice answered.

"Hi, Mrs. Grant?" I tried, trying not to shake with fear.

"Yes, this is her," she said, agreeably.

I'M A TERRIBLE PERSON, my brain thundered. Wait, wait…there was one chance…

"Is your husband home?" I asked, my stomach ready to drop.

"No, he's at work," she said. "Let me give you his number…"

I waited, though every second pained me. I had to know for sure. She read the digits, and I matched them with those on my company's contact list.

Oh, my god, I thought. *I am an adulteress. A homewrecker. A thing I never, ever wanted to be.*

I wanted to say something, to apologize for what I had done. I felt like a monster, some lecherous hussy out to steal the husbands of perfectly nice women who just happened to be married to lying scumbags. I loathed myself, and hung up quickly before any words could escape my throat.

Sure, it was his fault. He should have told me. But I should have asked, and I didn't. Maybe he would have lied anyway, and that would have eased the pain a bit. But I hadn't even tried. Had jumped right in without a moment's hesitation. I could blame the pheromones, human biology, the flawed institution of binary marriage, but no. This damned thing was my fault.

I carried that stone in my heart for a long time after, and it made me paranoid when I met new men. I became an adept background checker, authenticating every detail possible before any attempt at even suggesting a rendezvous.

Even today, I use trust-but-verify, never quite letting his—or her—word stand on its own. I can't afford to. Not if I want to avoid feeling the way I felt that one time.

I never saw Don again, but I've prepared speeches for him many times. They are not printable here.

But my harshest words remain reserved for myself. I can't expect good behavior from others if I can't demand it from me. Every time.

Except for This One Time...

by Cristee Cook

During 2016 and well into 2017 we've watched many artists and musicians leave the world. Epic storytellers, trendsetters, and style makers who taught us all how to be a little more cool and a lot more open-minded: Prince, David Bowie, Chris Cornell, Chuck Berry, Sam Shephard, Harry Dean Stanton, and Adam West, top the much-too-long list of losses. Each time, I've watched me news feed light up with tributes. I've listened to friends reminisce about defining moments that made this musician or artist one of their favorites. I've had empathy. But I've never related to the sensation that I somehow lost something personal to me. I've never felt like I'd lost a friend...except for this one time.

This time, it was Tom Petty who died.

Tom Petty died 21 days ago.

I can't get my thoughts clear about it.

I haven't cried.

I've listened to a Tom Petty song every day since I can remember listening to songs. I can't tell you when he showed up in my life because he's always been there. His career spanned my entire life. When I say that he's always been there for me, I mean it.

I won't regale you with tales of specific moments that one of his songs, or concerts, helped me out. It's a cliché. It's hard to explain how a person you've never actually met could be considered a friend or confidante. I can see how ridiculous that sounds as I write it. But the person that the world knew as the rock star Tom Petty...well, that guy, I think, was a solid foundation for many people. Because of his capacity for creating universal and life-affirming lyrics, and his expert delivery of good old rock and roll songs, he aided in the positive transformation of so many. This is the magic of music and Mr. Tom was a profound channel.

It's hard to explain how I feel now. Except for this one time, I can usually verbalize the internal storm.

Two days ago a friend shared a video with me of one of my favorite bands covering *Wreck Me*. It was a perfect tribute. I felt elation that someone thought to tape the moment, the pure love I have of both the band playing it and the original song, and the recognition that this is as close as I'll ever be again to Tom Petty's original spark. That even though we'll always have the 40+ years of music he left us, it doesn't sound the same now. Because without him here, our continuum has changed. And even though he always told me otherwise, nothing is actually alright anymore.

Good night, baby

sleep tight my love

may God watch over you from above

Tomorrow I'm working

what will I do

I'd be lost and lonely if not for you

So close your eyes

We're alright for now

Except for This One Time...

by Matthew Broyles

Musicians often perplex non-musicians. For people who either can't or don't pursue musical activities of their own, there is a sort of bewildered awe when they watch someone who can do a thing they haven't been able to. I have the same reaction when I watch physicists doing equations or gymnasts flipping their bodies in contorted patterns that would probably break my back.

But since music is generally regarded as a recreational activity—we 'play' music, after all, not 'work' it—people get confused when a musician doesn't really feel like performing. When I'm on vacation, for instance, I never bring a guitar. Since music has been a vocation for me to varying degrees over the years, taking the tools of my trade along on an escape from regular life is nonsensical.

As a sort of corollary to this, I find that professional musicians can have a complicated relationship with karaoke. Singing is a basic human instinct, one that has nourished our spirits for millennia. It makes total sense to have an outlet for non-professionals to sing whatever songs they want along with other people.

However, when part of your job involves singing as proficiently as possible, the idea of just jumping up in front of a backing track feels a little shabby. To me, anyway, and to some other musicians I know. I mostly keep the worlds of musicians and barroom karaoke in different mental buckets, entirely separate phenomena that are fine in their place, but probably shouldn't mix.

...except for this one time.

When I lived in NYC, I had a progression of temp jobs around town, for a wide variety of companies. One of these was a garden variety securities firm. Nothing special, except that the manager was a bit more impish than your average fiduciary exec, and hired similarly off-kilter people. I enjoyed working there, because I was less afraid of alarming anyone with my weirdness, which sticks out at times despite my best efforts to hide it in workplace scenarios.

It happened that I was there during the holiday season, and so I got an invite to the company Christmas party, held at a club not far from the office. Open bar, I figured what the hell. Upon arriving, my spine stiffened a little at the sight of a karaoke machine lurking in the corner. I'd let slip to a couple of co-workers that I was a musician, though at that time I hadn't released anything for them to listen to.

My singing voice is odd, a baritone with range limitations and quirks that I've learned to turn into advantages, but it's often not well suited for standard pop hits, which tend towards the higher spectra. Hearing people talk about cranking up the sing-alongs later in the evening filled me with dread. I'd talked about the album I was working on, and I'm sure they'd developed a picture in their head of a fairly competent singer. But I knew my limits, and feared getting thrown in front of a track I had no business singing. I made plans to escape before the foofarah got going.

Damn the people for being too damned interesting to talk to, and the wine for being too good, and my tolerance for being so low. About the time I realized I was drunk, the lights dimmed and I heard the synth-brass intro music from the karaoke machine.

Oh, crap. I was standing not ten feet away, surrounded by hooting financial services employees, similarly inebriated and clamoring for someone to get up and belt something out. Blessedly, the receptionist was feeling squirrely, and rushed to perform her favorite Spice Girls tune, to the delight of everyone. She wasn't bad, and I felt an odd sort of rush watching her: I could do that, I thought.

The compliance officer did a reasonably passable version of *The Gambler*, and I watched with interest, not ever having witnessed much karaoke in person, and certainly not done by people I knew. It was kind of fun, watching these staid office drones release their inner musical demons. I began to feel silly. If this guy was comfortable showing this side of himself to people he knew, why should I be afraid of giving them a little taste?

Surreptitiously, I browsed the song catalog, and breathed a sigh of relief at spotting Lyle Lovett. Okay, that I could do. Bucking up, I put my selection in the queue, and when the time came, the guy called me over. My heart thumped in my ear.

It was ridiculous. By then, I'd played countless gigs as a professional musician. Why was I scared of this? As the screen counted off, I took a deep breath, and launched into the opening words of *She's No Lady*, to boisterous applause. It was a respectable rendition, if I do say so myself, and whether by dint of the alcohol or the audience response, I warmed to the prospect of doing more.

My recollection of the rest of the evening is hazy, but I do have a distinct mental picture of me and at least ten other people singing *Love Rollercoaster*, a tune well out of my range, not to mention my wheelhouse. Nonetheless, it is a good memory, and a reminder of what unexpected things can happen when we make an exception now and then.

We make rules for ourselves for good reasons. But there is a time to break them. Knowing when that is and isn't can be the key to happiness.

But It's A Classic!

But It's A Classic!

by Anna Bardin

I have this friend, Sue. For years now, we've gotten together periodically with some sangria and the occasional illicit substance to watch old noir films, and every time, we have some version of the same debate.

Both of us are taken by the style and mood of films from Hollywood's golden age, particularly the way men presented themselves back then. Much as I love to see some skin, there is something undeniably sexy about a man in a finely tailored suit. Sue and I are heartily agreed on that.

What we disagree about is whether we would want to be any of the women in these films. Fashion-wise, I'm fine with all that. But my hackles do get raised to hear the presumptuous tones used to speak to women back then. We didn't have a very good deal in relationships, which tipped the power into men's hands at every turn.

Sue finds the modern empowered female shrill and unsexy, despite the fact that she sort of is one herself. None of us raised GenX can easily roll back our expectations of workplace equality and insistence upon sexual self-determination.

However, I sort of see her point at times. Watch Lauren Bacall, and see the definition of allure. Holding back, making him work for it. It's something that can get lost in a world where dates are as much about setting clear boundaries and fishing for red flags as they are about romance. Obviously there are reasons we date as we do now, but I sometimes mourn the loss of mystery.

Striving to have it all…self-assertion, playful pliability, vulnerable openness…this is the delicate modern mating dance. And the mix alters with the target. Some men crave breakability, others toughness, and women's desires vary likewise, changing sometimes by the day. There are times when I want to be overwhelmed by superior (consenting) strength, and other times when I want to be the steamroller.

For many, it can be confusing, especially since so many of us still have that classic fairy tale model in our heads of how it should be. We forget that the reason princesses were wooed in such a formal, careful manner is because their fathers held tremendous power, and could potentially send a squad to cut a suitor's goolies off. Many women in the old days were rather stuck for choice, not so much wooed as haggled with for their attentions.

And let us not forget the Vaseline on the lens. Classic films show idealized versions of humanity, just as many modern films do. Carefully staged sepia set pieces, suggestive of life but not directly reflective of it. We believe the old days were innocent because the movies made in that era omitted a lot of the ugliness. And even with that editing, honestly I see treatment of women that shocks my modern sensibilities. Lord knows what the bare truth was.

So no, thank you, I won't be pining to live in a simpler time, Cary Grant notwithstanding. I would much rather create a world in which the best defense isn't a good offense. Where love does not have to hide for fear of power.

Utopian? Maybe. But we've come a long way already. Perhaps the next golden age will be of sexual liberation for all. I very much look forward to seeing the movies about that.

But It's A Classic!

by Matthew Broyles

It happens on a fairly regular basis. I'm walking through the grocery store, or participating in a jam, or just flipping through the radio, and a song with which I have absolutely no connection cranks up. It's not necessarily that I hate the tune, but it does nothing at all for me. Yet through some labyrinthine path of pop culture happenstance, the song in question has become a Classic, and therefore inescapable.

In younger years, these tunes had achieved their status before I was born, and so I could shake my head and just blame the generation gap, even though there is seldom any correlation between a song's age and my emotional response to it.

What began to alarm me was when songs that came out during my own adulthood suddenly started becoming Classics. Like, I remembered them coming out, and going 'meh,' but nonetheless here it is playing on this bar jukebox, with people going, "Dude, Classic..." all around me.

Wait, how the hell did this third-rate piece of major label cookie-cutter slop become a goddamn Classic? I certainly wasn't consulted.

This has made me wonder about Classics of the past. Are these songs the best from a given era? Of course not. They're just the ones that were marketed better. Placed in movies and on strategic regional radio, given nice posters for the record shops.

Is that what a Classic is? Something so omnipresent that people can't imagine life without it? That seems rather grim to me, if not outright scary.

I recall the Beavis and Butthead conundrum:

"Why is this guy on the TV?"

"Because he's famous."

"But why is he famous?"

"Because he's on the TV, dumbass."

Once something becomes a Classic, you can't tell people that it's not. Any assessment of relative merit is overshadowed by its overwhelming ubiquity. This is compounded in the age of the robot DJ and the marketing pie chart, which target our lizard brains to comfort us with familiarity, softening us up for the pitch.

Now, I can say all of this, and it makes sense to me, but then I have to remember that I don't believe in objective values when it comes to art. Every time a person listens to a song, they are bringing their entire life's worth of experience to that listening. And because each of us has had a different life, of course we're going to have different responses to the song in question.

With that in mind, is my objection to the establishment of Classics simply a manifestation of the fact that I don't tend to live in the majority mindset? Perhaps these Classics have earned that designation because they accurately reflect the emotional state of the public at large.

I'm not sure about that, though. I know plenty of people who sing along to songs that they have no idea what the actual lyrics are, much less what they mean. Of course music is not a purely verbal art form, so their reactions are based as much on rhythm, melody, and aesthetic backdrop as on any meaning the author was trying to convey. If it goes thumpity-thump and you can sing it loudly when you're drunk, that may be enough to make it a Classic.

In my years of playing with a hillbilly party band, I noticed this phenomenon. Most of the time, people had no idea what we were saying on the mic, but if the chorus was catchy enough and the beat made their feet move, that was enough to make them freak out. This has been exploited by many songwriters, who load up the verses with their quirky bits, and then keep the choruses simple. I can't fault the approach, as some of those are my favorite tunes as well.

The thing that strikes me, though, is the odd mix of authoritarianism and democracy in the establishment of what is or isn't a Classic. Obviously you can't make the public like something they don't like. Not completely. Working in record stores, I saw huge marketing pushes from the labels for a tune that went absolutely nowhere, because people just didn't like it. But I've also seen damned good songs disappear into the ether because the powers that be didn't put enough muscle behind them. Seeing a finely-wrought tune fade away while a dumb paint-by-numbers production acquires Classic status makes my head explode.

The only thing that gives me a bit of hope is the occasional rise of an unexpected Classic. *Man of Constant Sorrow* comes to mind, a traditional tune that most people recognize these days, yet largely obscure prior to its inclusion in *O Brother Where Art Thou* in 2000. There does seem to be a contextual requirement for Classic status, and if the timing is missed, it can take years for something to catch in the public consciousness.

And perhaps, as with so many other aspects of living in this society, I have to resign myself to not knowing what the hell is going through most people's heads when they nod along to something that leaves me cold. Not just pop songs, but arty Classics that many of my peers insist I should like.

Maybe it goes back to that subjectivity. If we are truly listening with our honest hearts, of course we will hear things differently than those around us. We are individuals, and I believe there are different Classics for all of us, whether the floating jukebox of popular culture keeps them on regular rotation or not.

But It's A Classic!

by MC Dalet

Okay, confessions of a wayward professor: I could care less about half of the Western canon of great literature. Sure, I know the benchmarks, the major authors, and why their work is important; but I find my anthologies of English and American literature to be chock-full of pretentious, long-winded puffery to which no contemporary student ever really connects, mostly because it is also boring. There, that is now stated plainly and on the record. It probably won't land me a job in the university, but it's true.

I have faced a fair bit of taste-shaming as an academic. It does seem antithetical, really: I am a professor of humanities and English; I have a specialization in American literature; and I fucking hate Herman Melville. One of my doctoral mentors once told me that there are two texts every humanities scholar should read once a year – *Beowulf* (in the original Old English) and *Moby Dick*. I'm down with *Beowulf* (I said I could care less about half of the canon, not all of it). *Beowulf* has action, a monster, moral quandary; what is more, the text itself is a fascinating site of religious conversion. It is great fun to examine how the monks who transcribe the pagan source material attempt to Christianize it on the fly. But *Moby Dick* can suck it. I respect the attention to detail, the way that the agonizing length of the story reflects the isolation of Ahab's crew at sea and the vengeful captain's relentless pursuit of the White Whale; but I don't need to know how to whale, how to build a whaling ship, or how to slog through prose in desperate need of an editor to enjoy a good revenge tragedy. I think I'll just watch *Star Trek II: The Wrath of Khan* Guess what. . .when I assign that one, most students actually watch it so that we can actually proceed to the big money, how to analyze a story.

While I'm chucking Melville to the curb, you can take William Faulkner, Henry James, Earnest Hemmingway, most of Willa Cather (I don't discriminate based on gender), Restoration comedy wholesale (let's not forget the international picture), and James. Fenimore. Cooper. (There. I did with periods what Cooper does with commas.) I've read them all. I never will again if I can help it. This is not a rant. Each of these authors' canonized works has set up camp in the anthologies because they are good work, they brought some innovation to the art of storytelling, and they double as soft historical documents. I do not suggest we forget history. . .or these authors. . .or their work. However, I suggest that for many of them, the time has come to slide back, remain preserved as the precedent-setters for contemporary storytelling that they are, and wait for graduate students or super-avid readers to find and potentially admire them, maybe. Plenty of scholars have discussed the need to re-stock the canon so it is not so Euro-centric. That is not this discussion.

What I'm really getting at is evolution. Consciousness evolution. The evolution of storytelling; hence social evolution. Educational evolution. Our stories are more complex now. They invite more reader participation. They can be packaged in different media. Sure there are blockbuster movies and trash TV, but there are also literary films and serial dramas whose narrative intricacies outstrip even Melville's and Faulkner's passages. And we cannot expect students to love reading or to engage in literary analysis if they are bored stiff, or worse, don't read past the second chapter. Substituting *Khan* for *Moby Dick*...not really kidding about that. "But it's a classic!" Yes, it is; but it doesn't get my students excited about literature.

The curse of the academic – of all adults, but I find it most prevalent in the academy – is the imposter complex. I used to think that my obsession with teaching popular culture was just that, an obsession fueled by laziness. I used to feel like I was getting away with something, like I wasn't a "real" scholar. I'm coming around to the belief that that is poppycock. The humanities, and the study of the stories we tell are ultimately meant to empower us with the ability to understand our human condition, find our place within it, and write our own story. For this, we need to understand the conventions necessary to engage our contemporaries. Yes, as Bob Marley says, "If you know your history, then you will know where you're coming from." But I find my students are so inundated with information and narrative, that they do not know where they ARE in the present – where they belong, or often, what they authentically feel, once all the "you should"s and "you ought to think"s are stripped away. One first has to find one's self on the map before one can find where one is coming from, or where one is going.

So I chose to begin with what is present and real to them, and to me. Then and only then can we look back and discover where these stories our society tells came from. I can get from *Breaking Bad* to *Macbeth* in one move, and my students follow me. Try going the other way, and we never make it past Act I. For now, I remain on the fringes. The old guard still holds to "teaching the classics," but those same folks (noted literary scholar Stanley Fish, I'm looking at you) claim that the humanities do not need to justify their existence, an attitude that could kill the discipline that is, in my experience, vital to the survival of our species. I'd rather face the "slings and arrows" of the old guard to ensure that the next generation embraces the PRINCIPLES of humanistic inquiry than go down with Ahab's ship.

o

Art and Theft

o

Art and Theft

by Anna Bardin

I used to piss my father off a lot when we watched television together.

Well before the end of a *Columbo* or *Starsky & Hutch* episode, I had already deduced who the perpetrator was. I knew it irritated him for me to say so, but frankly I was annoyed when the protagonists took so damned long to figure out what a little kid had already spotted.

This is hilarious to me now, because of what I write. When you start reading an erotica story, you already know what's going to happen from the moment you meet the characters. I mean, duh. What makes it exciting is not knowing exactly *how* it's going to happen.

Part of why genres exist is because to a degree, many of us like a certain amount of predictability. We don't like to say that, but obviously when you pick up a book in the Mystery section, you know there will be a mystery inside. Same with Romance, Historical Fiction, etc. Within a reasonable range, we already know what's going to happen. Again, the journey is the thing.

I have many writer friends who go on about needing to reinvent fiction, challenge conventions, and defy expectations, and that's all fine. But when you read what they're writing, honestly a lot of it has already been done before. Well, of course it has. You can't communicate if nobody knows what you're talking about, so we use symbology and archetypes that people recognize in order to get our point across.

There's a reason the same plot devices and character types have been used over and over again throughout the history of storytelling. For all our technological and social advancement, we are pretty much the same species we were back in the days of *Gilgamesh*. We have jealousies, passions, weaknesses, all these cracks that writers can pry open and instantly connect with readers.

The specific details of the plots and characters change, but less so the nature of the devices themselves. Science fiction, even, is not all that far separated from the fantastical tales of gods and spirits in olden times. Our imaginations are captured by the unknown, but of course they must be anchored by the known. Feelings, motivations, explicable reasons for events to progress in a way that makes sense to us.

Writing, like other art forms, has its basis in theft. Every event we witness, every relationship we experience, every book we read, goes into the big hopper in our churning brains. The process of writing is about mixing all of those elements into a form that is both engaging and, hopefully, original. But take that last word with a giant salt tab. There is nothing truly new under the sun.

DNA combines in novel ways to create individuals totally unique in the history of humankind, yet in the macro lens, there is strikingly little that differentiates them from one another. Two eyes, one mouth, survival instincts, mating impulses, all existing within a fairly predictable range. We are different, but not that different. Is that bad? Or is it instead comforting? Part of writing is reaching out, wondering if someone else is thinking what you're thinking. Seeing if they understand you, and can relate.

We steal from the past to create the future. If a young erotica writer borrows and reshapes one of my stories, that is as it should be. I didn't invent sex, nor any of the ways to perform it. What I bring is my own combination of experiences, hopefully unique enough to capture a reader's imagination. To tickle a thought that had already existed at the edge of their awareness, teasing it out and giving it more solid form, that they can explore the idea further if they choose. But at some level, it had to already be in there, else they wouldn't have picked up my story in the first place.

There is no innocent artist. We are thieves by nature, appropriators of cultural events, observers and interpreters of others' behavior. And if we weren't, none of what we make would be worth a damn. If you don't see at least some part of yourself in a story, it means nothing to you. Art is necessary because of how it frames what we see every day. And to do that, we must steal what is around us. With no ingredients, there is no pie.

And who doesn't want pie?

Art and Theft

by Matthew Broyles

In the 11th century CE, an Italian monk named Guido d'Arezzo codified the seven-note scale system that, in modified form, is still used today in most western music. With the subsequent development of the chromatic scale, Europe was given twelve notes to play with, and using those, several centuries' worth of music has piled up.

Sometimes when I'm writing a song, I can't shake the feeling that I'm stealing it from someone. And that feeling is usually correct. The idea that I have come up with a totally unique combination of those twelve notes is preposterous, especially when building them in the framework of melodic pop music.

This used to cause me a great deal of angst. Why create something that's already been created? Innovate or go home, dangit.

But just as old symphonies can be reinterpreted by modern orchestras, so too can the notes of the past be given fresh perspective through a modern lens. *Ohio* sung by a group of African-Americans like Leon Bridges, Jon Batiste, and Gary Clark, Jr. carries an unavoidably different weight than when sung by four white guys. Not better or worse, but different.

This is why covers can be powerful. But go one further, and realize that even an original song is, at some level, a cover. Twelve notes can only be arranged in so many different ways. Old bluesmen knew this well before the dawn of the music industry copyright machine. Say what you need to say, using whatever chords feel right. Borrow 'em from that other guy and put your own story on them.

When we get worked up about musical theft, it almost invariably boils down to money. Gordon Jenkins sued Johnny Cash for *Folsom Prison Blues* not for artistic reasons, but because Cash was making bank and Jenkins wasn't. Same for Willie Dixon and Led Zeppelin. Homage is great until someone makes a mint. Then we want our piece of the pie.

People lost their minds when the sampling thing kicked in during the dawn of hip-hop. Can't they come up with their own riffs? Sure. But the tradition of reworking old riffs is as old as music itself.

Everyone knows how *Amazing Grace* goes. But that's just how it sounds now. In the old days, church lyrics were written separately from music, and at any given gathering, the song leader would indicate which words would be sung to which melody. It was only in 1835 that those lyrics got joined to a tune called *New Britain*, a melody freely available to be used on any other set of lyrics. *The Star-Spangled Banner*, likewise, was a set of lyrics attached to an old drinking song, *To Anachreon In Heaven.*

So how does a song go? Any way we say it should go. I love Chase Holfelder's YouTube channel, which converts major key songs to minor keys, because it shows the fluidity of musical interpretation. Same with Postmodern Jukebox, the kings of pop deconstruction. Music is meant to be jacked with. I get so pissed off when someone insists on a cover band playing a tune note-for-note. You want that, go listen to the goddamned record. If I'm listening to a cover, I want a twist.

This is why mash-ups are so amazing. The ease with which *Stayin' Alive* can be matched with *Back In Black* mocks our insistence that music is wholly original. Twelve notes, man. Sure, you can try to throw them together in haphazard ways and create unlistenable noise-art, but at some point there has to be a harmonic connection to draw people in. Tom Waits can toss the entire junkyard into the rhythm section, but at the center of the chaos, there's still a singable song, one that owes a debt to all those that came before.

Accepting that theft is an intrinsic component of art is difficult in our litigious age. Musicians make little enough as it is, and I know as much as anyone how rare it is to actually get real money for something you've created. I can't really blame songwriters for charging in to nab whatever portion might be theirs. But there is a grain of disingenuousness therein. The spring of music flows best when it runs unobstructed, and insisting that your combination of notes is wholly unique in the history of composition doesn't pass the odds test.

David Gilmour said that a song is only his until it's released, and then it becomes property of the masses. His lawyers have different opinions on that matter, naturally.

Still, the next time you lambaste someone for ripping off a melody or lyric, keep in mind that they are carrying on a tradition as old as music itself. Art is theft, and always has been.

○

I and We:

Community in the Age of Individualism

○

I and We: Community in the Age of Individualism

by Anna Bardin

"I" is a very important word to me.

People have called me selfish, and perhaps I am. My approach to life has been to make sure that there is never a "we" that I can't get out of easily.

Some "we"s are inevitable. Office departments, gender groups, generational cohorts... one can never be entirely "I." But when possible, it is my preferred designation.

Many see this attitude as a criticism of their life decisions. I assure you it is not. If something makes you happy, I'm the last person to try and talk you out of it. I have friends who would be miserable if they were not deeply entrenched in their "we," be it family, church, softball teams, what have you. More power to them, you do you.

So when I receive judgment from people for being single and childless, I get a bit haughty. Did I tell you not to get married and have kids? No. I attended your wedding, and bought that nice gift for your baby shower. I want you to be happy, and I guess I thought that feeling should be mutual. Bitch.

Now, don't get me wrong. I know the joy of giving yourself to someone else. I'm an erotica writer, for crying out loud. Surrender to the oneness is among the chief ingredients of sexual pleasure, and requires relinquishing the "I" for the "we." But for me, that moment is sacred on its own, and should not necessarily be lumped in with the kind of "we" that domesticity and cohabitation entails. If that component charges your batteries, fine. It freezes mine up something fierce.

I'm aware, though, that a society can't exist on "I" alone. Especially as an urban dweller, the interlocking gears of the infrastructure that makes my "I" preference easy to maintain are plain to see. I'm a cog myself, at one of those corporate entities that increasingly run our world.

Would I prefer to be a rugged individualist, dependent on no one? Probably not. I like buying clothes made by someone else. I don't want to harvest my own spinach, or slaughter my own chickens. I'm perfectly happy promoting an economy where everyone does something different, and we augment each other's lives by our specialized labor.

Yet I still chafe when someone uses the "we" word. Like, you got a mouse in your pocket? Who's "we"?

Obviously this depends on context. There is power in group action, as evidenced by the movement currently swelling against sexual abuse, driven by a collective will to punish that behavior socially and economically. If being part of that particular "we" helps to make the world a better place, then by all means, sign me up.

Maybe that's the key. Making sure that "we" is self-selected and conditional. Malleable, escapable. If membership in a "we" entails a lifetime subscription, then no thanks. But if all parties are committed to the conditionality and changeability of a "we," then let's talk.

No one is an island. But I think there is room in life where those of us who wish to occupy a tiny fjord of our own can do so without incurring the ire of those further inland. You can come visit, and we can be "we" for a while. Just remember that you are a guest, as I am in your life. "I" and "we" are playmates, not enemies. Let's party.

I and We: Community in the Age of Individualism

by Matthew Broyles

Full disclosure: I am a crappy capitalist.

I come up with at least three unprofitable ideas before breakfast, some of which become unprofitable life pursuits (this page, for example). With that in mind, it's not all that surprising that I lean towards socialism.

But there, too, we find a sticky wicket. Socialism focuses on making a cohesive unit out of many disparate parts, and the fact is that I am also crappy at being an integral part of a community. My preferred mode of operation is solo most of the time, and I chafe at having to meet others' expectations.

Sociologists and psychologists alike go on about how western culture has become one of individualism. One can quibble with that, noting how strong the pull of tribalism still is in our society, but in the main, I don't think it's outrageous to say that most Americans are much more focused on making themselves happy than they are on serving a greater good.

If we weren't, entire industries would crumble. Self-help, self-improvement, the vast creature comfort machine that caters to us, emphasizing want over need, whim over plan. Advertising slogans tell us we not only want their products, we deserve them. That is a sentiment aimed at an individual, not a collective.

Yet for all of our me-focused thoughts, a nation is still a collective. Especially an industrialized state, where labor is divided into specialties. I do know a few generalists, who can fix a car engine as well as they can mend a button or de-fragment a hard drive, but they are quite few. We are encouraged to specialize, and indeed must, as our civilization develops ever more complex technology which cannot be fathomed by a few YouTube tutorials.

This is a key struggle in the United States today. Cattle ranchers inhabit a different world than SEO analysts. Professional dancers and oil rig workers do not rub shoulders. In specializing, we lose touch with the other gears in the machine, and indeed begin wondering whether they are even necessary. A friend of mine was told that she doesn't understand the world because she's "just a piano teacher." As if these folks want to live in a world without music.

Unless we value every contribution from every corner of our diversified economy, we will see all others except ourselves as extraneous. When I play a venue, I respect the staff, because what they are doing for the music industry is just as important as what I'm doing. Plumbers, electricians, bartenders, all intrinsically necessary to create and maintain a space in which humans can have a much-needed night on the town with some nice tunes. Which, yes, are also necessary.

Now, as a pinko socialist, I'm apt to find certain professions lacking in necessity. Hedge fund managers, let's say. People whose sole function is to game capitalism for maximum individual profit. That these people have more of a voice in our government than a wastewater treatment plant employee or a park ranger is bothersome to me, and I believe the prominence of such predatory jobs is part of why we continue to place profit over sustainability, at our peril.

The subjective nature of value comes into play here. There are people with no books in their homes, just as I have no floor jack in my garage. Or even a garage. What makes some people wake up early on a Saturday makes me want to stay in bed. Likewise, what keeps me up on a Saturday night puts others to sleep. We cannot all agree on what is essential all the time. Invoke Maslow's hierarchy, maybe, but even then, you will find plenty of people who would choose artistic freedom over reliable food and shelter.

How, then, does the I become we? If we cannot reach a consensus about what is most valuable in our society, then we end up as we are now, endlessly battling over which cog to dismantle, which piece of the machine is taking up energy that could be diverted to other tasks.

It's a conundrum I feel personally when I wonder if I'm doing my part to advance the social and political causes I believe in. Every commitment to fundraising and organizing for a collective good is another several hours where I can't create the works that enable me to breathe, to feel fully human. How much trade-off is too much? That calculus shifts depending on the day, and guilt follows when the pendulum swings.

We cannot be either all individual or all communal. This is one reason communism fails, and I would posit that it is why capitalism is in such an untenable state, following through as it is to its logical conclusion. There has to be a middle way, one that satisfies both the need for self-actualization and the imperatives of collective survival. If we do not find it, then we face a future of alternating dystopias, each overthrowing the other when the weaknesses of ideological purity show their ugly faces.

We occupy a space in history that will be much examined in years to come, by descendants we may never meet. But we owe them our careful consideration of whether "I" comes before "we," and to what extent. It's a debate I have daily. Maybe if we all work on it together, in good faith, the question will answer itself.

○

Would You Rather

○

Would You Rather

by Anna Bardin

Actual drunken conversation with my friend…

Her: "Would you rather sleep with a man who voted for Trump or never have sex again?"

Me: "I thought this was supposed to be a hard question."

On the real, I will diddle myself for the rest of my days rather than let a mouth-breather get his mitts on me. Is there even a debate here?

Apparently there is. I know women with misogynist husbands and boyfriends who consider carnal contact with another human a sufficiently valuable necessity to overlook pretty much everything that comes out of their mouths. I can't imagine the activities are much good anyway, if consideration of a woman's enjoyment is that low on the guys' radar. Ladies, you're better off with a bottle of wine and a vibrator.

Thankfully, I'm not alone in this. They had to build trumpsingles.com because most of the women on the regular dating sites wouldn't touch a man who had orange spray tan around his lips from the voting booth. I'll take my fictional fantasy crushes and a magic wand, thanks.

I don't know if anyone's done research on whether sex toys have sold more than in past years, but I'd be willing to put at least a fiver on it. Guns sell more under Democratic administrations, after all. Makes sense that if women have to be ruled by crotch-grabbing orangutans, we need some damn escapism.

Blessedly, that is not the binary choice before us. In fact, these times make it rather easy to identify the good men in amongst the orcs. Increases the competition to get with them, I'll tell you what, but the relief of getting busy with a man who actually wants to make you happy is all the sweeter when it happens.

I'm not exaggerating when I say that a dude in a MAGA hat between my legs is about as sexy as a pig fart. I would honestly rather sew myself shut. I will get me to a nunnery before any hands which have brandished tiki torches in righteous white boy indignation get anywhere near my lady business. Celibacy is Disneyland compared with that.

Really, though: Fuck off, you Nazi goatfuckers.

I'm sorry, what were we talking about? Oh, yes…would you rather watch a Trumper's face contort as he expels his noxious, legally protected DNA inside your precious, government-owned sanctum, or would you rather do pretty much anything else in the universe?

This is a question?

Would You Rather

by Matthew Broyles

Would you rather be right, or win?

I keep getting asked variations on this question when I debate with fellow lefties. It's similar to the sort of thinking one has in a long-term personal relationship. There's a lot to be said for preserving the peace, and sometimes giving up a little righteousness is an acceptable price.

Let's look at that assessment for a moment. Leaving aside the question of what is right in the first place, the edge in 2016 went to the ability to induce fear rather than a sense of being right. Ask an average Drumpf voter what the man's policy positions are, and they haven't a clue. Fear of Pizzagate and the ascending power of women and minorities appears to be enough to sway them.

Of what use is sound logic when "OOO!! SCARY!!" is more effective?

So then let's ask the question again: Would you rather be right, or win?

What could those of us on the left do to leverage Americans' proclivity towards voting out of fear rather than sense? We tried the angry-man-with-nuclear-codes thing, which I would have thought was scary enough. Maybe just *saying* it doesn't do the job. Another "Daisy" ad, perhaps. We are a visual rather than verbal culture, after all.

Pictograms, then. Emojis, gifs, whatever works. Instead of refining their talking points, the DNC needs to get their graphics and videography people working on the most frightening images they can conceive. Blast those suckers all over the teevee, post 'em on FB, hell, put RT or InfoWars logos on 'em if it helps.

It feels dirty, doesn't it? Well, this is a dirty nation, with dirty congresscritters doing dirty things to their dirty constituents in their dirty towns with their dirty city councils and dirty cops hiding their dirty laundry under their dirty American flags. Maybe the inclination to stay clean is totally wrong. Maybe, like kids at the playground, a little dirt never hurt. Maybe eating worms is the way to get people to pay attention to you.

You don't think I'm serious, but I am. Possibly. Honestly, I'm not sure what it would hurt to try. They go low, we go high, and then we lose, and everything goes to shit. Would you rather be right, or win? After a year of waking up to stomach-clenching news from the swamp, I'm thinking we just find some alligators that eat Republicans rather than attempting to import some swans. They're pretty, but in the end, they're food.

We think that this is like *Revenge of the Sith*, where if you have the high ground, you can chop off the limbs of your enemies. Okay, maybe you can, but then their bosses go and build them prosthetic suits, and they end up turning you into laundry on a space station anyway.

What does it hurt to run a dirty campaign? Once you win, you can govern how you want. Doesn't have to be dirty. Save that stuff for election season.

Use all the ominous horror movie music. Jump scares, scraping violin strings, the works. Make the inauguration of the opponent look like *Saw XIII: The Hackening*. Exaggeration sells, as does fear and oversimplification. Go for it. Own it. If it seems like too much, you're probably right where you need to be.

Okay, having thought about this, I am now totally serious. I would rather win than be right. At this point in history, that is my choice. If the corollary to being right is being ruled by a deranged game show host, then I have no interest in being right. I want to win, dammit.

People talk about how liberal Hollywood is. Then let's leverage that shit. Stephen King, go. Guillermo del Toro, have at it. Turn 'em all loose, every horror director and CGI'd blood-dripping fang. Just go for it. What the hell do we have to lose? We've tried being right. It sucks. Freakin' Liam Neeson the bastards. Do not stop until you have scared the pants off of every voter, until they clutch their ballots with trembling hands, desperate to escape the bone-crackling carnage that awaits them the second they pull that red lever.

Would you rather be right, or win? I know my answer now. Let the cartoon blood flow.

○

These Kids Today

○

These Kids Today

by Anna Bardin

I like 'em.

Except the ones I don't.

Now, if you'll excuse me, I have to get my old lady nap...

These Kids Today

by Matthew Broyles

My son frowned at me the other day. He does that a lot, but this time it was because I told him that when I was a kid, the worst thing you could be called was gay.

"What's wrong with being gay?" he asked, quite reasonably, as many in his age group do when confronted with homophobia from their elders.

So when I hear people my age and older talk about how the young people have no respect anymore, I have to ask: Respect for whom?

My recollection, at least from my vantage point in a small Texas town in the 1980s, is that the only people who got respect were football players and coaches, and the rich. Who were all white. And of course there weren't any gay football players. Right?

The culture I grew up in was built on disrespect. Disrespect for Native American homelands, disrespect for non-Christians, disrespect for women's opinions, disrespect for immigrants, disrespect for intellectuals, disrespect for foreigners, and certainly disrespect for the damned homosexicans.

Our society is not based on respect. It is based on obedience and conformity.

When we see all the chaos and upheaval amongst the modern straight white man—and as a modern straight white man I see a hell of a lot of it—we must understand that it is happening because PEOPLE AREN'T OBEYING.

Gays aren't ashamed of being gay. African-Americans aren't ashamed of being African-American. Feminists aren't ashamed of being feminists. What the hell is going on? Does no one have respect anymore?

I hear people complain that the young people are rude to them, and the first thing I think is, well, what did you do to piss them off? Did a casual racist remark escape your lips? Did you eye them with suspicion because of their smooth faces and apparent lack of concern about impressing you?

Because I don't have these experiences. I talk with young people all the time, and I find them to be far more open-minded and less reflexively judgmental than my age cohort was when we were young. Xers were the lords of disdain. To hear a fellow Xer complain about young people being snarky and rude is like hearing Pepe Le Pew complain about a foul smell.

Maybe I'm sheltered, but I'm not seeing this great groundswell of rudeness among the youth. I'm just not. What I do see are sneering Boomers with MAGA hats calling for the banning of everything and Xer parents shouting down referees at little league games.

Watch some videos of the Civil Rights era, or the way men casually bossed women around in old movies, and tell me people had more respect then. What people had was fear. Fear of breaking harshly enforced social norms, lest they become ostracized and possibly killed.

I certainly had fear. How quickly the whole crowd would turn on you if you liked the wrong person, or even the wrong band. The eggshells were paper thin. When we talk about safe spaces, we have to ask, safe from whom? I know exactly whom. The assholes. Who, by the way, were just elected to run our country.

It isn't Millennials who gave us Drumpf. It's old people with no respect. No respect for different lifestyles, no respect for unfortunate life circumstances, no respect for women's veracity, no respect for the environment, and certainly no respect for the young, who will inherit the blasted morass the old farts leave behind.

Talk to me about how the older generation has respect, when over half of them elect a boastful, misogynistic racist with no conception of history or international policy. Tell me how disrespectful the younger people are, when they voted in huge numbers for the first African-American president, and tried to elect the first woman chief executive

When I look at my son, now twelve years old, I see a person with far more tolerance and respect for the vast panoply of humankind than even I have. And when I worry about his future, it's not his actions I worry about.

It's ours.

○

This Is Your Brain on Social Media

○

This Is Your Brain on Social Media

by Anna Bardin

I was sitting in my doctor's waiting room last week, scrolling through my various social media feeds, when the Low Battery alarm chirped, showing only 10% left. I cursed, knowing I needed to have my phone active for the next few hours until I got home, so I stowed the device and stared at the ugly mass-produced Parisian café paintings on the walls.

Trapped there in what seemed like a never-ending morass of boredom, I thought to myself: What did I do in these situations before social media?

Oddly, it took me a while to answer that question. I've only been on Twitter and Facebook since 2008, and on sites like Tumblr less than that, but the dividing line between pre- and post-social media Anna feels like BC/AD. It really feels like something fundamental has changed in my brain ever since I started being able to have constant access to a never-ending stream of opinion, humor, news, and entertainment 24/7.

Friends have done the whole internet detox thing, going a week or more without checking their feeds, and while that seems to make a sort of psychological sense, I honestly don't know how I would do it. That's odd, because honestly, when I get home most nights, I spend far more time reading and writing books than checking my fidget clicker.

But maybe that's the thing. Social media is not a conscious, full-attention activity, but rather a boredom reliever. I'm on there way more when I'm killing time than when I actually have things to do, but looking at the amount of time I spend on there makes me realize just how much time I have to kill each day.

Meetings come and go, tasks get done, chores dispatched, but in the spaces between, internet. What filled those spaces before? I honestly have a hard time remembering.

I know I daydreamed a lot. Still do, but maybe it's more augmented now, with thoughts from others mixed in amongst my own. I used to carry a notepad around, to sketch story ideas or reflections on events. Those things have outlets now, through publishing and the big broadcasting engine of the online social salon. Maybe I have made the internal external.

If that is so, what do I think about it? She asked, to a virtual room full of readers from around the world. It's nice, that part, knowing that anyone could read my words and relate. I remember finding out that emails I'd written to friends had gotten forwarded to others back in the day, and being pleased that they meant enough to be passed on.

We want to share. It's a human impulse, to extract the insides of your head and show them to others, asking, 'do you have this part in there, too?' Finding out that you're not alone in your neuroses is a wonderful thing.

But then we have the dark side. Addiction, compulsion, jealousy. Wondering why this post only got one like, when that other one by your friend got a hundred. Sorting out the bizarre demographics of online celebrity. Why does this person have the blue check mark? Why does their hot take count more than mine? It's junior high, but global.

When I post something I'm particularly proud of, I admit hitting the refresh like a lab rat, waiting for my reward, the flood of approval, and being disappointed when it doesn't arrive in the quantities I'd envisioned.

The difference between that and book sales is the time horizon. I don't expect to know right away if one of my books is selling well, since retail data takes weeks to wind its way through the system. So I don't wait with bated breath, clutching my phone, jonesing the high. By the time I actually get a ping from the Amazon gods saying that people have bought my work, I've kind of forgotten I was waiting for it, so it comes as a pleasant surprise.

Perhaps that's the crux. The sense of instant gratification. So we're back to Buddha, reminding us that the higher our expectations, the more often we will be let down. When we stop believing the internet is supposed to provide daily rewards, we stop being sad when it doesn't.

So what to do with those idle moments, the ones that feed the giant social media machine? Save my mocking of shitty doctor's office art for my own amusement, storing it up for use at the next party? Obsessing over plot details until I stop liking the story anymore? What do we do in the moments when we're not doing anything?

It could be said that what we do in those moments helps to define us. And if social media is any indication of our collective psyche, we are an anxious lot. Can't blame us, really, unless the instability of that mass intelligence is how we got here in the first place.

Maybe if we put down the phone and let the silence speak, we will hear ourselves more clearly. Whether we like what we find is another discussion. One better had with a shrink than with the world at large.

This Is Your Brain on Social Media

by Matthew Broyles

It's happening more often.

I'll post something political (who, me?), and the comment thread begins to fill. Since I've pretty much alienated most of my card-carrying GOPers by now, the resulting discussion is largely commiseration and harrumphing, along with some often incisive analysis of why the thing is why it is.

But then it appears: The fracture line.

It could be anything; a Berniac reference, a casual generational snipe, a regional generalization, but within moments, ALL OUT WAR has erupted.

And I'm not talking about disagreement. I mean name-calling, blame-throwing, stuff you would say to someone who stole your kid's lunch money. I've seen it between people who I know for a fact are both gentle, considerate individuals. But in the garish, cartoon world of social media, the person they are talking to has somehow become the antichrist.

Over what? Usually not very much, at least in my estimation. At least nothing worth GOING ALL CAPS about, since nominally, these folks are on the same side of the culture wars. But we all know that the worst kind of war is a civil war, and some of the ugliest rancor I've seen in recent years is not between right and left, but between left and left.

I believe that social media, which gives us a square av and brief bio with which to represent ourselves to the entire world, has made us see other humans as little more than their online profiles.

Further, I believe that the proliferation of bots and astroturfing accounts to play merry hob with our elections and social discourse has made us cynical about interacting with people we don't know online.

Additionally, the retweeting and forwarding of memes and talking points makes us immediately categorize everyone who uses one of these ready-made arguments on the spot. It makes us believe we have argued with this exact person before, and, weary from the last argument, we cut straight to the fed-up spiel, not giving the discussion a chance to naturally escalate to that, if it were going to.

I've done it myself. When the libertarian goon squads descend to tell me that taxation is theft and the like, my brain immediately flashes back to the hours upon hours of discussions I've had with libertarian friends, many of whom no longer wave that flag. Worn out by the prospect of repeating so much work to state my piece to the latest Rand convert, I jump straight to irritation. But of course this person is not the same person as the last one I debated, and will have a different set of whys and what ifs to nail down. It makes me tired to think about embarking down that path again, so I don't.

It could be said that I'm making the problem worse by passing on easily-digested nuggets of liberalia, adding to the repetition of arguments that some faction or another finds objectionable, so that when discussion does at last occur, the tone is more of retaliation than debate.

Yet one of the only things that keeps people sane is the confirmation that we are not the only ones. That someone else sees how bizarre or self-evident something is, and that we're not just taking crazy pills. At its best, social media connects like-minded people in dark times.

At its worst, though, it distills those people into caricatures of their beliefs. When I get a Friend request, the first thing I do is go through their profile, looking for telltales. Overly simplistic memes forwarded, masturbatory outrage groups joined, long-paragraphed posts cut and pasted from the traditional culprits…I'm looking for bots, for zombies, for the only clues I have in this environment to tell me who the hell this person is anyway.

The one thing I don't do is talk to them. This is a problem built into the platform. When you meet someone at a party, and you think they might be a fellow traveler, you can probe with questions and jokes, gauging response. This is not easily doable in the social media sphere, where everything you know about the person is based on the face they have presented for public digestion.

I've never done the online dating thing, but if it's anything like choosing whether or not to Friend or Follow someone, anxiety is built in. You don't want to look down at your phone, as I have done on occasion, and find out that a godawful verbal melee has broken out in your comment thread while you were away, because that person who seemed reasonable enough in their profile is actually mad as hell at a general demographic represented by one of your other friends.

Even in the midst of these conflagrations, I get the sense that if we were all in the room together having the same discussion, the knives wouldn't come out. Or if they did, they would be considerably less long and stabby. So much valuable interpersonal information is lost in the digital transfer. We don't feel like we're talking to another person, only a boxy manifestation of whatever's sticking in our craw at that moment.

I don't know the solution. But knowing the problem can be useful. I have deleted many angry responses to people I didn't know, because I realized a key fact: I don't know them. With that in mind, perhaps saving the big guns for people you know is the best practice.

This Is Your Brain on Social Media

by MC Dalet

Two things are true of technology: it is both highly mechanistic and fallibly human. Our technologies take a lot of blame. I have cast such blame myself. "Technology has made us stupid, reactive, and lazy," the argument goes; but the very nature of technology – what it is – is a series of inventions that enable human beings to augment and expand our natural abilities. I would say "transcend our natural abilities," but I'm not sure our consciousness will allow that just yet. But expansion and augmentation, certainly. Cars propel us through space much faster than we can run or ride on horseback. Word processors allow us to compose, revise, edit, and share documents much faster than working on a typewriter. Trust me, I'm old enough to know. The Internet and digital tools allow us to disseminate those documents, and to access all kinds of information much faster than the most adept library researcher using a card catalogue and microfilm.

It stands to reason, then, that our technologies also amplify and augment such human tendencies as confirmation bias, foolhardiness, and sloth. We are social beings, yes. We are human beings. So it follows that the technology of social media has the ability to bring out the best and the worst of our social habits. We humans are also a kind of elegant machine, our brain the motherboard; and embedded in our genetic CPU are many pieces of outdated software. The most prevalent of these, as far as I can see, is the tribalism program – the tendency to cleave to bias and stand in violent defense against anything "other."

The great irony is that, while the Internet (and social media as its sub-set) allows us the ability to chip away at our divisive tribal instincts because of the sheer amount of information, opinion, and experience available to us in the global frontier of digital space, the algorithms that govern the operation of social media specifically are designed to filter out diversity in favor of previously held preferences. While the brain on social media may be open to infinite possibilities, we are delivered a finite spectrum from which to choose. And our tribal program, it seems, prefers it that way.

Make no mistake, we cannot blame technology for our shortcomings because, even as users, we are complicit in programming "The System." We engage advanced external technology using our outdated internal, and very human, software. In all social media platforms, we are given the opportunity to show preference. Whether a "like" a "love" or a swipe, when our preference is given, it creates a quantum split, a new social media reality. The formulae designed with tribalism in mind, narrow and collapse possibilities even within the already narrow spectrum of "like-minded" content based upon quantitative information, key words, and previous associations. If we are passive, our brains on social media can default to the quantitative, and to the simplest interpretation of language, the likes of Orwellian Newspeak.

But human beings are not quantitative. We have emotions and are capable of making choices. And language is complex and subject to figurative use. Often it is the non-logical choice or the resonance of a poetically rendered phrase or lyric that opens the pathway to personal growth. We have the choice not to indicate preference based on our tribal predispositions, but rather upon the desire to learn more about where others speak from, even if we will never agree with their positions. . .or their key words. Sometimes just knowing whom you are confronting creates a more peaceful conversation. Perhaps seeing beyond the artifice of basic language and quantifiable identifiers would demonstrate that, deep down, we all have pretty much the same seed-level desires. We can, should we so choose, use our organic brain to reprogram our social media experience. Once one is aware of the Matrix, one can better navigate, and even influence, it. I could play trickster, showing "preference" for a variety of viewpoints so that my view of the world is not so digitally myopic.

But our judgements.

Here again is the idea that technology amplifies what is already present. Here again is social pressure. In both worlds – digital and flesh – we are so socio-politically polarized that I risk being absolutely ostracized by my liberal cohorts should I "like" a conservative post or publication, whether or not my motivation is guided by the liberally championed ideal of open-mindedness and critical research. Heavens knows that I risk abuse every time I try to engage my differently-minded acquaintances in what I hope will be a civil conversation about current issues and concerns. I was a weird kid in a small town. I took my share of teasing in middle and high school; but the verbal bullying I've encountered on Facebook puts it to shame. It's rarely from the friend with whom I initially engage, but from their friends. Tribalism. And I have yet to be defended by my real-world friend when the discussion goes south. So now, my social anxiety is amplified and augmented in digital society. How will I be judged? Can I stand the slings and arrows? So I end up posting pictures of my kids doing cute things and leave it at that. The irony: a platform that it seems emboldens most makes more of a recluse of me. But that's reactive. And probably laziness, amplified and augmented.

Perhaps it is important to prepare our brains. . .and our courage. . .and our hope – all of the things worth amplifying – FOR social media. What can we inject INTO the program, the System, that will actually improve it, and us? Digital space actually provides the incredible opportunity to have an observer/participant experience. Social media archives conversations that we can, with some distance, look back on and learn about ourselves in order to avoid future pitfalls. Your brain is in your head, not in the machine. The only way the digital can control good old-fashioned synapses is if we allow it. Once we pre-prepare our consciousness, then we might be able to transcend our current state.

o

How Do You Sleep?

o

How Do You Sleep?

by Anna Bardin

If there's one thing that unites my generation (the one that ends in X), it's sleep deprivation. Left or right, male or female, at some point every one of us will post something online about how we need more sleep.

One could put this down to being in a very busy time of our lives, what with career responsibilities, care for aging relatives and kids, and just learning how to stop acting like teenagers and go to bed on time, for pete's sake. And that wouldn't be inaccurate.

But I don't think that's the whole story.

I'm doing the things I'm supposed to do. I have a solid office job, a 401k, and stay out of debt as much as possible. Yet as I close in on my fifth decade, I find myself lying awake in bed at night, wondering what the hell I'm going to do when I reach what was formerly known as retirement age.

Like a lot of people, my ostensible nest egg got routed in '08, and a lot of the institutional problems that caused that crash are still in play. Another financial crisis is a matter of when, not if, and on our current trajectory, it will hit before I reach sixty-five. And if the P-grabber-in-chief is still at the helm, there's a good chance that unlike 2008, the calamity will stretch out much longer, potentially devastating my investments and even threatening my employment.

People in my cohort talk a lot about living in the moment, and it's easy to see why. Because we honestly don't know how we will survive into our dotage. Especially those of us without children, who are unlikely to have a spare room to crash in once our funds run out. Social Security will be dead and gone by then, that's clear at this point. Rather than wait to die in a poor house, I would honestly rather take a bottle of pills and get it over with.

This is not the sort of decision I ever dreamed of contemplating. As a kid, I figured I would slow down like my grandparents, settling into the steady rhythms of old age, not rich, but relatively comfortable. Now I see only horror. Illnesses blossoming into unpayable debt, safety nets gone, no home, no food, no income, only suffering.

It keeps me the hell awake.

Make more money, the teapublicans exhort, then you won't have to worry. So I look at the boss' office down the hall, and see her hair falling out from stress. Though she makes more than I do, her position in life is only a little more secure than mine, and her health is a wreck from being at work all damn day and night. I suppose if I want to hasten my death, that's a quick way to do it.

Not everyone can make a lot of money. We've seen to that, capping the salaries of teachers and other professions that aren't directly wired into the big speculation machine that is our modern economy. What of the rest of us? Go find a corner and die, says Paul Ryan with a s**t-eating grin on my TV. More room for the job creators, creating jobs from which no one can escape, except through death.

This is the world I wake up in every day, and the one which hovers menacingly over me as I try and sleep. What peace can be found in such a hellscape?

You want to know why I spend my time having lots of sex and writing about same? Well, firstly, because it's awesome, but against such a bleak backdrop of falling empires and pillaging monsters, it is the only joy left to me. Heavens help me the day that avenue of relief dries up.

Sleep if you can, while you can. It's not going to get any easier.

How Do You Sleep?
by Matthew Broyles

Chess teaches you many things. Especially when you play it with your children.

I've never been a competitive person. I'm one of those people that gets complained about, who wants everyone to win, to feel like they should be proud as long as they've done their best.

My son is not one of those people.

"Dad, in this world, there are winners and losers," he tells me one night after I beat him in a very close game. "And tonight, I'm a loser."

It tore my heart out, hearing him say that. I tried to convince him that losing a game was a tiny thing, a learning experience to help him become better, an exercise in dealing with adversity, yaddah yaddah. All he knew was that he lost, and that made him a loser.

I've devoted entire podcast series, songs, and thinkpieces to the idea that I don't believe in binary victory and loss. Failure is a verb, not a noun. We fail, but we do not become failure. I thought I had inculcated my only son with this wisdom, but he's been resistant to such notions.

Thinking back, I know there were things my parents tried to teach me that I didn't accept for one reason or another, usually because they didn't match with my experience of life. With that in mind, I look around at the world in which my kid is growing up, and it all becomes clear.

On the news, stories of greed, and of futile resistance to the might of money and power. The rich richer, the poor poorer. We are led by a real-life Gordon Gekko, the ultimate manifestation of domination for its own sake, defined by the only metric our society seems to reward, economic victory at all costs.

Morality is tossed into the bin on the rough climb to success, evidenced by the avalanche of revelations about our most prominent celebrities. We talk pretty words about being a good person, and watch good people get fed to the wolves for their efforts.

In such a world, who wants to run the risk of losing?

But I have to ask: How do you sleep?

When you've ruined the lives of innocents, laid waste to others' hopes and dreams, and stamped the faces of strangers simply because it gained you another few bucks…how the hell do you go to bed and not wake up in a cold sweat from the nightmare of what you are?

It's not in me. Even if I saw the wisdom in playing the game of late-stage capitalism by its inbuilt rules, I would go fetal the moment I realized that some scheme I perpetrated hurt an innocent bystander. Maybe that makes me weak. It certainly makes me vulnerable.

Perhaps my son sees that vulnerability, and fears it for perfectly understandable reasons. He hears me talk about how hard it is to fight the moneyed powers that be, and observes the reality of it every day. The kid is smart. Why wouldn't he want to be in a better position to resist the cold winds of economic and political reality, blasting through the cracks in the edifice of our civilization with increasing ferocity?

And maybe that's advantageous to me, too. I'm not getting any younger. If the kid's financial footing is as precarious as his dad's always has been, in whose attic will I stay when unforeseen calamity strikes? Perhaps I need him to be a better capitalist than me. Maybe he's right, and I'm wrong.

I know, I know, the kid is only twelve, and far from fully developed. But his head for pragmatism has always been stronger than mine, so I think economic realism stands a good chance of being part of his permanent makeup. And by itself, that's fine.

What I worry about is collateral damage. I don't begrudge anyone the ability to make money, so long as harming others is not an intrinsic part of the business plan, which it seems to be for most of our corporate overlords. It's this aspect of the binary win/loss equation that haunts me, and I hope it bothers him, too.

The boy beat me in Candyland a few nights ago. I mentioned that I didn't feel too bad about that loss, because the victor is chosen by the randomness of the cards, not strategy.

"It doesn't matter whether it's your fault or not," he reminded me. "When you lose, you lose."

I argued with that assessment, but honestly, my heart wasn't in it. He's not entirely wrong.

Knowing that, how do I sleep?

How Do You Sleep?

by MC Dalet

How do you sleep when I do not?
How do you sleep,
knowing you have conned your way to power,
abusing and exploiting ignorance,
while I dare not,
clinging to my credibility,
fearful your disregard for the American student will destroy my livelihood
in the liberal arts
and rob my children of a viable public schooling?

How do you sleep?

How do you sleep
while I pace my kitchen floor,
opening bare cupboards at 2 in the morning,
hoping each time
a miracle morsel will appear
to appease the angry emptiness of my growling gut
while you pick my pocket
with 500 pages
to pile more privilege upon those whose pantries bulge with name-brand multi-packs
more likely to reach expiration than consumption?

How do you sleep,
knowing that the only food I can afford to feed my children is
so far from organic
it's practically plastic?

How do you sleep?

How do you sleep. . .
how the fuck do you rest
after pushing US
to the brink of nuclear annihilation
to feed your Twittering ego,
while I wake, wide-eyed,

to be living under an apocalyptic threat
I was certain was decades departed?

How do you sleep,
knowing my children
-- and yours –
know a danger we swore they'd never face?

How do you sleep?

How do you sleep,
peddling pedophilia
while I wakefully watch over my daughter
while she sleeps,
praying she never knows
the horrors you endorse for vengeful votes,
begging that she never has to mark herself with a hashtag,
sobbing silently
(as not to disturb her still-innocent sleep)
at the very thought?

How do you sleep?

How do you sleep,
while I watch
woefully
out my window
wondering if those flashing lights at 3 AM
are coming to kill my black neighbor
or flog the father of my daughter's best friend
in the feudal fight
to make America white again?

How do you sleep?

How do you sleep
while Nazis march on American streets,
guns fire,
ruffians rule,

California burns,
refugees cry for human dignity,
oil spills,
bots bully,
enemies threaten the gates from within,
and the most patriotic people I know
suffer incurable insomnia,
incapable of comprehending
a country under callous control?

How?

How do you sleep
while I write this,
red-eyed,
wondering how I can possibly tell my son
to have faith in democracy,
in decency,
in a nation that allows you to get one bloody wink of repose
while you divide us
in some maniacal meiosis
until I am divided against myself?

How do YOU sleep?

I can't.

Not anymore.

When dreams are gone, what good is there in sleeping?

o

Happy Holidays

o

.

Happy Holidays

by Anna Bardin

Like most people, I have a lot of holiday memories. Most of the time they blend together, a supercut of feelings both warm and awkward, running consecutively, blurring into a general sigh of contentment.

One memory, though, stands out.

My father died in the spring of 1992. The previous Christmas, he had been sick, but we didn't know the extent of it at the time. Getting through my last semester of high school and first semester of college with a gaping, Dad-shaped hole in my heart was one of the hardest things I've ever done. By the time we all convened at my grandfather's house for Christmas in 1992, I was exhausted, both physically and emotionally.

I'd driven all day from north Texas to rural western Arkansas, chugging coffee and popping uppers to keep myself awake. I hadn't gotten a full night's sleep the whole year, and the makeup required to conceal the dark circles under my eyes was getting expensive. Pulling into Grandpa's driveway, I could think of nothing but sneaking in through the back door and going to the guest room to sleep for a week.

But of course everyone else was already there, and hearing me drive up, they emerged from the house with the traditional greetings. Spending four months away from my brothers had helped dispel the old tension between us, and they seemed legitimately glad to see me. My mom, even, was not as crazy as she had been earlier in the year, despite her continual clinging to fundamentalism in a desperate bid to give meaning to her husband's passing. Aunts, uncles, and cousins were on their good behavior. It was all very nice.

Until we tried to eat dinner.

As soon as I saw the long table, with the same number of place settings as usual, I began to feel anxious. Would someone try to sit in Dad's chair? I had been at the kids' table all my life, but now there was a vacancy. What if my older brother tried to graduate to the big table? I felt a stirring of rage at the thought. Not because I wanted the spot, but because it smacked of opportunism. I don't know why I felt that, he was just as devastated by Dad's demise as I was. But I was still mad at the universe for taking my father, and everyone seemed complicit in the whole damned scheme.

I could have talked to Tommy about it, let him know that it was bothering me, but I kept it squashed inside, simmering.

At last, we gathered around, holding hands in a circle as Grandpa gave the blessing. Though not religious, something about our patriarch's invocation of the divine in that room always felt comforting, and it eased my anxiety a little. This was normal. Maybe it would be all right.

But no sooner had we said "Amen" than my mother, the goddamned widow herself, suggested that Tommy sit next to her at the adults' table.

Competing impulses shot through my blood. I simultaneously wanted to punch my mom in the face and collapse into a heap on the floor. Some part of me knew that the first option was unreasonable, not least because I had never struck my mother in my entire life. So my quivering body took the second choice, and I burst into a full, racking sob, my eyes welling up as I backed against the wall, knees threatening to buckle under me.

Everyone stared in horror as I completely lost my shit in front of the whole extended family. Thank goodness for my younger brother Richard, who held me upright, keeping me from dissolving into a pool of tears on the floor. It was an ugly cry, dignity thrown right out the window, and I had no choice but to let it take me. I had cried so much that year, but this felt like all of those times put together. Somehow my late father's seat at the Christmas table was the last thread keeping my old world intact, and now it had been severed.

Richard walked me to the living room and sat me down on the couch, where I soaked his shoulder, weeping uncontrollably, holding onto my former rival for Dad's attention. My sorrow was infectious, and he began to cry, too, although more manfully, staying solid and strong for me.

"It's okay, Anna," he kept saying, rocking me back and forth. "It's okay…"

It wasn't okay, and he knew it. But those were the only words he could manage, faced with his inconsolable sister who had just ruined Christmas dinner for everyone.

After a while, I heard the sounds of normal weather conversation emanating from the dining room, and I knew they had moved on. Then I got mad.

"How the FUCK are they eating dinner right now?" I asked, less to Richard than to the universe.

How was anyone doing anything normal? THIS WAS NOT NORMAL. It pissed me off further than Mom hadn't even come in to check on me. Was she glad he was dead? Deep down, I knew that wasn't the case, but my mind was unmoored from reality, just as this moment was. NOTHING IS NORMAL ANYMORE. WHY CAN'T THEY SEE THAT?

After another long cry, I finally felt some semblance of control return to my body. Then shame kicked in. I felt guilty for keeping Richard from eating, and told him so. He shook his head, looking at me like I was stupid for saying that, and I had to laugh. The shift was instantaneous, and while I was still sad, the familiar condescension from my brother warmed my heart. Okay, maybe some things were still normal.

I didn't eat anything, retiring quietly to the back bedroom to compose myself for an hour or so. A while later, I heard a gentle knock on the door. Opening it, I smiled to see Grandpa holding a plate of food for me. I nearly broke down again at the sight, but I was cried out at that point, and accepted the food gratefully, sitting on the little wicker chair as he sat on the bed opposite me. After a long moment, he spoke up.

"I was going to give this to Tommy," he said, reaching into his pocket. "But I think it would mean more to you."

Grandpa produced a small, battered pocketknife, one I recognized. Dad had replaced it long ago with a fancier one, but Grandpa had kept the old one in the utility drawer. It bore Dad's initials, carved presumably with another knife. He held the knife out to me with a sort of reverence, and I took a deep breath. I could tell it was important to him, this gift, and I swallowed all protests as I took the wood and metal memento into my palm. It was light, an insubstantial and rusty old thing, but at that moment it looked like Excalibur.

I don't know why I didn't cry again as I held it. Maybe Grandpa's stoic formality made me buck up inside, to want to be worthy of such an honor. I felt suddenly stronger, as if some of Dad's life essence still remained in the old blade, seeping into me the longer I gripped it.

"Thank you," I said, voice steady and sincere. "I'll keep it safe."

Grandpa nodded, a knowing smile spreading across his wrinkled face. Without another word, he rose and closed the door behind him as he left me to eat in peace.

With the first bit of disposable income I earned after graduating college, I bought a frame to put that pocketknife in. It still hangs on my wall, and from time to time I take it out, feeling the nubbly wood and the indentations my dear departed dad inscribed it with when he was just a kid.

Christmas is no longer sad for me. While relations with my family are often strained, I feel as if we understand one another. In exposing my barest self to them that day, I said all I needed to say.

Happy Holidays, and may honesty fill your heart this season.

Happy Holidays

by Matthew Broyles

Humans seem to have a need for certain days to be special.

We go about our daily rounds with dogged determination, but every so often we require a day to not be like the others. It's part of why we have weekends, though the gobbling maw of late-stage capitalism has eaten away at those to a large degree. But at appointed times of year, even the moneygrubbers have to slow their roll for a few hours.

For some, these respites are not restful, triggering anxieties about holidays gone by and apprehension about being in the same room with hated relatives. For others, it is the closest they feel to loved ones, free from the grind that too often gets in the way of meaningful human interaction.

Personally, it's an opportunity for me to compare and contrast. Since I have spent almost every Christmas of my life in both my grandmother's and parents' houses, the occasion cannot help but recall past Christmases. The kids' table that was once my domain, now given over to the grandkids. The shrinking adult table as attrition thins the ranks. The subtle changes of faces and expressions through the long years of struggle and triumph.

Sometimes it's a very sad comparison. Remembering the naïve idealism I possessed at holiday gatherings in my twenties, and contrasting it with the more grounded sarcasm that I and my cousins now employ. I hear the new generation's excited babble from the living room, and part of me cringes, waiting for time to dull their enthusiasm for life. Another part, however, hopes that their energy and insight will push them higher than we could go.

My early memories of Christmas are of middle-aged conversations about topics I cared nothing about, absorbed as I was with whatever new shiny things had been unearthed from beneath the tree. Adult voices, seemingly knowledgeable about the larger world that existed above the heads of us kids.

With alarm, I realize that I am the age that those people were then. Did they feel as unqualified to navigate the crashing rapids of adulthood as I do? Were they making it up as they went along, as I have? Over the years, as I grew older, I got more details about their lives, and knowing what I do now, it's fairly obvious that they were bumbling through as best they could. Maybe that's all anyone ever does.

It makes me wonder about future Christmases. My son and his cousins, grown up, recalling with laughter some quirk of mine or of my siblings. Will I be there? Will we all? Impossible to say from this vantage point. Entropy never stops, and you never know who's next in its path.

I remember thinking about this at a relatively early age: The kids meet at their parents' house until the parents die, then the grandkids meet at the kids' house until those parents die…there is a constant splintering of old family units into new ones. When my paternal grandparents died, I saw one of my Christmases dissolve, replaced with a bunch of new ones that didn't involve me directly. The same will happen when fate finally catches up with my 99-year-old maternal grandmother, and thence to my parents.

Logically, it would seem then that at some point, elderly Matthew would be at the focal point of a family node. But with one child, that feels odd. Especially when I have cousins who do not have children at all. Maybe some novel form of family agglomeration will arise, a collection of people with no direct ancestor present to head it up.

Indeed, I see friends whose family are either dead or estranged, forging their own holiday traditions with other friends. This makes sense, as in the United States, only 55% of adults are married. And an increasing number of them don't have children. The traditional composition of a holiday gathering is bound to change accordingly.

Perhaps I'm already behind the curve on this, having been raised in a still-intact nuclear family descended from generations of same. Would a Christmas get-together of friends minus family feel the same to me? I may as well ask if a holiday held somewhere other than the two houses in which I still celebrate those traditions would feel different. Obviously it would. And inevitably, it's going to happen.

Just like assuming that everyone should be wished a Merry Christmas, family-centric views of holiday celebrations are tonedeaf and presumptuous. Different people have different days that feel sacred to them, and whom they wish to spend those times with will vary.

So when I wish you Happy Holidays right now, know that I mean it in the broadest possible sense. Whatever days you find holy, enjoy them with whomever you choose, however you deem fit.

Me, I'm just going to sit around the table with the ghosts of Christmases past, listening curiously for the whispers brought by the winds of the future, and remembering that we are on a ball spinning in space at a thousand miles per hour, in a solar system moving at 514,000 miles per hour, in a galaxy moving 1.3 million miles per hour through the blackness of space.

No wonder we need a day every so often to slow the hell down.

Happy Holidays

by MC Dalet

My feelings about the American holidays – let's just call them that – are a mix of three distinct emotional states: joy, anxiety, and wonder. At 43, as a husband and father of two children, these states are often simultaneous. They are cyclical. Sometimes they comingle, all three distinctly present at once. Once upon a time, in a winter decades ago, there was only joy. This year, wonder is winning out, but the wonder is the result, ultimately, of anxiety.

I'll admit it: I always get a youthful tingling inside when the holiday season rolls around. It starts at Halloween. The weather turns crisp and invigorating, breaking the harsh heat of a Southern summer that's overstayed its welcome. Costumes. Candy. Good clean fun. Then Thanksgiving food and high-stakes football. By the time the lights start cropping up, I go a little Buddy the Elf. I have a genuine fondness for the holidays, but it's driven more by memory than the waking present, I think. After all, they come with a healthy dose of stress when you're an adult; doubly so if you are an adult living paycheck to paycheck, with little to no wiggle room. Triply so if you are said adult with children to whom you feel a responsibility for making the merry months magical on a meager budget. It is easy to have joy when you are a child and your responsibility is to receive. Provision exacts a price, and as a father, I am inescapably aware of the numbers on the tag.

As a child, my holidays were joyful, predictable, and comfortable. We ran the same circuit of my parents' families each year, on the same schedule, driving the same route, and stopping at the same service stations for gas, snacks and bathroom breaks on the way. Our progress through the Christmas season could be accurately tracked by familiar landmarks that themselves changed little over the years. When we landed at our final destination, we ate a traditional Southern Christmas dinner (a repeat of Thanksgiving, dish for dish) opened presents from family on Christmas Eve under the watchful eye of a portrait of the White Jesus, fell asleep watching the Santa tracker on the local news station, our stockings hung by the wood oven with care, and awoke to find those vessels – handmade by Aunt Lesteree – filled with stock treats, and beside them presents from Saint Nick wrapped suspiciously in the same paper our parents had used the night before. We awoke in Granny and Grandpa's house, nestled somewhere outside Southwest City, MO, a town with one street and a population of 660 souls. My experience led me to believe that Norman Rockwell had gotten his depiction of America and its most precious holiday just exactly perfect.

While my Rockwellian view of America slowly faded as I matured, the holidays lay suspended in an idealistic bubble. When I came home for winter break my first semester of college in 1992, baptized in the chaos of life outside my own small town, wearing my flannel, Prozac and Alice in Chains CDs in tow, I lost my angst in the embrace of the familiar company, the holiday route, the landmarks, and a handmade stocking. During the "acid winter of '94," I drove myself to Granny's, the Counting Crows' *A Long December* on infinite repeat. I sobered up, followed the route. I did not need a psychedelic façade so long as I could wrap myself in the familiar embrace of the known. The same orange and pack of cashews awaited me on Christmas morn, and for a blessed moment nothing was wrong.

The early years of my marriage were a negotiation to be sure. My holidays were rote, and never extravagant, while my wife's family transformed the holiday into a high-dollar production, Hallmark on the outside, with Clark Griswold expectations driving the play. My routine was broken. There was fusion, the unknown. The new familiar became the drive from one family to another, in the dead of night. Christmas Eve at Granny's, Christmas morning with my wife's family, with four hours in between. This drive was filled with the familiarity of our relationship. In our early days of courtship, we'd drive, often aimlessly, for hours. Our final destination was always home. Though headed for a parental home, the drive itself provided the embrace of the familiar. We read *Harry Potter* to each other by the light of a candle secured in a cup holder. We listened to the Grateful Dead. We arrived as adult children, responsible for receiving. Then came our children. And anxiety.

It is not hyperbole to say that every holiday season is a financial squeeze. The older one gets, the greater the gifting responsibilities. Adding children to the Christmas budget is the same game as adding them to the grocery bill, but in a concentrated dose.

This year has been especially challenging from a financial perspective, and I'll admit to having a bit of an implosion wondering how I could give my kids a holly jolly Christmas. You can invoke all the Hallmark it's-not-about-the-gifts sentiments you want, but two facts remain: 1.) culturally, our society spins a Santa narrative that equates behavioral goodness with gifts, and 2.) biologically, children receive, adults provide. Because of the intricacies of reception, children don't have a clear sense of what things cost. This can work in an adult's favor or against it. Regarding the narrative, it is difficult not to be nervous when the cousins with whom your children share Christmas morning have parents that are loaded. My reactive brain wonders if they will judge themselves not-as-good based upon relative haul. What story, what truth, will they believe?

So in the end, what I'm struggling with is not the money, the lack thereof, of even the gifts and our cultural emphasis on things as worth. To be honest, much like myself in my youth, my kiddos don't ask for extravagant gifts. My daughter's humble Santa list is easily manageable, and the boy is two. Give him Hot Wheels and he's thrilled. What bothers me is mine and mine alone: the nagging "what if." What if, for whatever reason, they don't have the happy holidays I always enjoyed. It is the uncertainty -- the antithesis of the familiar route, the stock stockings, and the small town bubble. This is where the wonder takes over – a wonder neither positive as joy nor negative as anxiety, but an energy of discovery.

I am not responsible for providing my children the SAME experience that I had, or that my wife had, as children. The world has changed. I have changed. She has changed. And that's a good thing. Familiarity is a false security. It is comfortable, but not synonymous with joy.

It took our adoption of Chanukah and its lessons some five years ago to educate me on the true magic of Christmas, that this is a time of miracles. A miracle, by definition, defies expectation, shattering and transforming the familiar into. . .something else. Something better.

It was a miracle that I never knew my own parents were as stressed and strapped for cash as I am when my brother and I were my kids' age. It was a miracle that, without being told I should, even as a child, I did enjoy our ritualized time together more than the gifts I received. And it was during the holiday season three years ago that we learned that, despite many odds, we would have a second child. And I can tell you that the love he has brought our family is a gift from Heaven. It is a miracle that I can release my own childhood to realize that my children are just thrilled that the holidays are here, overjoyed by that alone. I see children who love surprises, who simply ask what is next. We are a family free to make our adventure up as we go.

So this year, as we light our Chanukah candles and prepare to trek to family Christmas, I release the anxiety, move through the wonder of revelation, and return to the joy that all winter holidays are supposed to welcome. I release the need for the familiar in favor of the happiness of change and the light of miracles.

○

Dear 2018

○

Dear 2018

by Anna Bardin

Let me make this as clear as I can.

So, I don't know what sorts of things years are into. Like, what gets you going with the hey-hey and the wowee-wow. But 2018, I'm telling you right now that I am willing to do *anything* for you if you can be less shitty than 2017.

ANYTHING.

Mostly. I think. Like I say, I dunno what it is you like. Maybe dudes. If so, I have like-minded friends. We'll talk.

Just…think about it. After 2017, I am no longer above bribery.

(winks, nudges, says no more)

Sincerely,

Anna

Dear 2018

by Cristee Cook

The anticipation of your arrival has given me pause. Here we begin another chapter in which we all make grandiose promises, hoping and wishing that this year we'll really stick with to our goals. This seasonally paradigm is an invitation to disappointment and failure, and I just don't think I can do it anymore. I don't like making promises to a year. So, I want to let you know that I'm resigning from resolutions. Effective immediately.

I've decided instead that I want to continue.

I want to continue my personal trajectory of growth and expansion. To continue to choose to bravely face and do hard things: to create new art and have new experiences, even though I don't know where all the resources will come from, or how it will all work out. To use my words with all the love I feel, especially if I have to say something hard. To push myself beyond my own limitations and try anyway. As Samuell Beckett said, "Ever tried. Ever fail. No matter. Try again. Fail again. Fail better."

I'll even go as far as to say that I don't think I believe in failure anymore.

I don't think I believe in judgement anymore. I don't want to judge myself. Or others. We're all just doing our best. I sincerely hope we all make it.

And I don't want to hear all the reasons I must choose things based on outdated conditioning. Enough with telling other people how to live. I'm sorry for the times I've bought into that conditioning, and especially for the times I've perpetuated it.

So, no more lies. Enough with dangling the promise of major life changes just because the calendar changed. Enough with the idea that growth and change can't be a daily endeavor. I, we, can all do this life thing with grace and love if we choose to.

What would it take? What would that be like? And how does it get better than this?

Dear 2018

by Matthew Broyles

I must admit, on this day last year, I wasn't entirely sure we would all make it to January 2018. The idea that this nation and the world have survived an entire year of rule by Cheeto Mussolini is preposterous on its face, yet here we are, not all that much worse off.

Not yet, anyway. A lot of the groundwork for the next financial crisis has been passed through our foetid Congress, but not yet implemented.

Which makes me rather apprehensive about 2018. That said, there are some things worth anticipating.

The midterm elections are of course foremost. Having dispatched pedomaniac Roy Moore in Alabama of all places, the possibility of placing a hefty Congressional block on the Angry Creamsicle is damned tantalizing, and something I intend to put my precious time into. I personally know a few of the people running on Democratic tickets locally, so that's a start.

Creatively, I have several writing and musical projects that could reach fruition in 2018. The successful crowdfunding of my second novel in 2017 gives me hope that there will be a ready audience for anything I put out in the coming year, which is a heartwarming prospect indeed.

If I were to ask 2018 anything specific, I would ask it to be stable enough to get us to November without undue chaos, despite the probability that a wrecked economy would better ensure an opposition party landslide. But the toll a societal meltdown would take on all our lives is not a price I'm eager to pay for political victory.

My son will turn 13 in 2018. When I talk to him about the future, he picks up on my forced optimism. Certainly we have a lot of time to get through before he is of adult age, but we're not that far from needing to make plans about education, driving, jobs, and such. Friends of mine have children who've graduated ahead of schedule this year to get a head start on college, and it wouldn't surprise me if the boy did the same, in which case our time horizon grows even nearer.

I will turn 44 in 2018. Assuming the current retirement age of 65, I am more than halfway through my working life. But of course retirement is a luxury we GenXers will not likely experience on our empire's downward trajectory. As a creative person, I don't expect that I will stop creating until my body keels over, so 'retirement' is not applicable there. Still, I have at least 21 more years of needing to work a job of some sort in order to eat. That's a little less time than I've been doing it thus far.

Smack in the middle, both chronologically and economically, I hope desperately that 2018 will not bring some manner of calamity that will derail either my steady growth or my son's. I hear my 99-year-old grandmother's stories about life in the Depression, and wince at the possibility of having to live through such times. Or worse, of my boy having to.

Dear 2018, be gentle. We're all doing the best we can. We err, we slip, but most of us mean well. I hope you do, too.

Dear 2018

by MC Dalet

I don't think I will survive you.

I barely survived 2016; then 2017 changed everything, chipped away at me. I will not make it through your passages, which will most assuredly be rugged.

I am not rugged. Not yet.

You see, when I say "I," I refer to my personality, my belief system, my manifestation in the world. The I whose last thread of innocence fell when "good people" carried Nazi flags through the streets of America and finally glanced at its bug-out bag when Tom Petty stopped "running down a dream." Though my core desires remain largely unchanged, my perspective has been forcibly altered. Me as I know me will not outlive the year to come.

I want to say your predecessor was cruel, that it had the energy of death, of endings. Artists I respected passed, killed themselves, or were exposed as pederasts. I learned that despite all the diversity training in the world I do not and cannot truly understand the extent of my white privilege, all while being made to understand the true scope of hatred that exists in the world. I was asked to hold secrets and thus hold to myself disasters unfolding. I witnessed the Center shake, collapse, and finally fail to hold.

But there was a gift: 2017 removed a veil from my eyes. I see ugliness and acknowledge its real-ness. So it is of the world; so it is of myself. Having veils removed may be enlightening, but it is painful, like having one's skin peeled away.

How many skins, like serpents, do we shed in a lifetime, if we truly grow? Each time the death-birth ritual leaves us tender and exposed, but newish. And I cannot help but wonder how I could see at all with the thick, rough, obsolete skin hanging loose, repelling the light from my retinas, my pupils full open but unreceptive until the bulging blockage fell away, leaving me light-blind and helpless for a time. . .until I adjust, acclimate, reboot. A short circuit. From chaos comes clarity.

So this is what I ask of you, 2018: clarity.

I grew up in small town Oklahoma; I've stood on the Right. I am an educated, intuitive, and empathetic artist/scholar; I've stood on the Left. Both have blinded me. Both have left their scars.

I cannot find the center from the side. I cannot leave the side as "I."

Dear 2018,

I beg you, destroy "I" that my Being may feel we and become me. Peel another layer so my soul can see with its eyes. Awake me not with false doctrines bent on being correct, but with a desire to know the truth at all cost. Even my popularity, my comfort, my identity.

Show me what I don't know I don't know.

I pray you, finish what this half-decade started and devour me. Pain? Give me more, but do me a favor, will you? Grant me the antidote. Do that, and I will swallow it and choose not to suffer. Touch only me in your destruction. My kin have their own requests, their own fears, their own correction. Just bring me closer to mine.

2018, I will not survive you. Not in my current form. I will die and be reborn in your bowels.

So push me further. Set me in front of the monsters so I can see them. Make me see them so that I can choose to stand my ground and tell them to "Go away!" And if they consume me, may my heart be so true that they have no choice but to spit me out, unable to stomach the light I have begun to shine. My old self would join them not to be torn asunder. This time, I will to choose the fight. Finish the job, '18. Make me a warrior, and I will look, as now, only to the future.

Acknowledgements

from the editor's desk

○

Obviously, the lion's share of the thanks for this tome's existence goes to the writers themselves. Huge kudos to Anna Bardin, Chris Dashiell, Cristee Cook, Eva Moon, Doremus Jessup, Marged Howley Dudek, James Michael Taylor, Ashley Van Arsdel, Scott R. Rey, Dr. Adrian L. Cook, Mandy Dnah, Paul Williams, Grace Joonie Hall, and MC Dalet for all your thoughtful words and the willingness to share them with the world.

Additional large thanks to Joey Keeton for keeping the website up. Don't want me putting my hands on the techy stuff, nosiree.

And big, BIG thanks to everyone who clicked, read, shared, reblogged, or otherwise partook in our crazy experiment over all these months. We love having you along for the ride. Heck, if you get squirrely, join up and you can get a title in your inbox every Wednesday your very own self. Always glad to hear new voices.

Thanks for reading, and keep up the good work. All of it.

Lightning Source UK Ltd.
Milton Keynes UK
UKHW050624280519
343447UK00004B/573/P